Building a Schoolhouse

Laying the Foundation for Success

Volume 1

SUSAN SIMON, MA, MED

Building a Schoolhouse
Laying the Foundation for Success, Volume 1

Published by Wheatmark®
610 East Delano Street, Suite 104, Tucson, Arizona 85705 U.S.A.
www.wheatmark.com

ISBN: 978-1-60494-030-5
LCCN: 2007943279

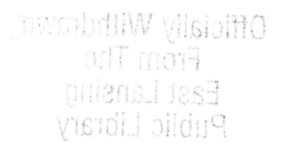

CONTENTS

Introduction 1

1. Trust...5
   One Step at a Time

2. Leadership...39
   Kisses

3. Empowerment 82
   The Yellow Cart

4. Environment...124
   Middle School Blues and the Walkout

5. Optimism...167
   The Gift

6. Accountability...196
   Fire! Fire!

7. Ritual, Tradition, Ceremony 238
   Saying Goodbye to a Friend

Index 265

This book is dedicated to my loving parents, Marge and Ralph Simon. Their constant encouragement, careful listening, and belief in me has supported every step I've taken along my life path. They taught me that I could dream any dream and accomplish whatever I envisioned and pursued. The spirit of this book reflects their unconditional love.

INTRODUCTION

I ENTERED THE teaching profession some thirty years ago because I liked working with people and I wanted to make a positive difference in the lives of others. I loved my years as a teacher because I was able to help my students discover their inherent creativity and assist them in developing new skills to support those natural talents. I found teaching to be a highly challenging and fun way in which to express and develop my own creativity as well.

In my desire to expand my circle of influence and impact more people, I became a school principal. This new role was quite different from my original role of teacher yet it contained many teaching opportunities. I now found myself in the position of helping teachers discover and apply their creativity, multiple talents and various experiences to their teaching, which ultimately impacted many more students than I was able to reach as a classroom teacher.

During my seventeen years as a school principal, I came to appreciate the incredible dedication and hard work of the teachers with whom I worked. I saw my mission as one of role model, resource person, confidant, mentor, friend, manager, and educational leader. I loved working with students, teachers and parents to collaboratively establish school environments that were supportive of both the teaching and learning processes. Over the years, I learned more and more about good teaching by observing passionate teachers plying their trade. There is real magic in watching a teacher who feels passionately involved with her teaching inviting and helping her students to grow academically, emotionally, and socially.

The schools where I was principal were fun, exciting and supportive centers of good teaching and high achieving students. They were wonderfully supportive communities where everyone loved coming to work each day. After a few years of receiving feedback about how well our staff, administration and parents worked together, I began paying closer attention to what we were doing that seemed to work so successfully. What were the basic components that allowed us to create a supportive school community where teachers were constantly growing in their skills and successfully teaching all students who were making steady growth toward mastery? Why was our school, which had all the normal challenges a school has, viewed as exceptional in the community? Why were our teachers involved in important leadership roles, winning awards and loving their work, despite the increasing difficult pressures bombarding the educational system? Why were our students making steady progress, feeling happy and safe in their classrooms, discovering their own particular learning strengths and realizing their giftedness? The answers to these and other questions pertaining to success in school, for principals, students and teachers are found in this book.

Building A Schoolhouse includes my views and experiences of how to create, maintain and consistently improve a vibrant and successful school community. The ideas, strategies and action steps I share are guidelines for teachers, administrators and parents to begin the dialogue around the important teaching and learning issues that face them in their classrooms, in their schools and in their communities. Each chapter in this book is devoted to a different characteristic, quality or principle that contributes to the formation of an excellent school. Since we often learn the most and relate the best to personal experiences, I have begun each chapter with a true story, designed to illustrate the chapter topic. The chapter itself will explore the reasons for using a particular quality, characteristic or principle in the school setting. I will show what that quality would look like in classrooms and schools and discuss why that particular characteristic is important to ensure that all students succeed. Finally, each chapter is loaded with strategies and action steps that a teacher, administrator or parent may immediately use to positively influence their success rate and, at the same time, maintain joy in their profession.

I believe *Building A Schoolhouse* will be a valuable resource to teachers, administrators and parents as they work together to create viable learning communities. Faced with constant and often strident challenges to their teaching and leading, many teachers and principals are losing heart and leaving the educational arena. We can't afford to lose good educators because of lack of support, feelings of despair, loss of passion for their job or constant pressure to conform. Educators must find a balance between applying the methods that will allow them to meet the demands for high accountability while at the same time developing those teaching and leading strategies and personal qualities that allow each teacher and principal to uniquely contribute to every child with whom they work.

Building A Schoolhouse demonstrates ways in which people can work more successfully with one another in order to realize individual and group goals. These are universal qualities and characteristics, which lead to stronger relationships, creating greater happiness and more success in life. Whether you focus on the stories, action steps or content of each chapter, *Building A Schoolhouse* will present you with opportunities to explore your connections to students, to schools and to your own passion for what you do. This book is designed to impact educators and parents on both the personal and professional level. Hopefully, readers will be drawn into a self-reflective process of examining their goals, successes and challenges as educators and parents. At the same time, the topics presented provide a rich source of questioning and discussion for faculties and school communities. The ultimate goal for both personal and group inquiry is improved educational opportunities for all students in healthy, motivating and supportive school environments. *Building A Schoolhouse* is designed as a resource and guide, assisting educators and parents in navigating the increasingly complex job of successfully educating students.

The reader need not begin with chapter one and read sequentially through the book, although the chapters are intentionally sequenced. You may choose a topic of particular interest and begin there. Or, the reader may wish to read the stories that introduce each chapter and powerfully illustrate the chapter topic. Strategies and action steps may be your starting point for reading this book. Choose a few action steps to try out in your classroom, school or home and see if they really do make a difference. However you choose to approach using *Building A Schoolhouse*, my hope is that you find inspiration within these pages to continue your work for children in the most powerful and successful way that is possible.

1. TRUST

....

"One Step at a Time"

AFTER TWENTY-FOUR YEARS of leading a fast-paced, hectic life, I decided to leave the east coast and move west in order to experience a more casual and slower-paced lifestyle. I accepted a principal's job in Arizona and prepared to move. Little did I know how intense an experience I was about to enter at the troubled school that I would soon lead. However, a few months before taking over the helm at the school in Arizona, I had an experience that was to fortify and strengthen my efforts to build trust among the school community and help me work through the many disheartening setbacks in that process. It was all about learning to trust in taking One Step At a Time...

I had been in Hawaii for almost two weeks, spending time in nature to think through some of the major life changes I was about to undertake when I moved from Pennsylvania to Arizona. Toward the end of my stay on Maui, I decided to drive up to the volcano Haleakela and hike down into the crater. I had read about the beauty of the volcano and I loved hiking so it seemed like the perfect thing to do. Nature has always provided me with great insights about life so I had no doubt that I'd learn something useful on this hike. The adventure that most drew my attention was a long hike across the crater floor. The guidebook suggested starting at the top of the crater and then hiking down the trail to the lower trailhead, a seventeen-mile trip.

I woke up early the morning of the hike, knowing that the drive up Haleakela took time. I needed to get an early start to complete a seventeen-mile hike. The drive up the mountain follows a winding two-lane road that ultimately took me to the top of the 10,000 ft. volcano. As I drove slowly up the twisting mountain road, I encountered fog at the higher elevations. I hoped that this wouldn't interfere with my hiking. It was mid-morning when I finally arrived at the ranger station. The ranger advised me that it was probably too late to do the long hike and arrive at the end of the trail while it was still daylight.

I was disappointed that I had arrived at the trailhead so late. Why didn't I get an earlier start? After berating myself for wasting so much time, I realized that I was really afraid of hiking the long trail by myself. I had deliberately taken extra time so that I couldn't do the full hike. I decided to go to the upper trailhead, hike down into the crater for a few hours and then hike back out the same trail. This would give me a good sense of what it felt like to hike in a volcano. I was mad at myself for "wimping out" on the long hike. Fear is a powerful force. It had guided my actions. Why couldn't I have admitted I was afraid to do the long hike by myself when I got up that morning? I could have avoided all the self-criticism. I needed to begin to trust in my knowing.

Although I had read about Haleakela, I wasn't sure what to expect when I arrived at the top. The trailhead to the Haleakela trail sat on the lip of the crater. Standing at the rim provided a panoramic view of the crater and the trail that wound its way down into the volcano, becoming a tiny ribbon of white far off in the distance. My first view of the crater reminded me of a moonscape. It was desolate looking, strewn with outcroppings of volcanic rock, massive boulders and mini-craters imploding throughout the volcano. What surprised me the most were the beautiful colors spread out before me. I had expected mostly black and gray but instead I saw muted shades of green, brown, yellow and red. These subtle colors blended together to form miniature volcanoes, fields of rocks and oddly shaped mounds spread out across the horizon as far as I could see.

It was a vast space, completely empty of people, except for me. I was awestruck at the beauty that lay before me. Here I was, standing at the brink, ready to begin my great adventure! I was excited and energized and a little frightened but so glad I had come. Symbolically, I was taking the first step on an unknown path, not sure where it led or what challenges might arise along the way. I was soon to take that same first step, toward the unknown, when I moved from the east coast to the west. Facing my fears and trusting myself turned out to be the focus of this trip to Hawaii.

Many Haleakela hikers are disappointed because clouds often move into the crater, obscuring all visibility and turning an otherwise warm day into a chilly, damp one. There were no clouds this day! It was perfect! The sun was shining and there was a pleasant breeze blowing. I was able to see for miles ahead of me as I began walking down the steep initial portion of the trail. This completely amazed me as I had expected to be climbing over boulders and rocks as I made my way down the trail. Here I was, walking in the sand with no obstacles on the path ahead.

I felt happy as I began this wonderful hike, knowing that I had partially conquered a fear in being here and embarking on this journey into the unknown. The sky was so blue. The warm sun felt nurturing. I was on vacation in Hawaii! How could life be more perfect in this moment?

Often, when hiking, it's necessary to keep your eyes on the trail so as not to trip on roots or stumble over rocks. Since hiking in the crater was so effortless I was able to focus on all that was around me. I stopped occasionally to pick up rocks and examine them or to sit and marvel at the colors that surrounded me. It felt as if I were walking on top of the world. I wished my friends or family could share this incredible experience. However, there was something primal about being the only person in sight for miles, walking through the crater of a volcano. I felt quite miniscule and insignificant in the grandeur of all that surrounded me, but I was enjoying every minute!

After an hour or so of hiking down into the crater, I stopped and looked all around me. All I saw for miles were rocks, mounds and hills. The trail was visible ahead, snaking its way down and down and down into the volcano. I noticed that there were still no other people visible in the crater, either below me or above me. It suddenly felt empty and barren. I was so isolated. The reality that I was alone, in the middle of a volcano, immediately created a state of fear. My gut twisted and I heard these questions in my head. What are you doing here by yourself? Are you crazy? What if you get lost and no one finds you? What if you get hurt? I realized that no one knew where I was. Should I get out of the volcano as fast as I could? My heart raced as I nervously turned around in a full-circle, scanning the horizon for people. Empty. What had been a fun, exciting adventure was now marred with fear and uncertainty. I sat on a rock and told myself everything was OK. Danger didn't lurk behind every boulder. What had just happened here? Taking several deep breaths, to calm my jittery nerves, I temporarily pushed my fear aside, stood up and continued along the trail, determined to enjoy the experience.

After another hour of hiking, I found a large boulder, just off the trail, that I could lean against and rest. Of course there were no trees or big bushes in the volcano so there weren't any shady spots. It was early afternoon and the sun baked my already red shoulders and slowed my steps. I continued to look around, still amazed to be in a volcano. I ate a snack, drank some water and leaned back against the rock. Suddenly, all was still. Silence surrounded me. No wind. No scurrying animals. No hiking boots crunching rock. I paused mid-bite in my sandwich, my eyes darting around the crater. Sit perfectly still, I told myself. I closed my eyes and listened. Nothing. Total silence. A tiny sound of breath reached my ears. I heard my steady and regular breathing more clearly with my eyes closed and soon my heartbeat followed, thundering in my ears. That was all I heard. Life. Is it possible that my life is the only sound, I thought? These eerily quiet minutes stopped the world around me. Peaceful feelings flooded my heart and coursed through my body. I tried to hang on to the moment, knowing it was probably the only time in my life that I would experience total silence.

Whoosh!! Whoooosh!!! This sound stole the silence. I didn't recognize the sound until I saw a bright white cloud moving into the crater. My first thought was, "I've never heard a cloud before!" I actually was hearing the wind blowing the cloud into the crater. If I hadn't been in total silence, I wouldn't have had the experience of hearing a cloud blow into the volcano. Suddenly, the sunny, hot morning was obliterated. I now sat in a white fog that totally blocked my view of anything that wasn't within one foot of where I sat. The air became quite chilly and damp. Luckily, I had a sweatshirt with me, which I put on. However, I still felt chilled to the bone. Was it the weather or the eeriness of the situation? After sitting there for a few minutes, deciding what to do, I stood up and found my way back to the trail. The fog became thicker and I couldn't see anything beyond about six inches around me. The fog magnified my fear. Which way was out? Everything looked the same in the eerie whiteness. The cold, white cloud particles brushed against my skin. I stood still, lost in thought, trying to decide which way to go. Silence covered me. I was alone in this white world with no signs to guide me out. The wind broke the silence, but stirred the fog into thicker swirls of white nothingness. I stood still, fearing to stay, afraid to continue, without being able to see what lay ahead.

Finally, I decided to go forward. I hoped that I would walk out of the cloud by going deeper into the crater. Since I was hiking at such a high elevation, it could be possible to walk through a cloud. I kept my eyes on my feet and the trail immediately in front of me.

Since I couldn't see ahead or behind, I had to find the next little part of the trail by looking at my next step. I could see only the next step. I had no idea how long I would be in the fog or what I would find when I left it. It seemed to me that nature was giving me a physical opportunity to walk into my fear. Since this trip to Hawaii was all about confronting my fears, it felt appropriate and natural to find myself in the middle of a volcano crater, lost in a cloud of fog, attempting to reach the unknown that lay ahead.

It suddenly occurred to me that all I had to do with any challenge, uncertainty or fear was to take the next step and the next step, until I finally found my way through. Worrying about what lay ahead for me was a waste of time and energy because it was beyond my knowing. This seemed like an important concept since I was spending quite a lot of my time worrying about upcoming changes in my life, trying to figure out what might be around the next bend. What I could immediately work with was the path that lay at my feet at any given moment. I felt that I could walk into the unknown and be able to quell my fears and survive all that was to come.

Almost immediately, after coming to this realization, I walked out of the cloud! At first I could see about a foot ahead, then five feet ahead as the sunlight began peeking through the fog. Finally, I walked into the hot sun with the entire crater spread out before me. My fear immediately lifted. I felt lighter and buoyant. I ran down the trail in a burst of joy, having left the uncertainty. I looked around me. Were these beautiful copper-colored and golden-brown mounds here before? Had the sky been this blue when I began the hike? The world surrounding me shined gloriously colorful. The cloud was nowhere in sight. Where had it gone? It now felt like anything would be possible for me as long as I remained calm and took the next step. This idea comforted me and I felt that nothing would be impossible for me to accomplish in the future.

I hiked deeper into the crater for a mile or so then turned around and headed back out. The trip back up the trail was quite different than the trip down. No more clouds blew through the crater! I met several other hikers along the way and enjoyed visiting briefly with them. I was surprised at how many people I saw on the hike out of the crater. Nature spoke to me alone on the way down. Now that I had received her message, I was ready to interact with people again. When I arrived back at the rim of the crater, I felt victorious. I had conquered my fear and moved forward! Missing the seventeen-mile hike allowed me to be totally present to receive an important lesson. It had been a good day at Haleakela!

When I'm confused, worried or uncertain about what will happen in my future, I think of the hike in the cloud in Haleakela. It reminds me to focus on what I can do now because life is lived in the present moment. Fear can come and go as quickly as a cloud blows through a volcano crater. I can sit in the fog of fear or take one step at a time toward clarity.

Trust

Definition: *a firm belief in the reliability, honesty, ability or strength of someone or something.*

Trust is a core characteristic necessary for the successful implementation of academic goals and school vision. Teachers and principals demonstrate their strongest leadership skills and bring their individual talents to their teaching and leading when they work in a trusting environment. Students learn the most in classrooms where they feel confident that their teacher will treat them with the utmost respect and care, nurturing any self-doubts or insecurities and turning them into strengths based on successful classroom performance. We must open ourselves up to interactions with self, with others and with the subject matter in order to lead or teach or learn. This opening of self, which invites scrutiny from others, is personally risky and sometimes frightening. We're never quite sure how our self-expression will be accepted or judged by a colleague, friend or foe. There-fore, we learn as we grow into adulthood, to be more cautious with our sharing of self. This caution is often warranted and protects us from hurt. Unfortunately, at the same time, this reluctance serves as a barrier that most often blocks how much light might be allowed in to shine on self. We often keep the door closed for fear the light will be too bright and will expose all of our flaws that we have successfully hidden away.

When principals don't step forward and boldly serve as the voice supporting the personal growth of their students and teachers be-cause they expect ridicule or opposition, the school falters. When skilled teachers hold back on their teaching because they fear criticism or judgment, their efforts will fall short. When students don't allow themselves to become one with their learning because they fear fail-ure or humiliation, they cheat themselves and their growth process. Trust is a fortress surrounding our deepest fears and insecurities. It creates a safe environment in which we can learn more about self and our purpose in life, bringing our talents and gifts forward within a secure structure. As we experience the joy of self-expression without fear, we're able to gain enough self-confidence to boldly step forward into situations that aren't as well protected. This is the moment when learning about self and the outside world occurs. The stronger we become in our risk-taking actions, the more trust we build in our own knowing and ability to appropriately respond to any life situation. Trust is a characteristic shared between people that supports personal and professional growth and achievement because it creates a safe space to be human.

Learning thrives in environments that build trusting relationships, which pave the way for excellent teaching by teachers and achieve-ment by students. Trust or the lack of it significantly impacts class-room dynamics and school-wide climate. Schools where trust exists are centers of possibility and growth. Those without trust are difficult places in which to work and learn. Trust finds its home in relationships. Teachers begin building relationships with their students on the first day of school. Some begin even sooner than that by sending introductory letters home or sponsoring an open house to come and meet the teacher before school starts. The act of teaching requires relationship building with people and with the subject matter. Most teachers are successful in developing trusting relationships with their students. These relationships set the stage for student risk-taking and active involvement in the learning process.

Students will expose their vulnerability only in an environment where they feel safe. Therefore, trust building is one of the most important tasks of the classroom teacher. Once established, trusting relationships must be constantly nurtured and monitored. It's easy for one negative incident to abolish all the good that has been created. When you observe students actively engaged in their learning, speaking up in front of the class, trying out new ideas, and learning from mistakes and missteps, you know the teacher in that classroom has developed trusting relationships with his students. Learning is much more difficult, and certainly not as collaborative, in classrooms that lack trusting interactions.

Any learner must feel safe before he will venture into the unknown, risk answering a question or speak out for what he believes. Emotional safety is at the heart of trust. If I feel emotionally safe with you, I probably will grow to trust you. Students who know that the teacher respects them and won't humiliate them or put them down in any way will take risks. Many students have had experiences or interactions with peers, parents, teachers or principals that have been critical and judgmental. Some students take a very long time to develop trust. Some never do. Teachers must take the initiative in gently leading their students to a place of trust regardless of how long it might take to achieve this goal. For some students, the teacher is the only solid role model and the only hope for developing trust with an adult. It is a serious responsibility and an awesome gift to contribute to a relationship. Those teachers who are most requested by parents to work with their children seem to have a natural ability to create trusting relationships quickly at the beginning of the school year and then consistently maintain and strengthen them as the year progresses.

Teachers build trusting relationships more quickly with students who have had previous positive experiences in this area. Students who have not met with previous success in trusting others will take more time, great patience, and loads of acceptance to reach that space. Students like the teachers who respect and like them back. They gravitate toward teachers and adults who recognize who they are, point out what they can do, and help to encourage them to make it through the many challenges they face. Children are very astute and will quickly discover which adults in their lives really love them. They intuitively know when someone is on their side and they can see and hear beyond the words that are used. Teachers show their students that they accept and respect them in hundreds of different ways throughout the school year. Consistency is a key to showing a student that you support and care about him. When class size is too large, teachers have less time to spend with individual students. Some kids can get lost in the shuffle of very large classes. Teachers use the strategies of paying attention to and getting to know each student to build relationships. Schools that drive teachers into a purely academic focus, at the expense of personal relationships, do a great disservice to the students and teachers. Going through an entire school year feeling no trust for your teacher sets up a significant handicap for students. Learning will be stunted in such circumstances. Fortunately, most students develop very positive relationships with their teachers each year as they enter a new classroom. However, a few students will not develop trust with adults or peers because they have been hurt in the past and they won't allow for the possibility of that hurt to happen again. These instances, when mistrust rules, are very painful to student and teacher alike. The student wants to trust, but can't. The teacher works tirelessly to build trust, but to no avail. Often these students become the disenfranchised dropout group. They've gone through years of school making no meaningful or lasting connections. They're adrift and unable to trust in self or anyone else. Success in school often eludes them. These are the students whom the system fails. Luckily, the great majority of our students are successful in learning to trust. This critical student and teacher relationship becomes a platform for growth and achievement.

Trusting relationships between teachers build powerful partnerships in improving education. Teachers grow personally and professionally through the interactions they have with one another. Schools in which teachers collaborate and support one another are centers for outstanding teaching and the academic advancement of students. The difficult job of teaching is most understood by those people in the classroom every day dealing with all of the challenges that face them. Some of the most effective and informal staff development occurs when teachers work with one another on a daily basis. There is more consistency, feedback and follow-up when teachers work together than there is when an "expert" comes in for limited training. Principals and teacher leaders ought to encourage teacher collaboration on a regular basis in a school. The principal can support this happening by providing planning time, release time for classroom observations, and needed materials. It's in the principal's best interest to share his leadership with teachers. They will have a much clearer understanding of the job of teaching.

In addition to the professional advantages gained with teachers working together, there is also the personal payback. Teaching is often an isolating, frustrating and difficult job. At the same time, there are numerous success stories, new strategies and excitement to be shared. Teachers, who have a teaching partner or other teachers to go to with problems, and successes will feel more heard and understood. The multi-tasking principal can often only provide limited support to teachers. That's not enough. Teachers supporting teachers strengthens the fiber of a school. Also, knowing that you have many supporters and friends in the work environment makes going to work each day a more pleasant experience. Strong allegiances and friendships form when working together on the job. Many of these relationships become lifelong friendships. They strengthen teaching and teachers, and ultimately, the schools where they work. The principal plays an important role in establishing a school climate where teachers support one another and work together for the common good. However, it is up to the teachers themselves to see that this actually happens. Schools in which gossip, negativity and personal attacks take place won't be centers of achievement for students. Nor will they be environments in which teachers and teaching thrive. The pulse of the school climate can be taken by noticing how many teachers work together in supportive and productive ways. Sit in a faculty room and listen to the teachers. Do they speak negatively about other teachers? Watch interactions at a staff meeting. Are differing opinions respected or are comments made and eyes rolled upward? Spend any time watching the interactions within a school and you'll be able to determine if teachers value working together.

Principals and teachers must develop close working relationships and feelings of trust for one another. Principals set the example for communication and relationship building within a school. If you're a principal who wishes to change a negative school environment, begin by modeling the clear communication and positive relationships you wish to exist in the school. This requires a dogged determinism to stay focused on the goals and not to be deterred by the weight of all the requirements of the administrative role. The initial steps to take to build trusting relationships occur when the principal takes time to talk to teachers and to get to know them. It's difficult to trust someone that we don't really know. In addition to talking to teachers, the principal must spend significant amounts of time in classrooms observing the teacher in action with the students. It's useful to have a good sense of the strengths of the teacher and his teaching and communication style. Since principals see the entire school picture, they are often instrumental in bringing teachers together who might never have thought to collaborate with one another. The principal serves as a matchmaker, in this case pairing or grouping educators who would interact very successfully with one another. Principals who hold high expectations for teacher collaboration will work tirelessly to co-create school environments where teachers work together and support one another. Many principals shy away from creating schools as centers of collaboration because they think they will turn their power over to the teachers. This line of thought shows a basic lack of knowledge about leadership. Effective principals know that they will be most successful in their jobs when everyone on the staff is acting from a place of power and leadership. Teachers love working with principals who know how to maintain their administrative authority while sharing and encouraging leadership at all levels of the organization.

When teachers and principals trust one another and closely collaborate, highly motivating activities and successful results occur. Closely examine any school that has multiple activities and opportunities for both student and teacher growth. You'll find close relationships and frequent encounters between teachers and administration. This collaborative role between teacher and principal also serves as an important model for the students to see in action. If adults are asking kids to get along and help one another, they must demonstrate this same phenomenon among the adults at the school. Sharing an ethic that honors collaboration will also draw parents into interactions with school staff in appropriate and supportive ways. Collaboration is truly a situation where living the strategy provides satisfying and meaningful results that can be emulated by others within the organization.

Trusting relationships play a major role in the academic success of the members in a school community. The best learning occurs through the teaching of excellent teachers. Teachers grow in their skills through training, experience, trying new ideas, collaborating and receiving feedback. In order to be successful, teachers must be well trained and supported. Additionally, they must plumb the depths of their personal interests and talents to discover what they have to offer. We display our strongest leadership skills and greatest giftedness in those areas about which we are passionate and knowledgeable. Therefore, it is imperative for teachers to come into touch with their deepest levels of commitment and interest, which is only accomplished in trust filled environments. The learning process requires the learner to put himself on the line in the light of other people's scrutiny. Belief in self allows this to happen. This is true for teachers, students, and administrators.

The principal-teacher relationship often serves as the basis for creating a school climate in which students are the primary focus and teachers are recognized as the key contributors toward student success. In schools where teachers have meaningful and trusting relationships with their principal, anything is possible. Great respect between principal and teacher creates the environment in which both parties put aside ego and work collaboratively for the benefit of the students. The students are ultimately the group most positively impacted in a trusting school environment. They willingly step forward into their strengths and interests as they discover and develop them. The learning process takes place both in places of safety and environments of risk. Our students should be able to manage their learning in both ways to become self-actualized and able to meet life's diverse challenges. Learners must come to a place of trusting themselves, their environment, their teachers and the fact that they'll have the skills to meet whatever problems or opportunities present themselves. Schools gifted with charismatic principals who co-create with outstanding teachers are exciting centers of learning for student and teacher alike. These collaborative education centers create an environment of safety and support and become families to those who belong and participate. Students will all be more willing to take risks in their learning and believe in their innate abilities to accomplish their goals when they bask in the love and support shared throughout their community. Schools that operate under these principles are havens in a chaotic world, providing a temporary place for people to live their lives of purpose and meaning in an environment of personal safety. If you've ever had the opportunity to co-create a loving, caring and supportive school, you are a very fortunate individual indeed.

Building trusting relationships in school communities certainly includes the parents. We know that parental involvement in education contributes to a child's masterful learning. Therefore, it is critical that educators create situations in which parents can have the opportunity to get to know and trust both the principal and the teachers. This takes time. It also requires that effective communication systems be set up between home and school. Most parents wish to be informed about their children's progress on a regular basis. Frequent and clear communication from the teacher to the parent will form the foundation for a long-term, positive relationship to develop. Parents who are actively involved in the life of the school, as volunteers or PTSA members or in other ways, will more quickly form relationships with teachers and administration. It's up to teachers to make sure they reach those parents who aren't as actively involved. Notes and information sent home on a regular basis helps inform the parents who aren't able to volunteer at school. Parents play a significant supportive role both within the school and within the community at large, serving as a deep resource for their local school. Parental support or lack of it can make or break a school. Developing positive and informed relationships with parents is absolutely critical in building bonds of trust. Educators and schools that shut out parents throw away a valuable resource and do harm to the students and the school community. Teachers need parents to assist in the challenging job of educating their children. Parents need teachers to help them raise their children to be happy and successful individuals. It's a win-win relationship for both parties. Teacher and parent collaboration is critical to student achievement.

If trust is so important to a school's successful operation, what exactly is it? How would I recognize it? What causes one person to trust another? What actions do I take if I wish to build trust in my relationships? Trust requires a firm belief in the reliability, honesty, ability or strength of someone. Therefore, when these four critical aspects are present, trust flourishes. The first aspect of trust is reliability. We all strive to have predictability and stability in our lives, particularly desiring these characteristics in our relationships. Most of our daily activities are spent in contact with others, at work, at home and throughout the community. Relationships touch us primarily at the heart and feeling level because they are so interrelated with our sense of self and what we're about. Therefore, when our relationships are positive and reliable, we feel happier, capable and more alive.

Reliability in relationships means that we can count on others to do what they say they'll do. We can rely on their honesty, caring, friendship, and consistency in behavior. A friend or family member in whom you place your trust must demonstrate consistency in words and actions, standing by you in both good and difficult times. Reliability means you know what to expect from another and you believe that he will act accordingly in most circumstances. Reliable people get the job done and they demonstrate this to you over and over in your interactions with them. Reliability stands on the shoulders of consistency. Dependable people are not perfect and they will occasionally fall down but they'll always pop back up and resume their forward movement. You begin to develop trust with someone upon whom you may rely. There is a comfort in this surety that creates a bond leading to friendship. People who are inconsistent and disappoint you time and time again are difficult to trust. There is no foundation for or experience of trust with them. Reliability is fundamental to creating a trusting relationship with another person.

Honesty is the second facet of trust. Telling the truth all the time is the communication benchmark to reach honesty. We seek honesty in our relationships to help us sort out all the challenges and questions that life presents. Honest communication doesn't necessarily mean that I blurt out whatever I'm thinking. It's not usually effective if it contains blame, shame, judgment or other communication blocking strategies. Truthfulness occurs when an individual attempts to express his views in an objective, non-judgmental, concise way. Objective feedback in the communication process is particularly beneficial to us because it provides us with information in a way that we can accept it or disregard it. Personal motives don't interfere in honest communication and the person speaking should provide insight that isn't influenced by his own agenda. Honesty is trusting that another person's actions will come from an inner place of integrity, guiding their actions towards themselves and others. Delivering honest feedback and opinions requires insight and tact. The human psyche is easily hurt by the use of ill-conceived words. Therefore, we must carefully monitor our interactions with others so as not to offend and cause damage while trying to provide help. Finding people in our lives who we can trust to be open and honest, yet sensitive to our ability to hear what they have to say, is invaluable. As educators, we must model honest communication with our students and teach them how to deliver their own in the best way and at the right time. We must also practice this ourselves with our colleagues and administration. So often, people fly off the handle and say things that are hurtful under the guise of giving helpful feedback. Words that harm, rather than help, lack in basic honesty. This doesn't mean that honesty is always positive. That wouldn't be honest! However, it does mean that we need to think how to share information, knowing that our words and actions significantly impact other people. Principals face this challenge frequently when talking to staff members about lessons or situations that didn't work. It requires speaking objectively to problem solve without accusing or belittling. Honesty in communication and consistency in action creates trusting bonds between people. Educators who wish to establish trusting relationships with students and parents must practice these skills in every interaction each day.

The third facet of trust is ability. Trusting in someone requires a belief that they have the ability and knowledge to do the job or carry out the role you're counting on. You wouldn't go to a general practitioner for brain surgery. The knowledge base and level of ability required to successfully complete the surgery wouldn't exist. For parents and community members to develop trust in the educational process, they must see visible examples of teachers and administrators who are knowledgeable and able to successfully complete their jobs. Outcome is obviously important in measuring the success of the educational system and the competence of those doing the work. Trust in another's ability develops over time. Parents begin to trust a teacher when they see that their children are happy at school and achieving. Communication between home and school provides parents with awareness of what is going on in their children's classrooms.

Principals responsibly ensure that all teachers on staff receive training in effective teaching strategies, actively engage in curriculum development and acquire knowledge about the state standards. Balanced staff development programs are essential for keeping all teachers current and growing in their teaching skill. Check out your school's staff development program to get a sense of how your children's teachers are trained. Is the program based on the latest research showing the most effective techniques? Is there consistent training throughout the school year? Are you pleased with the teaching that is occurring in your children's classroom? A principal who wishes to create strong bonds of trust between school and home must demonstrate that first-rate teaching occurs in every classroom of that school. He must support, encourage, and monitor his teachers working to improve their teaching skills and deliver sound educational programs. It takes time for a school to develop a reputation for excellence in teaching. Hard work, consistency, monitoring, feedback and making changes contribute to the process. Once schools develop a positive reputation, it continues to take hard work and constant evaluation to continue the forward movement. Trust builds over time, but can be easily destroyed in one instance of loss of focus. Mistrust comes forward much more easily than trust. Educators must remember that they have a daily responsibility to demonstrate the excellence, in their teaching, in order to continue building positive relationships with parents.

Bridges of trust must intentionally be built between teachers and administration and between teachers and their peers within the school. Teachers will form trusting relationships with their principals when they see that the administrators know what they're talking about, understand interpersonal dynamics and demonstrate their ability to serve as school leaders. It's very difficult to believe and trustingly accept a principal's evaluation of your performance if he doesn't know what he's doing. Principals who are lacking in basic administrative and leadership skills lead many of our schools today. Teachers in these schools often feel that they are operating on their own with their primary support and feedback coming from their peers. They don't trust the leadership so they stay away from the principal as much as possible. Teaching is still a profession where it's possible for a teacher to close his door and keep the outside world at bay. This is not desirable, but occurs in schools with weak leadership. Students and teachers pay the price for weak leadership in a school. Therefore, we must train and employ leaders for our schools who will understand how to build trust between and among all segments of the school community. This is the only way that significant change will occur. When teachers trust their principal, they are more likely to make changes, perform to higher standards, assume school-wide leadership roles, and develop trusting relationships with other segments within their school community. In schools where trust and respect exist, teachers will do just about anything the principal asks in order to forward the mission of the school and achieve its goals. The principal will find every way in which to support the teachers in their work of teaching all their students to achieve mastery. Schools where teachers trust the principal, and vice-versa, are motivating centers of learning and growth for everyone. Principals constantly develop strategies to support the teachers. Teachers grow in their skills as they stretch themselves to new heights. Students are the ultimate winners in this scenario because they attend a school where all segments of the community work diligently on their behalf.

Schools where teachers actively collaborate hum with excitement, new challenges, and innovation. They are centers of self-exploration and risk-taking in which teachers find ways to be more effective in their work. All segments of a school community must develop at least basic levels of confidence with one another if a school is to become high achieving. The hard work of trust building requires diligence and sensitivity. A school will only be as strong as the bonds of trust that develop between and among all members of the school community. If there are weak links in the organizational circle, the whole will be weakened. Consistent and inspirational leadership sets the tone and introduces the pace of growth. Find the teacher or principal whom no one trusts and you'll find the weak links in the organization. Educators who demonstrate their ability to do the job at hand create connections with parents and other educators that ultimately build exceptional learning programs in schools.

The final facet of building trust is strength. Recognizing another's strength of character is key to working with him and allowing him into our lives. Strength of character reflects upon the core values held by an individual. When another person holds the same or similar core values as we do, there is a higher probability that trust will form. On the other hand, if we don't share core values, we're less likely to form firmly trusting relationship. Therefore, it's essential that all members of a school community work closely to define, agree upon and communicate their shared vision and core values for the education of the students and the operation of the school. People who hold radically differing viewpoints may or may not be able to be absorbed in a meaningful way into the school community. Often differing viewpoints can be quite healthy and push us to look at other options. However, if educators hold radically differing values regarding the work of the school, it might be difficult to find common ground.

The strength of character possessed by a colleague is perhaps best demonstrated and tested in difficult situations. Those people whom we see go through one challenge after another and maintain their dignity and belief in self and life's purpose inspire us with their strength. We come to trust that this inner strength, which we've seen demonstrated in so many situations, will be present in our interactions with that person. This creates feelings of trust toward that individual. We come to rely on another's inner strength in both personal and professional situations because it provides us with the will and ability to move through difficult times, maintaining our own sense of possibility and desire to succeed. Parents, too, recognize the character trait of strength in teachers and administrators, knowing they will serve as excellent role models for their children as they proceed through the educational process. Relying on a principal's or a colleague's strength of character means we can trust that there is a safe place for us to alight during our own personal challenges and difficult times. Knowing that someone may be able to assist us helps to alleviate some of the fears that arise in new or difficult situations. Strength of character can easily be modeled and shared. The more positive impact we have on other people's lives the more they will try to find out what we do or have that works so well. Demonstrated inner strength is like a beacon shining in the darkness. It awakens our senses, provides direction, and leaves us feeling just a little safer than we did before we encountered it.

Reliability, truth, ability and strength are four routes toward building trusting relationships. When you hold a firm belief in a colleague's reliability, truthfulness, abilities, and strength of character, bonds of trust are usually formed. If you wish to become an individual whom others trust, work on these areas. You'll not only build your own bridges of trust but will help others, throughout the school community, do the same. In this way, you'll facilitate more focused and meaningful relationships, leading to better teaching and more successful learning.

Trust is so fundamental to the educational process that schools where trust is absent have no possibility to achieve the measure of success required of them. Schools bereft of trust are unable to build the type of lasting relationships that lead to formation of supportive community. Schools without community lack meaningful connections needed to ultimately create unified purpose of thought and action. Trust is a cornerstone upon which to build a successful school.

The following four strategies build trusting relationships:

1. Walk your talk and know what you're talking about.

2. Treat everyone respectfully and with kindness.

3. Establish seamless communication systems.

4. Help others recognize and utilize their talents to achieve success.

....

Strategy # 1 - Walk Your Talk and Know What You're Talking About

Action Steps:

- visit classrooms, the cafeteria and other "hot spots" throughout the day

- determine a specific purpose for your informal observations – e.g. student interactions

- stay abreast of best practices and new research in your field

- say "I don't know" if you don't and then find out the answer

- think about what you say or commit to before you speak

There is no quicker way to let others know you're trustworthy than to be it. This requires consistency, focus, self-knowledge, compassion, and action. Yes, actions do speak louder than words. Words following upon actions become very powerful in the moment and in building future structures of trust. After repeatedly demonstrating that we do walk our talk, our words take on greater importance. Leaders build their leadership capacity by modeling, saying what they know and then demonstrating more modeling to keep the cycle spiraling to ever deeper levels of being. In this way, reputation and trust are formed. Principals enhance their ability to reach goals in schools through developing trusting relationship with all members of the school community. This should be a major focus of any new administrator entering a school. Trust is the most important factor leading to effective leadership. It's not a technique that can be implemented quickly and slickly. It develops over time and is based on minute-by-minute, day-after-day actions and words of the principal. Those who would try to shortcut this process will find themselves, at some point, up against a wall of skepticism and discover how hard it is to regroup in order to once again head in a positive direction. It can easily take at least one school year for an administrator new to a school to begin to build the depth of trusting relationships with staff that so powerfully move the school forward. There will be many slips and backward slides along this path of relationship building. The faint of heart should not be in leadership roles as this precarious path is littered with good intentions that fell by the wayside as disagreements and fears created barriers to the formation of trust.

There are many simple, but often time consuming, actions that school leaders can follow to demonstrate that they walk their talk. Visibility is a key to successful leadership and trust building. Staff members who experience the involvement of the principal on a daily basis begin to form a relationship with their leader. Principals should visit every classroom each day, greeting kids and checking in with teachers. Leaders know what's going on in all areas of the school because they are everywhere and pay attention to what they see and to what they are told. They ask questions and watch behaviors. It's easy for principals to get buried behind stacks of paperwork in their office and rarely pop their heads out to see what's going on at the school. The "paperwork principal" often becomes a shadow figure in the school, appearing occasionally, but not really making any significant contacts. It's hard for teachers to build trust with a leader who isn't present, doesn't really know what they're doing, and hasn't taken the time to get to know them personally. Many well-intentioned paperwork principals wonder why the staff isn't warmer toward them or is skeptical or unwilling to go along with their suggestions. This shouldn't puzzle anyone. Human beings desire to be known, respected, listened to, and valued. If a leader rarely sees his teachers in the classroom or seldom confers with them, these important bonds won't form.

Effective principals get a lot of exercise walking around their schools. This visible time spent in the classrooms and other school centers is more valuably spent when it's focused. Although the principal casually touches base and greets teachers, the more serious role of leadership demands a focus on the academic program and teaching interactions with students. Principals often walk through the school with specific intentions – e.g. to notice student interaction in the hallways, to see how many teachers are actively and directly engaged with students. Intention and purpose go hand-in-hand to assist the principal in using his time most effectively. Principals demonstrate that they walk their talk through focused visibility.

The second important component of walking your talk is knowing what you're talking about. A leader may have a good match between what he says and what he does. However, if he has a weak knowledge base, doesn't know education and leadership as strongly as he should, there will be a credibility gap that prevents the formation of trusting relationships. School principals can't sit idly by and let their skills or knowledge become outdated. In order to be an effective leader, the principal must continually work to improve his knowledge base and skill level. A principal who works diligently to keep abreast of all that is happening in the educational arena serves as a strong role model for the teachers in the areas of training and staff development. It's also OK for a principal to say he doesn't have all the answers or know everything. Demonstrating his humanness is part of what makes a leader so trusted. We can much more closely identify with someone who experiences the same challenges that we do. Teachers develop respect and trust for their leaders who demonstrate that they know what makes for good teaching and how best to support teachers in successfully performing their jobs. Leaders who walk their talk, know their subject matter and successfully communicate this to teachers are well-respected and inspiring to staff. One of the quickest ways in which principals can institute change and build a culture of trust, within a school, is to walk their talk every minute of every day. There is always someone watching. The same principles hold true for teachers serving as role models for their students. Most young children are naturally trusting of the adults in their lives. However, as they get older, children become more skeptical. They carefully notice whether the actions of adults match their words. Older students will not hesitate to point out to a teacher that he's not doing what he said he'd do. They challenge others when their words and actions don't match. Being authentic through walking your talk is an important life skill to teach our students.

Strategy # 2 - Treat Everyone Respectfully and with Kindness

Action Steps:

- perform a conscious act of kindness each day
- establish classroom and school recognition programs to reinforce those who show kindness and respect to others
- look for and acknowledge the best in others
- treat yourself with respect and kindness
- teach your students that being kind is altruistic rather than self-serving

People are inherently good and capable and wish to be treated respectfully and with kindness. The human spirit, strong and courageous, seeks acceptance and honor for being. Teachers will tell you that they can reach any child through kindness and respect, accepting that student for who he is and what he has to offer the world. Some come more slowly to this place of trust because of past negative experiences, but they can all arrive there over time. One person connecting to another is fundamental to our individual and collective successes. It seems a very simple suggestion to ask that every person be treated with kindness and respected for their personhood. However, we all see daily examples of people treating others in mean, disrespectful and unkind ways. Insulting and judgmental words, hurtful actions, and personal put-downs all negatively impact relationships and individual advancement.

Respect and kindness are first learned in the home and reinforced as the child grows to school age. The school setting is an appropriate practice field for building and nurturing relationships, providing diverse interactions with others. Teachers are important role models to their students in the areas of showing kindness and treating others with respect. Students watch every action a teacher makes, especially noting those interactive experiences between teacher and student. Kids copy the language and actions that teachers and parents use. One little slip up by parents, teachers or principals can send a powerfully negative message that isn't soon forgotten. Adults must be so careful about the messages they send through their words and actions.

While adults tend to be more consistent in treating children with respect and kindness, this often isn't the case among the adults themselves. You can go to almost any school in this country and find examples of staff members who don't get along with each other and show very little, if any, respect or kindness toward one other. This is often the case between factions of parents and teachers. It's impossible to trust someone who treats you as an inferior person, acting in mean and spiteful ways. These negative and damaging interactions between adults in the school setting impacts the entire organization. The weakest link affects the entire group.

Students and teachers coming from varied cultures and diverse life experiences create diverse school cultures. If we expect students to treat one another with respect and kindness, these skills must be taught and modeled by each member of the school community every day. Nothing damages a student's self-esteem more than being put down for who he is, where he comes from or what he has to offer. Offensive comments or racial slurs can be extremely damaging to the psyche. Students who don't develop trust toward their peers or their teachers rarely achieve the level of excellence in school of which they are capable. Instead of focusing on their learning, they are often dealing with harassment issues and feelings of insecurity and ineptitude. We know that students who are picked on and made to feel inadequate often develop severe behavior problems that significantly and negatively impact their learning and the learning of those around them.

It's so easy to demonstrate and teach kindness. Make a vow to perform conscious acts of kindness and notice the results. Pay attention to how you feel when someone says something nice to you or performs a kind act. This is such a simple way to develop relationships and create supportive environments. So many people are so wrapped up in self that they don't often think about others. We wield power through our kind actions. Kindness should be embraced and shared for no other reason than it's the right thing to do. If we perform helpful actions for the sole purpose of having someone say, "thank you" or "you're so wonderful" to us, we may be disappointed in the outcome. There need be no attachment to outcome when performing kind actions. In teaching our children to be kind we must instill this ethic as coming from a place of goodness rather than a place of expectation. Give freely of your praise and helpful actions and you will end up blessed in many ways. But, more importantly, your family, organization and world will all be positively impacted. We all benefit when anyone with whom we are involved shows generosity toward us, and others in our group. Kindness is sown through daily small actions of ordinary people and inspires other similar actions. Kindness embraces us and helps us know that we're not alone. Support from another person encourages a return of kindness to that person, becoming the basis for friendship and close working relationships. Small acts of generosity are practiced each day by the principal and teacher who understand that there is no quicker way to build trusting relationships with staff than to respect them and treat them with the utmost kindness. Authenticity of actions will be readily apparent. Authenticity must stand behind acts of kindness and gestures of respect.

Respecting another implies honoring him for his personhood. However, respect is also built upon good character and sound actions. Typically, while working with colleagues, we come to respect another person because of his skills, actions, personality and the values for which he stands. Respect grows stronger when we see a colleague live a life of intention based on his values. In order to trust someone, we must also respect him. The two go hand-in-hand, providing mutual support. Respect is an especially important characteristic to teach in our schools because it forms the basis for healthy and safe relationships, especially among the students. Children must learn how to show respect for their peers if classrooms are to become physically and emotionally safe places for students to learn and grow. Younger students most often respect other students because the adults tell them to. However, as they get older, children begin to respect their peers because of what they see them do. These feelings of respect are not always built upon positive actions. They are often built upon negative activities in which the peers are involved. It is up to the adults to present opportunities for respect to grow among students based on actions that match positive societal values. Educators should honor students who do the right thing. These students ought to be the leaders that other students emulate. School programs that support and encourage students to respect their peers are an essential part of the curriculum. Schools in which students get along with one another and their teachers are less likely to have harassment issues and behavior problems. Accepting that everyone is different and has unique skills to share is a core premise of education.

Respectful relationships must exist at all levels of the school organization, especially between teachers and principal. It is the unified intention and actions of the teachers and administration working together that ultimately creates the successful end result of student mastery in the classrooms. Teachers can be great teachers and do a good job in the classroom without respecting their principal. Administrators can lead a school and not respect every teacher. However, in the absence of respect, school climate lacks the cohesiveness necessary to ensure overall excellence. Therefore, it is imperative that the leader of a school begins to develop trusting relationships with teachers as quickly as possible. He accomplishes this goal through developing shared values, getting to know one another, showing consistency in actions, demonstrating genuine caring and practicing constructive and clear communication. Respect for another person grows over time and becomes the foundation for trust. Schools without respectful and trusting relationships seethe with fear, judgment and feelings of lack. Teachers and administrators who respect and trust one another will work tirelessly to accomplish their shared goals. Students who respect other students and staff will form meaningful, supportive and caring relationships.

Strategy # 3 – Establish Seamless Communication Systems

Action Steps:

- respond openly rather than defensively
- clarify misunderstandings immediately
- recognize that you may have something new to learn from every conversation
- choose your words for positive impact rather than for destructive purposes

- give your students practice in debating or discussing differing opinions

If I am to respect and trust you, I must know you. The best way to get to know another person is through communicating with him. Seamless communication flows smoothly and effortlessly. All segments of the school community must develop effective ways to communicate with each other. Successful communication strategies seem simple, but they actually take focus and intention. One of the most useful strategies is listening. Listen, listen, listen. Pay attention to what people say and what they don't, say but might imply with their body language. Listen for their emotion behind the words. Emotion communicates abundant information. Listen to understand the speaker, rather than to form your response. Give straightforward and useful feedback when asked or when it seems important to do so. Word choice is another powerful strategy. Use words to support and encourage rather than to wound and harm. Never choose words that put down or humiliate. Our choice and use of words powerfully impacts our lives and the lives of those with whom we come into contact. We ought to pay more attention to our words and the intention behind those words than anything else we do in the communication area. Teachers are particularly influential with their students through the words they use, setting the tone for our classrooms and schools. Words can create safe or fearful environments for learning and working. Reactive responses often occur because we didn't stop and think before speaking.

Educators are usually cognizant of the fact that harsh words, directed toward students, may cause harm. It isn't always recognized that this same fact holds true in communicating with other teachers, parents or administrators. Adults may be wounded by words as easily as are children. Careless comments, gossip and ugly confrontations all lead to an environment with an absence of respect and trust. Communication systems between teachers and their peers and between teachers and administrators develop over time and take much hard work. Daily contact, if only briefly, is both informative and necessary. Talk to your colleagues every day and touch base with the principal. Make your thoughts known. Participate in decision-making. Take a stand. Clearly speak your ideas and beliefs. Be heard so that others may come to know you better. Be willing to risk questions, criticisms and comments when you step forward and communicate openly and honestly. Show kindness and respect when communicating difficult issues to another person. Communicate to create not to destroy.

Communication is just as important over contentious issues as it is in positive times. In fact, school staffs that are able to openly, honestly and respectfully communicate with each other during difficult times and through disagreements, develop the ability to collaboratively work on any issue. An environment that supports each person having a voice in the important issues, and being listened too with understanding, allows diverse thoughts and ideas to enrich the decision-making process. It also creates deeper understanding and feelings of greater purpose and personal power. Most people desire to work in a setting that allows them a safe space in which to voice their opinions. Schools, as centers of learning and discovery, ought to be beacons of open and respectful communication between people. Students and teachers should feel absolutely safe and free to ask questions, say what they think, and share diverse opinions. Step forward to co-create communities where open, honest, and respectful communication sets the standard for all interactions.

Seamless communication implies a smooth and effortless exchange of words and ideas. Educators who work in environments of seamless communication don't worry about others being defensive. They expect that they'll be listened to completely and without personal agenda. Voicing their opinions is expected and welcomed. Communication gives and takes. It's backed by respect for diversity and belief in human compassion. It's seamless because the various factions blend so well together into an interactive whole providing more strength than its individual parts. Individuals come to trust one another in relationships that develop through clear communication.

Strategy #4 - Help Others Recognize and Utilize Their Talents to Achieve Success

Action Steps:

- spend time getting to know your colleagues beyond the surface level

- be a cheerleader for other's efforts, accomplishments and hurdles overcome

- see the good in every person and respond to it

- provide constant feedback to students and teachers as they learn more about themselves

- encourage your teachers to try new things and expand their repertoire of skills

Exploring our interests, learning about ourselves, recognizing areas of strength, and bringing our giftedness and purpose into the world are at the core of human existence. There is no cause more important to the human heart than to determine why we're here and to feel satisfaction and fulfillment in our work and our relationships. We all travel on the life-long journey toward self-fulfillment. The path looks different for each person. Some will travel on altruistic paths, others on roads of greed and self-service. Some move with breakneck speed, others with slow precision. The need to participate on this journey is an inescapable truth about life. What does this have to do with building trust in relationships and creating great schools? Since life journeying to discover purpose is such a significant part of our lives, those people who assist us on this important self-discovery process, play a meaningful role in our explorations. Individuals, who support our growth, may serve as catalysts for this exploration to advance. They provide the necessary encouragement and feedback that allow forward movement. We come to respect and trust those people who aid us on this search for self.

Principals who wish to build trusting relationships with their staff do so by spending time getting to know the individual. Insight is gained through personal and professional conversations, formal and informal observations of the teaching process, and identifying those skills and talents that are embodied and demonstrated by an individual staff member, both in the classroom and throughout the school. Getting to know someone more deeply should not be viewed as a manipulative tool but rather a natural part of community building. Every principal should provide feedback that will assist the teacher to continuously improve his skill set and knowledge base. A visionary leader will see areas of strength that the teacher doesn't recognize or plays down as insignificant. Principals, who recognize the unique talents and skills of their teachers, provide specific feedback about what they see. Next, they encourage the teachers to utilize their unique skills to improve their teaching. If they are already using these talents, they are acknowledged for doing so and encouraged to continue to build upon them. If certain skills remain dormant or unrecognized, the principal often sets up situations that will support the teacher in trying out these new areas. Finally, an insightful administrator once again provides feedback to the teacher during the learning process of trying out new skills or honing those that have been underutilized. Administrative support, during the "trying out something new period," is a major factor in teacher's willingness to participate in the change process.

What occurs at the most fundamental level in the relationship between administrator and teacher is rather simple on the surface. The principal uses his leadership skills to identify talent in a teacher, discusses specific insights with the teacher, encourages skills application in the teacher's daily classroom life, supports the teacher's efforts to live into these new skills, and provides new opportunities and support for personal and professional growth. Building solid relationships with teachers ought to be a natural role played by all administrators in order to support the implementation of meaningful educational experiences in every classroom. The real effects of this administrative role are felt at the deepest levels of the human heart and psyche. Teachers grow to trust a principal who holds personal and professional growth and well being as the purpose for their interactions. Teachers want their administrators to support their professional lives and their personhood in a respectful, non-intrusive and honest manner. Teachers grow personally through their professional lives. Therefore, the principal who supports his teacher's professional growth, through application of their personal skills and talents, forwards the goal of creating a school environment capable of providing academic challenges to its students. I will have the utmost respect and trust in a colleague who is interested in knowing who I am, assists me in my personal and professional journeys, encourages me to be better than I am, and gives me feedback that recognizes my growth and achievement. It's called focused and informed caring between two human beings. When this level of professional relationship exists between principal and teacher, teacher and teacher, teacher and student, and student and student, there is positive impact on the teaching in the classroom. Teachers hold the key to student success. Administrators best support and impact student success through their relationships with their teachers. Respect and trust are built one step at a time through purposeful and honest relationships.

2. LEADERSHIP

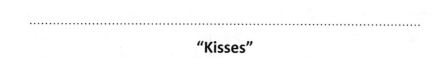

"Kisses"

THE SKILL AND depth of a leader are measured in the small ordinary encounters and events that crowd each school day as well as in the high-level, serious decisions and complex interactions that occur when working in such a person-rich environment. Communication underlies a leader's success. Leadership skills are learned and honed along the way. Here are a few I learned through every-day, ordinary encounters and complex interactions with extraordinary people.

Vignette # 1

I have discovered, during my many years as a principal, that chocolate is a powerful leadership tool. I noted this most clearly when I became principal of a school in Arizona. I took over at a school where teachers felt disheartened, older students disrupted classes, dissatisfied parents pulled their kids out of the school, and chaos was the tone of the campus. The members of the school community decidedly needed some attention from a caring leader. Little did I know, when I undertook this challenging principal's job that my leadership skills would grow through a chocolate connection. It all started because I have a sweet tooth and like chocolate. I brought a large crystal bowl to school, filled it with silvery Hershey kisses, and set it on my desk. Hershey kisses seemed perfect because they would allow me to grab a couple on the run and nibble them as I walked to a classroom or meeting. That burst of sugar and mouthwatering, chocolate delight was the perfect pick me up. The elegant crystal bowl provided a lovely, glittering elegant focus to my desk. It tended to draw people's eyes, thus removing the emphasis on all the piles of unfinished work, detailed phone messages and the lengthy things-to-do list that blended together in one un-ending jumble of leadership tasks.

I had intended to share the chocolate, of course. If I had brought it just for my own simple pleasures, I would have left the tiny morsels in their crinkly, plastic bag, deep in the back of my deepest, darkest desk drawer where no one else would discover them. However, in the interest of friendliness and not wishing to gain too much extra weight, I proudly placed them in their elegant container at the corner of my desk, which most people approached upon entering my office. It was clear to any casual observer that the chocolate was set out so that all could easily share it with me. I thought it would be a nice gesture of friendliness and caring, which had been so lacking in the previous administration.

Soon after pouring the silvery morsels into their lovely container, my secretary came into the office. "Would you sign these papers? I need to fax them to the administration…" Her eyes alighted upon the shiny kisses, leaving her momentarily speechless. A glowing smile creased her face as she beheld the glittering treasures. "May I have one?" she asked.

"Of course. Help yourself at any time. These are here for everyone to share."

She gingerly chose a kiss, pulled on the little slip that said Hersheys, carefully unwrapped it, popped it into her mouth, closed her eyes and said, "Mmmmmm," as the chocolate melted on her tongue.

"Take a couple with you for later," I said.

"Thanks, I will. These are so good! They're just what I needed." My secretary picked up a few kisses and began walking out of the room.

"What about the papers for me to sign?"

"Oh, I almost forgot," she said, handing the papers to me.

Later, during recess time, I was returning phone calls when the secretary popped her head around the corner. "There are two first graders who were fighting on the playground. Can you see them now?"

"Sure. Send them in." Two tousled little boys, Wil and James, ambled into my office. Wil wore smudged dirt on his face that had captured his teardrops as they ran down his cheek. James had a bright red handprint across his right cheek. "OK. I'll give you each a turn to tell me what happened. Don't talk if it's not your turn. James, you may start."

"I was running to catch the kickball when Wil jumped right in front of me and tripped me on purpose. Then he grabbed the ball. When I tried to take it away from him, he slapped me on the cheek," he said, rubbing his reddened cheek. I was about to ask for Wil's version, when I noticed that James had spied the bowl of chocolate temptations. "Could I have a piece of candy?" he asked in a polite and sincere manner while his eyes stayed focused on the bowl so abundantly filled with goodies.

"Wil, you were sent here for fighting. Do you think I should reward you with chocolate?"

"What if I promise not to fight anymore? Could I have some chocolate if I promise?"

Maybe I should have hidden the chocolate before these boys entered the office. "No, you can't have any today. If you two have good behavior at recess tomorrow, you may come in and have a piece."

Both boys beamed as they looked at the bowl and then one another. I thought that I shouldn't use chocolate for a bribe, but maybe that wasn't a bad idea after all. We settled the dispute and the boys left, without their chocolate. Of course, they didn't forget about my offer. They showed up the next day, at the end of recess, to claim their reward. Word apparently got out because primary students began to ask me if they could come to visit my office and have a piece of candy.

Later that afternoon, I met with Mary, a middle school teacher who was having a difficult time with one of her middle school students. He was disruptive in class and defiant toward her when she spoke to him. Mary was in tears when she related the stressful daily encounters she had been having with this challenging student. When she first began relating the behavior problems with him, Mary took a Hershey kiss from the crystal bowl, tore off the wrapper and crunched it into a tight little silver ball. She continuously rolled the silver wrapper between her fingers into an ever-tighter ball. Mary ate the chocolate as she continued telling me about her interactions with the troubled student. I noticed that in the course of our fifteen-minute meeting, Mary ate five Hershey kisses! I don't think she was even aware that she had eaten them, as she continued rolling the little silver balls around in her palm. After we decided on a plan for working with this student, Mary stood up to leave.

"Thank you. I feel so much better now that we have a strategy for working through this situation." Mary looked down at her open palm and seemed surprised to see the silver wrappings. She looked at me quizzically. "Oh, thanks for the candy. I really needed it!"

"Take a couple more with you," I suggested. Mary grabbed a few more kisses before she left the office. It was the end of my first day with the crystal candy bowl on my desk and it was nearly empty! Within the first few days, of so openly providing the chocolate temptation to all takers, word had spread throughout the teaching staff. From that day forward, teachers and staff members would quickly run into my office, say "hi" when I was there, grab a few chocolates and be on their way. I could also tell that they enjoyed the chocolate when I wasn't in the office as the declining level of kisses was evident when I'd return after being gone for a few hours.

The Hershey kisses seemed to take on a life of their own. They came to symbolize my open-door policy that said, "all are welcome at any time." Since this was a radically different message than the one sent by the previous principal, it made an important statement to the teachers, parents and students. Sharing candy is a friendly thing to do but it also demonstrates caring and an interest in the well being of another. The shining, crystal candy bowl soon became an important leadership tool for me as I began to gage the stress level of the teachers with how quickly the candy disappeared. On those days when the entire bowl emptied out, I knew staff felt stressed. I needed to be visible and communicating with them to find out what was going on and to offer my assistance on those days. The bowl of kisses proved to be a very accurate monitoring tool. I also gained a positive reputation for my caring attitude as evidenced by supplying the staff with Hershey kisses as well as my other good leadership skills! The importance and power of this sharing and caring message was demonstrated to me that first year on my birthday. My secretary greeted me when I arrived that sunny January morning and told me that I must sit at my desk from 9:00-9:30. At precisely 9:00 am, a long line of kindergarteners began streaming through my office. Each tiny hand held a Hershey kiss, some more squashed than others! As they walked through, each student set his kiss carefully on my desk and wished me happy birthday. Many also hugged me. Following the kindergarten students came the first graders, then the second, followed by the third. Eventually, six hundred students, from kindergarten through eighth grade, and their teachers flowed through my office that morning, each depositing a kiss and wishing me happy birthday! My desktop glittered! My spirit soared! Simple gestures touch the heart and make powerful statements.

Vignette # 2

"You can't have your office here," said Janice, the secretary. "The principal's office has always been in this back room," she said, leading me to a large corner room at the back of the main office. I immediately hated the room. The windows were up so high that you couldn't see out. The room was away from the main flow of traffic that moved through the office. I shook my head, turned around and walked back to the sunny front room where I had decided to set up my office.

"I like this front office better," I told Janice. "These wonderful big windows will let in loads of light and allow me to see everything that's going on. Since this office is so close to the front door, teachers, parents and students can drop in when they need to. It doesn't matter that it's smaller than that other office. It will work just fine for me."

"Well, OK," she said reluctantly. "I hope you don't regret this decision. Everyone will think they can just drop in at any time to see you. That could become a nuisance."

"It will work out fine," I assured her. "Just fine." It was a month before school would open, but word of my decision to take the front office spread throughout the small town in which the school was located. Teachers and parents began to drop by to introduce themselves and to welcome me. Everyone commented upon my decision to take the front office. To them it was a sign that I wanted to be both visible and available for anyone who needed me. This decision turned out to be one of the most powerful leadership decisions I've ever made. It was my first concrete action in walking my talk at my new school.

During my first few months at the school, I focused on opening and developing the channels of communication among the staff. Teachers who initially were suspicious of my frequent visits to their classrooms soon welcomed the specific feedback and positive reinforcement I gave them. I tried to follow-through on everything that I said I would do in a timely and consistent way. I didn't have to preach my beliefs. They became apparent through my actions. By winter break of that first year, the teachers and I had developed a growing mutual respect, based on shared vision and honest interactions. Building trust was a hard, long, up-hill battle because these teachers were all so fearful of being hurt again, if they grew to trust me. Gradually, the self-imposed walls of protection began crumbling as our relationships deepened and moved forward through our personal and professional interactions. By spring of that first year, I felt the staff and I had formed a good trusting relationship and we were moving ahead to improve our programs at the school.

The slight knock on the door caused me to stop writing and look up to see who was still at school at 6:30 one evening.

"Susan, do you have a minute," asked Molly.

"Sure, come in." Molly was a senior teacher on the faculty, revered and listened to by all the teachers. She had often served as the faculty spokesperson during our initial days together before open communication lines had been established. I greatly respected Molly for both her teaching and leadership skills.

"You're here late," I said. "What's going on?" Molly moved around in her chair, trying to get comfortable. Her shoulders hunched tensely up close to her neck as she took a deep breath and let out a long sigh.

"We've got a big problem," she said, looking at me with a worried look in her eyes. I couldn't imagine what she was talking about. Everything seemed to be going so well. After seven months of working together, we were well on our way to creating a trusting environment. We had just received approval, from the school board, to hire an assistant principal. I had lobbied for this position all year and was so excited about the additional leadership capacity we'd have the following year. I knew this pivotal position would allow me to move the school more quickly toward necessary change, which would bring us closer to realizing our vision and goals.

"The word is out around school that you have a favorite candidate whom you plan to select for the assistant position. The faculty feels this is unfair and they're upset that you're not including them in the selection process. Many teachers have good reasons that they don't want your candidate in this position. The staff asked me to talk to you about this." She crumpled back into her chair as if all the air had been let out of her body.

I was stunned and initially speechless. I stared out the windows into the darkness, close to tears. What had happened to seven months of consistent relationship building and role modeling? Could all that we'd built been formed on sand that now was washing away in the tide of doubt? Fear had reared its ugly head! When fear entered, trust left.

"I don't understand this, Molly. I don't have a favorite candidate and I've already spelled out the selection procedure which includes a committee of teachers."

"All I can tell you," she said, "is that the teachers feel betrayed again by leadership. They want their voices to be heard in this decision. In fact, there are about fifteen teachers who would like to meet with you individually to share their concerns. They speak for themselves and for the teachers who hold similar opinions but don't want to come forward. The teachers don't want to criticize your choice but they do want to tell you why they feel the way they do. Thanks for listening." Molly suddenly stood up and quickly left the room.

I felt like I was in a bad dream. My gut churned as anger overcame my normally composed nature. I pounded my hand on the desk in frustration. What had just happened? What had all those months of working late every night and during weekends created? Surely, all of that effort hadn't been in vain. Where was the trust we'd formed? Was it that fragile to be so quickly and easily destroyed? Apparently it was. I grabbed my coat and keys, turned off the lights and went out into the chilly, dark night. The darkness enveloped me and seemed to penetrate into my bones. By the time I got into my car, the anger had turned to tears and I cried all the way home. I felt so alone as I sat wrapped up in a blanket on my living room floor that evening, trying to drive away the coldness that I felt in every cell in my body. I hunched over, hugging myself and sobbing through my frustration.

"Let them find someone else to deal with their fickleness!" I screamed at the walls. "I can't do anymore. I can't work any harder." If this was what all of my hard work and consistent leadership had come down to, maybe I should resign. Maybe I had made a huge mistake moving to Arizona. I had rarely felt so desolate.

I came to school reluctantly and in a bad mood the following day. Initially, I spoke with as few people as possible, closed the blinds and remained in my office all morning. Teachers avoided eye contact and hurried by when they entered the outer office. I couldn't believe how rapidly the environment had changed from one of support and collegiality to one of betrayal and gossip. What was I to do? How ought I counter this negative event? When I looked up and saw the closed blinds blocking out my awareness of what was going on, I remembered why the teachers had been so excited that I chose that front office. They thought it meant that I would be visible, transparent in my actions and available to them. I had been all of those things, consistently throughout the year. Leadership requires that the leader walk her talk, especially during difficult times. How could I fix this? What was I to do? I loved these teachers and felt sad and angry that they would so easily feel betrayed by me, question my integrity and move into a space of fear. However, I was the leader and they were looking to me now for leadership. I stood up, walked over to the floor-to-ceiling windows and opened the blinds so that I could see and be seen.

"Janice, would you please call Molly and ask her to see me when she has a break this afternoon?" Walk your talk reverberated through my mind. Just continue to walk your talk and you'll lead them and yourself through this difficult time. Molly appeared at my office door about ten minutes later. "Come in, Molly." She gave me a weak smile as she sat down.

"I appreciate you coming in last night and telling me what the teachers are feeling about the selection process. I'm really surprised that they think I have a favorite when I've in no way expressed a preference. I was hurt at first and upset. I still feel upset, but if the teachers perceive there's a problem, then there is a problem. I'm sending a memo out detailing the selection process. However, I want to hear what those fifteen teachers have to say." I sat quietly, waiting for Molly to say something.

"I know this seems as if the teachers don't trust you but it's actually the opposite," she replied. "They feel safe enough to speak out and tell you when they think there is a problem. This is a huge risk for these teachers. In the past, they would have spread gossip and worked against you behind your back. Now, they want to be heard in an appropriate way."

"OK, Molly. I'll place a note at the bottom of this memo inviting any teacher who wishes to speak to me about the selection process to come meet privately with me. However, I won't entertain gossip or putting others down. I want to hear their concerns, expressed in a professional manner." I had always been available to these teachers and had listened with attention and caring. "Move away from your hurt feelings and anger and listen to them so you can see why and how the fear crept in," I said to myself. "This will be a turning point for the future success of this school." I pulled my mind back and looked at Molly. "What happened here, Molly?"

"Everyone has gone back to last year when things were so awful and they are reliving their feelings of betrayal and anger at being lied too. This really isn't about you."

It sure felt like it was about me! They were questioning my leadership. "Keep me informed about how the teachers feel after I meet with them."

"Thank you." said Molly. "This staff really wants to work with you to solve this problem."

I felt somewhat better after this meeting with Molly. Maybe we could work this problem out after all. During the next two days, I met individually with eighteen teachers. Each one professionally and clearly outlined their ideas about the assistant principal position. Most of them were very nervous when they entered my office. I clearly saw their fear and realized the courage it took for them to speak up "against" their principal in order to do what they thought was best for the students and the school. Most of the teachers seemed to feel better when they left the meeting, satisfied that their positions had been heard and understood. The next four weeks were spent in communicating and refining our goals and procedures for the hiring process. A committee of teachers and I hired an assistant principal four weeks later. Those were four of the toughest weeks I've experienced as a principal. I had to step aside from feeling personally attacked, be able to listen so deeply that it almost hurt and demonstrate compassionate leadership through trying to alleviate their fear and restore some modicum of trust. It has never been harder to walk my talk as a leader than in that first year crisis situation.

Leadership

Definition: *the action of leading a group of people or an organization*

Leadership is both an inherent talent and an acquired skill. Success in leadership is based on a solid and unwavering understanding and respect for people and human interactions. It grows stronger and fuller through professional and personal growth and is nourished through the empowerment of individuals and self. Good schools require effective leadership in order to grow and succeed. More effort and resources must be directed to training capable leaders both at the teacher and principal levels. The whole is only as good as its parts. Schools need every staff member to assume a leadership role to successfully manage the rapid changes that constantly bombard the system. When all members of the school community contribute fully, system-wide success is the end result.

Leadership, exhibited at all levels within the organization, leads to success. Every school that is successful has dynamic leadership guiding the school's forward movement. Effective school leaders share their influence, developing circles of power among the staff. When shared leadership is developed, nurtured, encouraged, and reward- ed, it proves to be a powerful force in school communities. School leadership is a big job requiring full participation. Excellent leaders display personal integrity, skillful communication, and knowledge in their subject area. Leaders are visionary planners as well as practical doers, combining a myriad of relationship building skills to ensure employee loyalty, collaboration and excellence on the job. They can be firm and authoritative as well as gentle and understanding. Leaders who inspire others to follow them are usually skilled in a variety of areas that allow them to " be all" to many different people.

No one can effectively assume a leadership role if she doesn't like people. A huge part of the leadership job is to inspire others toward greatness and accomplishment. A leader can force production of end results but the engenderment of loyalty comes through developing personal relationships. Coercion doesn't work in schools. Most school leaders have very limited ability to fire or dismiss personnel. Their daily work with people centers on creating honest and open relation- ships with clear and respectful communication. The school leader must be willing to show her own humanity, compassion and knowl- edge if she expects that from her staff. Role modeling plays a key role in the leadership in any organization but especially in schools where hundreds of people watch the leaders every move. This can be both intimidating and powerful.

Good schools become great schools when all segments of the school community take on leadership roles. The school principal should not be afraid to share her leadership. In fact, the only way she will have strong leadership power is if she shares it with staff mem- bers. Schools are typically understaffed and under-funded which creates great challenges for the principal and teachers. When the prin- cipal can effectively create and tap into the leadership ability of oth- ers on her staff, she'll be most successful in meeting these challenges.

Many administrators fear losing control when they give away and share power. The reality of the situation in schools is that the teachers are the true source of power within the organization. They are on the front line, in the classrooms, every day determining whether we graduate well-educated students or not. The wise principal will quickly see that she must invite staff into the leadership process and support and encourage them in their efforts. There really is no choice but to do this if the principal wishes to run a successful and supportive school. However, even with shared leadership occurring in a school, it is up to the principal to orchestrate how all the pieces flow together to create and implement the vision of the school. Schools with shared leadership but no one main leader often fall into patterns of dysfunction where all members of the organization struggle because of lack of clarity regarding specific roles and responsibilities. Schools require both a central leadership figure in the role of principal or head master or lead teacher as well as leadership that exists among staff members throughout the organization.

Teachers are the resident experts in schools. Most principals have been teachers but many haven't taught for several years. Even those principals who remain very current regarding curriculum and best teaching practices aren't functioning at the same level of expertise or specificity from which teachers operate. Most principals are generalists who know a little about a lot. Therefore, it's essential that principals rely on the expertise of their teachers to ultimately guide the school's vision and student performance within the classrooms at the school. If teachers are not involved in the leadership of the school, there may be lack of focus and the possibility for lackluster performance by both teachers and students.

Every teacher heading up a classroom is a leader. Some have better leadership skills than others. Some accept leadership roles with open arms and great enthusiasm; others stay as far away from assuming these responsibilities as they possibly can. Every principal faces the challenge of enticing both excited and reluctant leaders into the fold so that all segments of the community work together toward the shared goals of successfully educating students. It isn't necessary for all teachers to take a front-line, highly visible leadership role. Leadership opportunities exist in quiet, unobtrusive moments and situations. A teacher might observe that there aren't enough supplies to back the current reading program so she becomes active, behind the scenes, in remedying the situation. Plenty of room exists, within school organizations, for both reluctant and highly excited responses to leadership. The sensitive and wise principal will find ways in which to create leadership opportunities for all levels of participation. Most people grow in their leadership roles through practice in those roles. It's the only way to create system-wide excellence and cooperation.

Shared leadership makes the job of teaching a little less lonely because it creates support systems based on each person's role as a teacher. The art of teaching demands a teacher's time, energy, heart, patience, knowledge, and ability to stay focused on what matters in the classroom. Teachers have always naturally and openly supported each other at the same grade level, in adjoining classroom spaces, or just because they've become friends. Teachers go to one another when they have problems, concerns, frustrations and successes and are more likely to go to a colleague than they are to the principal. This fact makes it critical that teachers are trained and supported in leadership roles since they perform this function each and every day in a myriad of ways both in their classrooms and throughout the school.

Great leadership exists on all levels in a school. Shared leadership gives people a powerful voice. Most educators enter their profession because they want to change the world and make a difference in the lives of children. They do this through practicing their profession of teaching, gaining experience over the years and constantly working to improve their skill level and knowledge base. Teachers, like every other human on the earth, want to have a say in their work. After all, they've dedicated their lives to teaching. A principal would be foolish to think that she possessed all the knowledge about each grade level in her school that she needs to make sound educational decisions. It's impossible for a principal of a school to know everything she needs to know without the assistance and expertise of the teachers. Therefore, a principal who understands leadership will actively and intentionally provide teachers the opportunities through which their opinions are heard and utilized in decision making. The principal's intention must be genuine and based on respect for the teaching profession. Giving a sense of power or leadership responsibilities to a teacher, when the power isn't real, won't lead to any long-term success or build any trusting relationships so essential to shared leadership. People are personally and professionally empowered when they have a voice in their life's work that is legitimate and respected by their colleagues. Principals strive to create school environments that provide space for all voices and opinions to be heard, respected and utilized in the running of the organization. This includes students and parents as well as teachers and administrators.

We perform our best, when we find the work that we love to do and are respected and honored for who we are and what we know. The focus in schools should be on everyone performing and becoming their best. This philosophy rests at the heart of education. Parents and teachers work with children to help them determine what they do well and in which areas they might be most successful. Principals similarly should help their teachers to discover their greatest skill areas and bring them forward into the world. This is the key to improving instruction in our classrooms. Good teaching comes from highly trained, committed, and skillful teachers who feel that they have been empowered to share their gifts and talents in the fullest way possible. This seems like a simple concept but takes great diligence, on the part of the principal, to ensure that the goals of skillful teaching, possessing knowledge of content areas, building collaborative communication skills, and creating a passion for the work are constantly supported and recognized.

Strong leadership, at any level of the organization, assists people in finding their voice and expressing it freely and honestly with all members of the community. Finding voice means discovering the work about which you feel most passionate and expressing this to others both verbally and by the example of your work. Finding voice is finding self. It is expressing who you are without fear of ridicule or criticism. It is exploring all that you think you could be but may not yet have tried out. Good principals lead their teachers in finding their voice. They do this through example as well as by creating an environment where it's safe to pursue inner work regarding one's life passion. Discovering one's voice and consciously expressing it is one of the most powerful experiences we can have in life. One of the differences between a great school and a poor or average school is that in the former, teachers, parents and students have found their voice and are growing into their fullest potential as human beings.

Finding and expressing our voice leads us down a road of excellence where leadership skills come naturally and are embraced with comfort and enthusiasm. Our greatest leadership skills and abilities come forward when we participate in those areas where we feel the most passionate. When we feel passionate about something, we take chances and extend ourselves in ways that we wouldn't otherwise do. It's easier to move through fearful situations or experiences when we feel strongly about reaching a certain goal or attaining a specific objective. Leadership, whether school-wide or within smaller circles, allows us to express ourselves as teachers and leaders. Assuming a leadership role doesn't mean that a person must lead an organization or head a committee. Rather, leadership involves taking an active role in the envisioning, planning and implementing a project or activity. Smart principals will find out the topics or projects that their teachers feel passionate about and encourage the teachers to assume leadership roles in those areas. A teacher who feels great passion for History might be a good leader of the History Fair Program. Initially, this keeps the teacher in her comfort zone, but ultimately, challenges her to move forward into a different, more expanded, role. A principal, who is able to link a teacher's area of passion with an opportunity for her to express her voice in a leadership role, has strengthened the school's instructional program in many ways.

My voice clarifies and expresses my interest and passion. Interest and passion drive my motivation and personal actions. Motivation and personal actions lead to my greatest chances of success in whatever I choose to do. My leadership skills are most effective when motivation and action drive all that I choose to pursue. Therefore, it is essential that I have the chance to find and express my voice in both my personal and professional lives. Schools that aspire to excellence must work tirelessly to see that all members of the community are finding their passion and voice and expressing it openly and safely. Authoritarian leadership does not allow for this to happen. Schools with top down leadership and issues around who holds the power will never become centers where shared power and personal excellence are recognized and encouraged at all levels. Authoritarian rule often fears the power that might be assumed by staff members who enter leadership roles. Fear and loss of control often represent the driving factors that shut down any chance for shared leadership in a school. Parents checking out a new school's credibility should ask questions about power and leadership. "Do you have a leadership team? Who is on it? What leadership role do teachers play, on a daily basis, outside of the classroom?" If a school leader can't talk about shared leadership, the environment at that school may be one in which your child will not be encouraged to find her voice. What's happening on the surface level at a school is important. However, it's essential to look a little deeper and ask questions that will provide you with insight about the underlying structure of the school community.

The skillful leader stands both in the forefront and the background of decision-making. Sometimes the principal listens and observes, sometimes she actively participates, leading the way. There is a great deal for the principal to learn in her roles of listener and observer. These may be two of the most significant roles the principal plays. It is through listening and observing that the principal really gets to understand and see what is happening both on the surface and at deeper levels at the school. It's an excellent habit for a principal to touch base briefly with each teacher every day. Leadership by looking and listening provides a powerful source of information. Principals also garner much information from teachers, about pertinent issues, through quick conversations in the hallway or walking to the gym. Finding opportunities for connecting, even if only briefly, leads to better understanding and a clearer picture of what is occurring within the school, thus informing the principal's ability for more effective leadership.

Here are some steps to take if you are a principal, teacher, staff member, or parent who wants to expand your leadership role or become involved with leadership for the first time.

1. Find what motivates you and use it to accomplish your goals.

2. Step back to observe and focus your listening.

3. Remember that people come first.

4. Embrace change and take risks.

5. Develop all the skills you need to assume the responsibilities of your job.

6. Bring out the best in people.

....

Strategy # 1 - Find What Motivates You and Use It to Accomplish Your Goals

Action Steps:

- make time in your busy schedule to explore and develop your interests

- expose your students to a variety of topics and learning experiences

- incorporate what you like to do into your job

- volunteer for school committees or work groups that are focusing on issues that interest you

- find ways in which to take a leadership role in one of your areas of interest

If you wish to be a leader, it's important to enjoy the area in which you choose to lead. Assume a leadership role in an area in which you are interested and for which you have great enthusiasm and passion. Most people with leadership ability lead capably in any situation. However, we will be most effective, as leaders, and happiest if we're involved in areas that strongly motivate us each and every day. What motivates and interests you? Do you know? What do you love to do more than anything else? If there were no restrictions (e.g. lack of money, no time), what would you do with your life? Spend some time thinking about and answering these questions. The answers will give you some insight into areas in which you might be most effective as a leader.

Remember that being a leader doesn't mean you have to be a CEO or principal or president of a company. It means that you are taking an active role in guiding the change process. Playing a leading role takes on many shapes and looks different in various situations. Leaders at all levels are constantly improving and expanding their leadership roles. Becoming an effective leader requires ongoing growth, training, experience and intention. The leadership route is not always a smooth road to follow. Being a leader requires time, dedication, focus, hard work, and the commitment to work through the difficult tasks and times in order to move forward.

Teachers who wish to have more influence in their schools should become involved in those areas that directly influence the forward movement of the school. Teachers on every school staff demonstrate a great variety of strengths and interests. This diversity assists a building principal trying to build a cohesive, strong leadership team within a school. If the principal can mentor each teacher in recognizing and bringing her skills, interests, and passions forward, individual leadership roles will grow. If I have fifteen teachers each with a different area of expertise and interest, and I challenge them to become involved in supporting and promoting their area of interest for the school, I then have "expert leaders" in all those different areas. Not only am I increasing the knowledge base that will be shared, but I'm also ensuring that I will have a more highly motivated staff because they will be involved in something that drives their interest and passion. It's a win-win situation for all involved.

Teachers on a school staff, involved in leadership responsibilities, serve as role models to the students, parents, and their colleagues. Soon, more teachers begin to move into leadership roles until it is an accepted fact that being a leader is a natural role for a teacher to play in the school community. Sometimes teacher leaders come under attack from other teachers. Those who are attacking are generally teachers not involved in leadership efforts themselves. Fear and jealousy fuel their efforts to cause problems for those working as leaders. The principal must provide a work environment that supports and rewards each and every member of the school community for assuming leadership roles. Good schools have strong leaders both at the top of the organization and throughout its ranks.

Parents should also play an active leadership role in their child's school although they aren't as directly involved as the teaching staff. Once again, finding areas of interest and expertise will help parents find the spots in schools where they most effectively contribute. Parental input and support is essential to teachers and the principal who are creating a safe and supportive school environment where students and teachers meet with success. Schools that offer a full-range of student activities need parental involvement and leadership to facilitate all of these extra activities. A full school program requires widespread community support. The wise principal will find ways to utilize the abundant energy and expertise offered by parents. Parents who feel passionate about a topic or event happening at the school will work tirelessly to ensure that all comes together for that to occur. Parents have a great deal of passion and interest in the schools because they know the importance of a good education for their children. Parental involvement expands what teachers and principals do in the class-rooms and throughout the school. Administrators and teachers who choose not to involve parents in leadership roles make a huge miscal-culation that will not only impact individual classrooms, but also the operation of the entire school.

The ideal school community would have each segment of that community engaged in work that they love and feel passionate about pursuing. This would not only ensure an active and dynamic learning environment for all members of the community (students, parents, staff, administration) but would also greatly enhance each person's personal life. The beauty in helping students, teachers and parents tap into their areas of interest and expertise is that it helps them develop both professionally and personally. We want to continually improve the skills and knowledge base of our teachers. However, when we're able to engender people's involvement through their areas of interest, we also expect that they grow on the personal level. This combina-tion of professional and personal growth forms a power base both for the individual and the organization. Ultimately, when people make personal change and move forward with their lives, this also directly and dramatically impacts their professional life. The two cannot be separated. The fact that almost every professional interaction humans have with one another involves a personal encounter indicates the importance of tapping into and strengthening the personal side.

Ignite someone's interest on the personal level and you will discov-er her strongest area of leadership on the professional level. This work can be fun for a principal as she derives great joy in seeing adults and children find something they love to do that contributes to their com-munity and makes them feel good about themselves in the process. It seems like such a simple concept to buy into yet many administrators and teachers don't see it or realize its power. Creating a school community where all members engage in work that drives their passion is an awesome sight. Leaders should be working day and night to create these highly energized schools. Unfortunately, with the focus on teaching to a high stakes test, we are doing the opposite in so many of our schools by squashing teacher's efforts to work with their areas of interest and discouraging them from following their passion. Our children, their teachers, and society will ultimately pay a great price for this loss of leadership capacity.

Commitment is an important characteristic that usually accompanies people following their interests and passion, serving as a driving force that motivates them to accomplish tasks and bring their goals into reality. Commitment brings the personal edge to any project and / or assumed task. Personal drive becomes professional drive. Schools traditionally lack resources in all areas of operation. Teachers, parents and administrators, who are committed to creating a great school, fill in many of these gaps by sheer determination, driven by their level of dedication and commitment to the children and to education. Most of us are willing to fully commit to projects in which we strongly believe. That is not always the case with tasks for which we have no interest and in which we don't want to be involved. Therefore, if we wish to garner the strong commitment of members of the school community, we must engage them on the personal level. Their strongest and most lasting contributions will come through their personal commitment.

Strategy # 2 - Step Back to Observe and Focus Your Listening

Action Steps:

- develop an awareness of all that surrounds you by watching and listening

- watch a person's body language for clues to his or her current frame of mind

- teach your students, through role playing, to step out of the center of situations and learn to observe other's actions and re-actions

- practice the subtleties of knowing when to take charge or step back and let others be in control

- learn to listen from a completely objective place

Some powerful and forceful leaders stand in the forefront all the time, controlling and remaining in charge. A truly effective leader will be seamless in how she fits into the school scene at any given time. It isn't always necessary, nor desirable, for the principal to be out in front and in charge. Many times a more powerful and useful technique is to stand back and observe. A leader can use the powerful tools of observation and listening for expanding her leadership capacity. This holds true whether you're the leader of a school, a classroom, a committee, your family or any other group. A leader who is always front and center stage misses most of the meaningful action taking place behind the scenes.

Since leadership focuses on human relationships, it makes sense to pay attention to interactions among people. The principal, who plays a keen observer of people and their actions, will be a stronger leader because she'll have a better understanding of what motivates people in any given situation. A principal should do a visual check-in with members of her staff every day, briefly acknowledging their presence. The body language and personal appearance of teachers will tell the administrator a great deal about the teacher's frame of mind for that school day. Those teachers who appear to be in a less-than-good space can then be given whatever type of extra support would be helpful to them for that day. This personal connection lets the teachers know that their principal is interested in them, what they're doing and how they're feeling.

Typically, in meetings and other interactions at schools, principals stand out in a leading and sometimes domineering role. In schools where teachers practice shared leadership, principals can stand back and strategically watch the interactions among staff members. This can also happen in schools that don't practice shared leadership and can give the principal clues as to why teachers aren't assuming leadership roles. Watching people interact with their colleagues and with students and parents provides valuable information about their strengths and vulnerabilities. The observing principal will more often find ways to assist teachers because she'll have a clearer understanding of what they value and where their fears or concerns might lie. Principals must know and understand staff members in order to help them to become the best teachers possible. Teachers tend not to brag too much about their efforts and successes. It's up to the principal and other teachers to recognize and acknowledge the individual contributions teachers bring forward. Positive staff moral grows when teachers are recognized and acknowledged for all that they do, especially the small day-to-day efforts that so often go undetected by administration. Teachers, who receive kudos and appreciation from their administrators for the daily small tasks they do so well, will build stronger and longer lasting loyalty to those leaders.

Noticing details and small efforts serves the savvy principal very well. It is in the details that we really get to know the people with whom we work. If you're a leader, practice standing back and watching, consciously taking a few minutes to get out of the rushing mode to look around you. What is going on? How are individual teachers interacting with one another, with parents, with their students? Did you pick up some fear in a teacher's explanation of what they think should happen in a particular situation? Will a teacher's unusually disheveled look cause you to spend a few minutes talking to her to see what's going on, in order to give her support? When you're in a meeting with staff or parents, do you sit back and observe how the meeting is progressing even as you lead it? Paying conscious attention reveals an enormous amount of information that can be used to more effectively work with people, providing the leader with insight about possible points of contention or areas of stress. With this type of knowledge, leaders are able to lead more effectively and create a supportive and caring work environment at the same time.

Seamless leadership can fade in and out of prominence at any time and with any group of people. The effective leader is both strong and forceful and yet, soft and yielding. Great leadership blends both strength and gentleness. The art comes in knowing when to assume which stance. It takes great strength to yield and be soft and requires insightful knowing when to be authoritative and powerful. Leadership is a selfless ebb and flow of power, making it imperative for a leader to move away from concentrating primarily on her interests and focus more on the needs of the organization and the people within that organization. Out-of-control ego shatters leadership. The principal must remain mindful that her job of steward helps others to bring their leadership talents forward for the good of all.

Assisting others in their professional and personal growth is one of the most wonderful and powerful roles that a leader plays in a school or in any organization. It's truly an honor and a great responsibility to be in a role that gives you the opportunity to assist others in becoming their very best. Humility accompanies strong leadership. Selfless leaders understand that just because they're the person in charge doesn't mean they're the most important person. The school principal who takes on the job with the belief that she is in that position to help lead every member of the school community (students, parents, teachers, support staff, administrators) to develop and utilize their greatest skill areas will create wonderful opportunities for that to actually happen throughout the school. It is an awesome and humbling responsibility. The knowledgeable leader recognizes that brilliant and gifted individuals surround her, each trying to find the most effective way for self-expression. What a challenge and wonderful opportunity to be a leader charged with the responsibility for bringing individual giftedness forward!

The principles of standing back and observing apply to everyone who assumes a leadership role of any kind. It's not just for school administrators. Teachers, parents and students in leadership roles will benefit from following this strategy. Teacher leaders have just as much of a challenge as school leaders in effectively carrying this principle forward because they are so busy. When you're always rushing to the next task, it's difficult to pause, if even momentarily, and become the observer. However, observing requires only a few minutes of your focus. We miss so many nuances and small clues to a person's behavior and attitude because we're not paying attention. The speed of life pulls us into its frantic flow and we move along in a mindless way, reacting as we go. It's time to become mindful as leaders and pay attention to what we see as we're pulled into the fast stream of our job responsibilities. Slow down! It takes a conscious and intentional effort to pay attention. Begin the practice of acting intentionally today and one day observing your surroundings and the people who are present will become habitual. When that occurs, you will have taken a great leap in enhancing your leadership skills. Slow down. Pay attention. Think. Respond. Acknowledge.

Another way to gain insight into a peer's state of being is through listening. School leaders who master focused listening learn more in depth information about others. Calm and focused listening is one of the greatest gifts that individuals can give to one another. All people want to be heard and understood. Taking time to really listen shows that the listener values the person she is listening to and respects what is being said. When we listen to another person, in a focused way, we intentionally try to understand her point of view. This is more challenging in situations where the speaker has opinions that we don't agree with or understand. Our listening should be directed toward understanding not toward agreement. It doesn't always matter if we agree with someone else, but it does matter if we are really able to hear what she believes about a situation or topic.

Focused listening provides space for individuals to find their voices within their work setting. When an environment exists in which people are truly listened to and acknowledged for their ideas and skills, a safe place for expressing one's voice is created. In such environments, it is acceptable to have differing ideas and opinions and not be criticized for them. The most effective organizations have active dialogue among their staff members where it's expected that differing viewpoints will be expressed and discussed. True freedom of expression becomes the norm rather than the exception. If we trust that those with whom we work will allow us a safe space in which to express and be who we truly are, our gifts and talents will come forward and flower. Work settings filled with accusations, blame and judgment shut down any chance for individuals to express their true feelings through safe dialogue. If you're a leader who wishes to support your colleagues in becoming more incredible in their work and fully contributing members of the organization, it's essential that you create a safe environment for sharing and listening.

Teachers are usually very good at practicing focused listening with their students when they appear to really need a listener. Watch a teacher's body language when she's listening to a student. You will typically see an intense one-on-one focus with the teacher leaning in toward the student and listening with her full intention. It is clear that the teacher really wishes to understand what the student says. You are able to see the value that the teacher assigns to the student's words by her rapt attention. Teachers are also masters at hearing what the student doesn't say that is pertinent to the discussion. They can see and feel the emotion behind the words even if it's not verbally expressed. Teachers are emotion meters with their students, able to sense and understand the emotional state of their students at any given time throughout the day. Students are empowered by teachers who listen to them in a focused way. Spend time in a classroom known for excellence in student performance and good behavior and you'll find clear, honest and open communication ongoing in that classroom. Focused listening contributes to that picture. If you're clearly and carefully listened to and respected for your opinions you're more likely to respond to other people in the same manner. Focused listening provides a win-win situation for everyone in the school community. If you wish to improve your leadership and people skills, step back, take time to observe and focus your listening.

Strategy # 3 - Remember That People Come First

Action Steps:

- prioritize your goals, placing your relationships at the top

- remember that you work for a Human Service Organization where each person is important

- encourage your students to develop friendships with their classmates

- spend time getting to know your colleagues

- write lesson plans that consider the academic, social and emotional needs of your students

My first year as a school principal was focused on job responsibilities and paperwork. I worked diligently and for long hours making sure that I was doing everything I thought a new principal should do. This meant that I spent some time visiting classrooms, getting to know the students and teachers, but I spent a greater amount of time in my office trying to deal with the budget, schedules, and other management issues that are an important part of the job. I was a manager of the school that first year and I did a good job at it. I'm sure so much of my focus on management occurred because it was new to me and I wanted to be successful. Somewhere along the line that first year, I realized that maybe there was more to the job than just the paperwork. I'm not sure how that realization first surfaced. Maybe it came to me as I was spending increasing amounts of time with misbehaving students who were sent to the office. Maybe it dawned on me when I saw teachers leaving at the end of the day exhausted and sometimes discouraged. I realized that I was first and foremost working with people and not paper. This new awareness came upon me gradually and as it did, I found myself shifting my focus from paper to people. I didn't fail to complete the paper work; I just changed the priority of its importance in my job. Since then, I've consistently tried to follow the premise that people always come first.

Schools are human service organizations with a focus on people and their relationships. The work educators do in schools builds trusting relationships in which learners (child or adult) can find their talents and areas of interest and master skills that will help them succeed in their learning. If this is truly the work of education, then the focus in schools must be on the people. This holds true for anyone in a leadership role within the school community. It applies especially to the teachers who spend their entire day in interactions with their students. Although teachers generally put the students first, they sometimes forget this principle and allow outside pressures to determine their direction.

Placing people first means that there is nothing more important than treating each individual as a valued and important person, in situations that are harmonious as well as in those that are contentious. A leader can't afford to forget that individuals working diligently every day get the job done. Therefore, the focus of attention, support and feedback goes to the people within the community who are doing the work at hand. It's quite easy for teachers and principals to get enmeshed in the day-to-day minutia in their jobs. Reports are due, report cards must go home, lesson plans aren't ready, etc. etc. etc. Think of all the times you've been too busy at work to talk to a colleague who obviously needed someone to speak to. How many times have you hurried away from someone because you knew you'd have to stop and spend time? Sensitive leaders know that every single interaction with another person counts, whether it's a brief encounter or a lengthy conversation. The principal must be willing to stop and talk to a teacher on the spot. If time can't be spent with the person at that moment, then have a brief encounter and set up a time to meet later. The teacher who desired your attention will at least have had a chance to meet briefly and know that you realize the importance of what she needs to talk to you about – even if it turns out not to be important to you.

The issues of boundaries come into play at this stage of the game. Leaders must set boundaries around their time, their interactions, and their responsibilities. There are some people who are perpetual talkers, live in drama, and monopolize time. I'm not suggesting that the school leader should drop everything and spend hours with this type of person. However, I do suggest that the effective leader will know how to set boundaries and will do so. With an overly talky staff member or parent, this might mean saying, " I can only meet with you now for five minutes but let's see if we can work through the problem in that time." If you set time boundaries, stick to them. Teachers, students and parents will soon realize that their principal makes herself available to them and will listen whenever they need to be heard. This availability policy creates an atmosphere where teachers feel supported and listened to but don't take advantage of that relationship. Teachers feel reassured, knowing they can have the principal's full attention at almost any time. Most staff members and parents will not abuse this relationship.

Teachers place students first in the classroom, always planning their work around what is best for the student. "Begin with the student not the content" is a good place to start. "Begin with the teacher not the task" is a sound philosophy for the administrator to follow. It's critical that teachers cover academic content and teach skills in their classrooms. I'm not suggesting that they be ignored or down played. However, I am suggesting that educators should remember that they've entered the profession because of the people and their responsibility is to educate each individual who comes through their classrooms. Teachers also have an obligation to support and work closely with their colleagues, even those with whom they may have some differences of opinion, to forward the school's goals of educating all students.

Most of us understand if someone, with whom we need to talk, doesn't have time for us. However, when this happens, it doesn't always feel good. If we have something really important to discuss, and no one to listen, it can be devastating. Many reluctant students take a great deal of time and effort to get up the courage to talk to their teachers about issues important to them. It only takes one rejection to shut them up for a very long time. Usually, the teacher doesn't intentionally reject a student but it often feels that way to the student. The human psyche is very fragile and easily bruised. Most of us don't intentionally discourage and reject another person, but it can unintentionally happen very quickly and we might not even realize it has occurred. Adults also feel rejected and put-off when they're not listened to and can be hurt just as easily as kids.

Placing people at the forefront of your job means that you'll have a lot of work to do. However, when you routinely place people first, you begin to develop strong bonds of trust and respect. Eventually, the school community will become a center for clear and supportive communication where each individual knows they are important to the other members of the organization. In this type of setting, people work harder for the organization. Levels of performance and dedication are high. Ultimately, the leader will be able to accomplish much more within the school because of the high level of mutual support. People feel good working in organizations where they are held in high esteem and where their ideas and contributions are recognized and appreciated. "People come first" is a powerful motto for any organization to adopt.

Strategy # 4 - Embrace Change and Take Risks

Action Steps:

- change your routine at least once a week and do something differently

- examine your fear around a situation involving change to discover what is driving it

- make a "best case / worse case scenario" list when deciding whether to take a risk or make a big change

- do something you've never done before for a new experience and to gain insight about your abilities and fears

- structure safe risk-taking experiences, in lessons, for your students

Effective leaders identify their fears and work through them. Every human being, child or adult, faces fear on a daily basis. Our fears sometimes paralyze us and ensure that we stay in place, rejecting change of any kind. Most people feel more secure with the steady and predictable. Change usually brings fears to the surface where they can either be looked at and dealt with or shoved back inside. It is often easier, although not always personally satisfying, to block the fears and not face them. It feels better – for awhile. However, stuffing fears will usually begin to feel uncomfortable at some time in our lives. People in organizations face personally and professionally related fears every day. School and classroom leaders must recognize this because they create many of the situations that trigger fears. A leader best manages and supports change within her organization if and when she recognizes what the staff, students, and parents are feeling and dealing with on a daily basis. Everyone handles change differently. Some will embrace it openly and with excitement and others will fight it every step of the way. The leader plays a critical role as change manager within the organization and within the classroom.

Change comprises a large part of our personal and professional lives whether we like it or not, accept it or not, embrace it or reject it. Leaders in today's hectic world have the option of embracing change, trying to ignore it, or struggling with it. Most leaders, in fact, follow all three of these paths regarding change in their organization. Some changes are wonderfully good; others are harmful and difficult. Others are neutral. Change confuses. Change creates excitement. Change surfaces fears. Change swirls around our lives every day, sometimes kept at bay, sometimes warmly embraced. Paradoxes appear in the change process and this further confuses an already confusing situation. Change leads us into dark, unknown places that can cause us to doubt ourselves. It may also show us how resiliently we find answers. Change lives with us whether we've invited it in or not. There is no escaping it. It just won't go away!

Teachers and principals flexibly adapt and change on a daily basis. Schools are energetic organizations, always shifting and changing. School leaders gain power when they learn to use change as a tool to create successful organizations where all members of the community are supported in their efforts. Every person reacts differently to change. Some are reluctant; some excited. Principals and teachers must take care to insure that they understand the individual attitudes, of the people with whom they're working, in order to support the change effort. Leaders can utilize those staff members who find change rather easy as mentors for those people who are reluctant and fearful. A school principal comfortable and calm with the change process will help to influence other's reactions to it. The principal sets a school-wide tone by either making change an accepted, every day part of the scene or succumbing to the chaos of it. It is incumbent upon the principal, once the change process is happening, to support her staff. This will look different for each staff member much as a teachers' support for students will differ with each student. One size does not fit all when it comes to the change process.

Teachers, willing to make changes in their teaching, their classrooms, and their approach toward their students, are often more highly motivated and energized. Principals should encourage teachers to make changes every year. Changing grade levels or subject areas can be a completely renewing experience for a teacher, even though many teachers greatly resist this change because it often feels like a huge risk to them. In schools where principals and teachers have created safe environments for change and trial-and-error, more teachers are willing to take chances with the change process. Teachers supporting teachers in the change process leads to more widespread growth throughout the organization. Also, teachers who share the fun of trying something new spread this excitement to others. Peer influence among teachers plays a stronger role in motivating teachers to change than encouragement by the principal. Even the best teachers need to make changes from year-to-year. No one can remain stagnant and do a good job in the classroom because each class presents new challenges that require a new perspective. Schools where students excel support, encourage, and acknowledge the change process. The sense of accomplishment that comes from trying, and mastering, something new goes a long way to motivate school personnel to continue to make themselves and their school more effective in helping students. Growth will not occur without change. Change will be most effective when it is instituted from a proactive and creative attitude by the staff and principal. Our reaction to and participation in change is significantly influenced by our attitude. Our attitude is under our control and we always have choices. Therefore, we do have some measure of control over the change process after all. We hold the power to decide the approach we take in dealing with change issues. Fear closes doors. Support and encouragement create new avenues for success.

The change process often accompanies risk taking on the part of the individual or organization. Risk taking is a particularly important concept in schools because students who learn the most successfully take risks in their learning. Teachers who become the most dynamic in their profession have taken risks in their personal and professional growth. Principals who become the most loved and followed leaders are risk-takers in their leadership role. Schools will not become centers of excellence in the absence of risk taking. How do we create the circumstances for risk-taking to happen in schools? How do you encourage fearful students or teachers to take risks? When risk-taking is absent in a school, what do you do?

Risk taking requires individuals to expose their vulnerability. This is very hard to do, especially if you've had a previously bad experience with trusting other people to respect your self-revelation and they didn't. It's not surprising that most people reluctantly take risks. No one guarantees that everything will work out. It's sometimes easier to maintain the status quo, even if it's painful, than to face the unknown with all its uncertainties. The unknown often comes laden with wonderful things that we never imagined would present themselves. It is also strewn with difficult experiences that we would rather avoid. Students and teachers make the decision to become risk-takers or not every day in our schools. Instances abound in our classrooms for students to step forward into the adventure of learning. This requires letting go of the safe and stepping into the uncertain. How well any one student succeeds will depend on her teacher and the environment of the school and classroom. Creating safe and supportive classroom environments where students willingly expose their vulnerabilities to their peers and teachers is the most significant step educators can take to affect the end result of student learning. Classrooms do not become safe and supportive settings for the risk-taking of students if the principal and teachers have not already created that same system for themselves. It's not enough to expect only students to become risk takers. Every member of the school community must also be involved in their own growth through trying new things and venturing forth into unknown areas.

Risk taking occurs in environments that are free of judgment and prejudice. It blossoms in settings that celebrate diversity of thought and acknowledgement of uniqueness. Risk taking plants its seeds in classrooms and schools where there are no failures – just experiences that didn't work out. These growth experiences become lessons that contribute to the next risk to be taken rather than serving as barriers that stop forward movement. Failure thinking proves detrimental to student accomplishment and success. It must be removed from our classrooms and our schools because it undermines all that contributes to human beings moving forward in life. Criticism will often immediately shut down risk taking, especially in someone who reluctantly took the risk in the first place. So many people build up the courage to take a risk, take it, are criticized for the result and then won't take another risk. Teachers must be hyper-vigilant to ensure that students don't shut down because another student or the teacher made a disparaging remark. Principals, too, must utilize a communication system that doesn't judge and criticize teachers in those moments of greatest vulnerability.

The risk taking that we hope to see in schools is not reckless and unfocused, but rather, a strategy utilized by educators to lead students into deep learning experiences that will be meaningful and lasting for them. Risk taking and change don't require us to throw out everything for the sake of the new. It challenges us to find the balance between retaining what has worked very well in the past and moving into new arenas in the present and the future. Leaders at every level in schools must demonstrate their willingness to embrace change openly and take risks frequently. The changes and improvements that must occur in our schools will not come forward without these two important components of leadership. Future growth depends upon working with the change that permeates our lives and taking the risk of trying something new especially when there are no guarantees.

Strategy # 5 - Develop All the Skills Needed to Assume the Responsibilities of Your Job

Action Steps:

- identify your weak skills and take action to strengthen them

- ask your peers or principal for guidance in situations where you're unsure what to do

- study the subject areas you teach so that you can be an expert in those areas

- be open to learn new things because they might become major areas of interest that lead you on to new pathways

- teach your students the connection between improving their skills and becoming successful

Many people are natural leaders. They know how to relate to people, develop expertise in their content area, and get things accomplished. However, if you wish to be a successful leader at any level in the educational system, it's important to develop the skills that you'll need to be successful. Communication is one of the most important skill areas to enhance in order to be an effective leader. It's amazing that most teacher and principal preparation programs don't have requirements for communication courses. Since teachers and principals spend the great majority of their days in relationships with others, communication is an essential skill to master. Teachers and principals understand and utilize open and clear communication that reflects their integrity. Think of people you respect for their leadership abilities. Now, think about their communication style. How do they interact with others? What is so powerful in their communication? You can learn a great deal from observing good communicators. Since effective leadership means getting people to work well together toward a common goal, a leader must possess these sophisticated communication skills. Without them, leadership fails. Teacher leaders demonstrate these skills as well in their interactions with students, colleagues, and administration.

Equally important as communication skills is content knowledge. If you're going to be a good leader, you must know about the area in which you are leading. It's not necessary to be the consummate expert but at least minimally well versed in your subject area. For the principal, this would mean knowing education topics, curriculum, best-teaching practices, leadership, communication, and management issues. The principal doesn't have to be an expert in any one of these areas with possibly the exception of leadership and communication. Administrators rely on teacher expertise to help them run the organization. This is one of the reasons that it's so important for teachers to assume leadership roles in their schools. They bring their deep knowledge of content and subject area to the picture and act as on-site experts to the staff. Therefore, if many different teachers are involved in school leadership that ensures many different areas of expertise are brought into the picture. A wise administrator draws on the talent and knowledge of the staff to move the school's vision forward.

The more expert teachers become in their subject area and in their teaching skills, the greater their leadership contribution to the school. The smart principal will encourage and demand good staff development training for all staff members. This strategy will not only lead to improvements in the teaching in individual classrooms but will also help the entire school. Every member of the school community forms an important spoke in the wheel that drives the organization. When individual members of the organization improve and become stronger, the entire organization becomes stronger as well. Teachers who don't work to improve their skills and knowledge become weak links that adversely affect the running of the school. Therefore, staff development is one of the most important areas on which a principal should focus in order to bring about lasting change and growth to her school. Teachers who are informed and skilled ensure that students are learning and succeeding. They also serve as mentors and role models for their peers. The teachers who are the most powerful leaders in a school are also usually among the best teachers because of their commitment to personal and professional advancement and life-long learning. They are always looking for ways to support their natural curiosity and desire to be effective in contributing to the world. Service motivates educators.

Good schools develop and support powerful staffs of teachers. Effective leaders are not threatened by teachers who know more than they do. In fact, they rely on knowledgeable teachers in order to keep their information and skills current. The more that each member of the school community is empowered in a leadership role, the more successful the school and its personnel will become. Success breeds success. Excellence strives for greater excellence. Leadership leads through sharing. If you are a leader who empowers students, teachers, parents and staff members to discover and assume their personal leadership roles, you will have succeeded in creating a magical environment where everyone meets success and feels proud about their contributions. This is the greatest success a school principal may achieve.

Strategy # 6 - Bring Out the Best in People

Action Steps:

- make an effort to recognize at least one positive characteristic in each person with whom you work

- compliment your students and colleagues when they are successful or show good effort

- share differences of opinion without tearing down the other person

- work with your principal and colleagues to develop teacher recognition programs

- teach your students how to acknowledge their peers and give them guided practice in doing this

Every human being is unique and gifted. Everyone has special talents and contributions to make during their lifetime. Some seem aware of their abilities and easily share them with the world. Others are less sure and confident and keep a low profile, often reluctant to risk sharing themselves for fear of recrimination. It is critical that both the confident and the reluctant person identify their own gifts and talents and bring them forward into the world. This can be any world in which they exist – the world of their family, of work, of their church, of the local community, etc. Each person's giftedness is needed on a daily basis. Effective leaders know that a significant part of their work helps people recognize and identify their talents and then feel safe enough to bring them forward. Many teachers go into teaching because they wish to stay in their classrooms working with their students. They often turn off the outside world. Some do this because they don't feel comfortable in the outside world, other just want to be left alone to focus on the job of teaching. Teachers, who choose to focus their leadership efforts in the classroom, rather than the school at large, should be supported in their desire to focus on the art of teaching. However, they do have a significant role to play in the school at large. The principal should encourage this role.

Teachers adeptly discover the talents and giftedness of their students. They spend countless hours helping students explore different areas in order to find where they show the most interest and feel the most comfortable. The educational process educates youth in a variety of subject areas, skill sets, and experiences so that they can find what motivates them. Teachers then work with students to help them feel confident in sharing their areas of interest with others. Why is it that teachers are so good at this work with kids, but not so effective with themselves and their peers? Why are so many teachers reluctant to talk about and share their areas of strength with each other? Is the classroom a safer place for a teacher to discuss and share her talents than out in the school at large? Why would this be true?

It's difficult to bring out the best in someone if you don't know them. Leaders get to personally and professionally know and understand the people with whom they work. Principals discover the talents and skills of their teachers through watching them teach, talking to them, seeing how they interact with other teachers both informally and while serving on school committees. Principals should model their interaction with teachers on some of the same principles that teachers use to get to get to know their students and discover their talents. One of the first strategies a teacher uses is being friendly and genuinely interested in individual students. Principals must take the time to sit down with teachers individually and get to know them. Understanding what motivates and interests teachers helps the principal to support their contributions to the organization. You can't know what drives people if you don't spend time with them. Typically, an administrator doesn't have much time to spend in dialogue with individual teachers. That makes it even more critical that the principal stays present when meeting with a teacher. Being totally present means that you focus on what is happening during the interaction regardless of the time it takes. During this time, your mind and listening totally focus on the other person and the conversation. You aren't thinking about what you have to do next or the meeting you've missed. Communication that is focused through a leader's ability to remain present can be very effective in short interactions. Once the relationship between two people has been built, this time together will be even more productive. The principal who demonstrates a genuine desire to get to know teachers and keep in touch with them creates the foundation for life-changing relationships to develop. We become more willing to share ourselves when we trust the person with whom we are sharing that which we hold the closest.

Getting to know a teacher better and watching her teach also allows the principal to begin to see areas in which the teacher may not be currently involved but could become very successful. As the principal begins providing the teacher with informed and specific feedback, a professional and personal relationship, based on mutual respect and interest, begins to form. The feedback from the principal will strengthen the teacher's belief in self and re-enforce the good teaching skills that have been demonstrated. Through the dialogue and feedback loops that grow between teacher and principal, the administrator can begin to discuss skills that the teacher possesses. The leader can encourage and challenge the teacher to use her skills in new situations within the school. Usually, teachers more willingly embrace change and take new risks when they have the backing of a principal in whom they have great trust. The school leader's role is similar to that of a coach who helps her team members develop their skills and perform them successfully through practice, reinforcement, encouragement, and feedback. A principal, held in great respect by her teachers, wields great power in helping those teachers make changes and grow into the very best and most creative people they can become. When people we respect and trust want to lead us into new territory, we follow them. This is the ultimate power and responsibility of the leader.

The principal must take an active leadership role in creating a school climate where teachers are publicly recognized by students, parents, administration and most importantly, by their peers. There are heavy doors to break down, in some schools, to create a receptive climate for acknowledgement and celebration of diversity. Leadership teams can greatly assist the principal in establishing the norm of expecting excellent performance from staff and celebrating the examples of it in the classroom and school. It takes time and patience but eventually a school climate can be created where recognizing and honoring the skills of our peers is both acceptable and expected. We hold students to these guidelines in the classrooms. We must expect the same of our teachers and staff. The problem comes when a principal acknowledges or favors only a few teachers. All teachers deserve recognition for their unique skills and strengths. Teachers play a significant role in creating supportive environments for their peers within schools. They hold the ultimate power to help facilitate a culture of acceptance and recognition that supports professional growth or to continue closed and territorial school environments that discourage the human spirit.

Leadership is a privilege and a huge responsibility. It requires a steady presence, respectful interactions, knowledge, self-less giving, steely nerves, unlimited patience, firm decision making, keen powers of observation, humor and a love for people. Leadership finds its place in those hearts, minds and souls that desire to work with others to accomplish like-minded goals that contribute to a better world. Good leaders inspire us to be the best we can possibly be and to achieve all that we are capable of realizing. The greatest gift a leader has to give is assisting others to discover their talents, develop their skills and follow their passion, bringing it into the world, in service to others. Inspirational leaders positively change lives and contribute to a better world.

3. EMPOWERMENT

"The Yellow Cart"

Vignette # 1

THE SCHOOL YEAR had been in session for one week. Students settled into their new classrooms, getting to know their teacher's expectations. It didn't take long for the pace of a typical day, unique to each classroom, to become routine. Betsy, who taught kindergarten, had always believed in beginning to empower her students the first day they walked into her classroom. This year she decided to immediately assign classroom jobs to these inexperienced youngsters to give them opportunities to learn responsibility and feel good about their ability to accomplish a task. Students feel empowered when they succeed at a new skill or task. Kindergarten students love to try new things and be given responsibilities.

It was Monday of the second week of school. "Everyone put away your crayons and come and sit on the carpet over here, near the bulletin board," said Betsy. The twenty-seven students quickly scurried up to the carpet, sat cross-legged and stared at their teacher. "We have something very exciting to do today," Betsy told her students. "You're all going to be assigned to do special classroom jobs."

"Yeeeeaaaaa!" Cheers broke out. Boys exchanged high-fives and a few girls hugged each other. Betsy smiled.

"Now, I want you to listen very carefully while I tell you what classroom jobs I will assign. Can you all sit up straight and pay attention?" "Yesssssss!" they responded, shoulders back, heads held high, hands placed quietly in laps. Betsy then described the messenger's role, the paper collector's job, paint pot washing and several other classroom jobs that students would take turns completing. The students sat quietly at first but wiggled and clapped their hands together, in delight, with each job that Betsy presented.

"Now, I want to tell you about the most special, but hardest, job of all," said Betsy, standing up and walking across the room. Twenty-seven heads and bodies turned to follow her actions. Betsy went behind a room divider and came out pushing a bright yellow handcart, sporting ruby-red wheels and a sky-blue wooden handle. "Ooooo! Wow! Yeeaaaa!" cheers rose from the students who were now standing and jumping up and down, waving their arms wildly in the air.

"OK. Everyone sit back down now." All settled back onto the carpet. "This is the milk and cookie wagon," said Betsy in a solemn and serious voice. "This cart will be pushed to the cafeteria every day to pick up milk and cookies for snack time. You must have a cart driver's license to do this job. Does anyone here have a cart driver's license?" Students looked at each other, shrugged their shoulders and shook their heads "no." "Well, I'll choose two students to be the drivers and we'll see if they pass the test and get their license."

"ME! Me! Me! Oh! Oh! Oh! Me!" twenty-seven voices shouted, their hands flailing wildly about as they volunteered to drive the special yellow cart.

"Sarah and John please come over here." Two smiling students jumped up and ran to the sunshine yellow cart. Some students sighed and sank to the carpet; others raised their shoulders then pushed their fists toward the floor, displaying disgust and disappointment with the decision. "All of you watch now so that you'll know how to drive the cart," said Betsy. "Everyone will have a turn driving the cart during the school year." That immediately brought every little body back to full attention. Betsy spent a few minutes instructing Sarah and John in the art of cart driving. They stood side-by-side, small hands gripped the wooden handle and practiced circling the classroom. Turning seemed to be the most difficult skill to learn. One awkward turn led to the paint easel toppling to the floor. Everyone froze. Sarah and John looked at their teacher with their eyes asking the big question – "Will we lose our job?" "It's OK," said Betsy. "This is practice and you're learning." Smiles transformed the solemn and worried faces as the driving duo took another turn around the room.

"Well, I think they're ready to go to the cafeteria. What do you think?" Betsy asked the class.

"Yea! Let them go!" someone shouted. The class cheered as Sarah and John maneuvered the cart through the narrow classroom door. They turned and looked back at their class, with huge, mischievous smiles on their faces as they began their great adventure.

The bright yellow, wooden cart, with the two large red wheels, careened down the hallway and narrowly missed crashing into a line of students returning to class from the gym. The two kindergarteners pushed the bright yellow cart, each one struggling to be the controlling driver on this important milk and cookie run. The wooden cart was empty as it headed toward the school cafeteria for its daily snack pick-up. In addition to the line of students who were nearly run down by the hotshot drivers, other students laughed and commented as the cart whizzed past them.

"Hey, you almost hit the wall," laughed a passing girl, not much bigger than the student drivers.

"Do you two have a driver's license?" asked the music teacher as she walked down the hall.

"No," they laughed. "This isn't a car! It's a cart and we have a cart driver's license." The yellow cart, with the bright red wheels, rounded the corner near the office and approached the cafeteria. The speeding duo arrived in record time. The large, steel cafeteria doors presented the first real obstacle to be overcome by these adventuresome kindergarteners, as they and the cart came to a screeching halt.

"You open the door and I'll push it through," Sarah commanded John.

"No, I'll push it. You open the door," replied John, trying to bump Sarah away from her hold on the cart.

"You pushed it around the corner. It's my turn! Let me have it!" shouted Sarah, pushing John aside. The argument continued for a few minutes, becoming increasingly violent, until a teacher, passing by, graciously offered to open the door. The wooden cart was ushered through the light gray cafeteria doors, raced past the serving line, crudely maneuvered through a narrow passageway near the freezer and came to sudden halt in front of the tall, silver refrigerator with both drivers maintaining equal control. "We need milk!" two voices called out in unison.

The custodian came around the corner, mopping the floor as he walked and said, "Just hold on a minute and I'll get it for you." He finished his mopping and walked over to the pair.

"How are you two today?" Mr. Smith asked as he opened the large upper door of the huge refrigerator.

"O.K. We need milk. We have to hurry!" John said with urgency in his voice.

"Here, I'll get it for you," replied the custodian, taking a tray of tiny milk cartons out of the refrigerator. "How many chocolate? How many white?" he asked. John dug deep into his pocket and pulled out a scrunched up piece of paper, handing it to Mr. Smith.

"Looks like you have a lot of chocolate drinkers today," he said as he counted out seventeen chocolate milk cartons and ten white milk cartons, placing them on a large silver cafeteria tray. "Here you are," said Mr. Smith as he placed the tray in the bed of the yellow cart. Sarah began to arrange the cartons in neat rows.

"Hurry up," said John. "We have to go!"

Mr. Smith gently laid a tray of peanut butter cookies across the top of the cart. The tray was supported by and balanced on the sides of the wooden cart.

"Be careful with these cookies," said Mr. Smith. "They might slide."

"OK," said Sarah and John in unison. "We have to go!"

Mr. Smith helped the kindergarteners turn the cart around and head toward the heavy doors. "Wait, I'll open the door," he said, as the pair vied for steering position behind the handle of the yellow cart. "You're doing a great job!" Mr. Smith told the students. "Be careful going down the hall. Don't go too fast or the cookies will spill."

"John is the one who goes too fast," Sarah said smugly.

"I don't go too fast!" John replied. "You're just a slowpoke!" With that comment, John gave a shove to the cart handle, Sarah grabbed hold of it and off they went. They glided effortlessly through the open cafeteria door and turned left down the long hallway. They had only gone a few feet, when Sarah spoke up, "Hey, we're going the wrong way! Our room's the other way." Sure enough, the pair was headed toward sixth grade.

"Why did you turn this way?" asked John in an accusing tone. Sarah gave John a withering look but didn't respond. They did a quick swerve in the middle of the intermediate hallway, as the peanut butter cookies slid to one side of the tray, and headed down the primary hallway to their classroom.

"You're going too fast!" shouted Sarah, hanging onto the wooden handle as the cart flew down the hall. The pair dashed around the curve, leading to their classroom, as if the cart was driving them and they were just hanging on for the ride. Their reckless journey seemed to challenge anyone who might be in their way. Luckily, in this one instance, a class of students was not coming down the hall! However, in their out-of-control swerve around the curve, several cookies jumped off the tray and landed on the carpet. The cart suddenly stopped which sent a few more cookies over the edge. Since no adults were in sight, this wasn't a big problem.

"Look what you did!" Sarah said accusingly as she began to pick up cookies.

"Just wipe them off," said John, brushing the cookies on his jeans. Sarah had neatly lined up all of the peanut butter cookies on the tray just as the principal came down the hallway.

"Hi, what are you two doing?" she asked.

"We're taking our snack to the classroom," they chimed in unison with big smiles on their faces.

"Well, it looks like you're doing a great job!" said the principal. "I'm glad you're not racing down the hall." She walked away, headed toward the office. Sarah and John looked at each other, smiled, grabbed the sky-blue, wooden handle and raced down toward their classroom. When they arrived at their classroom door, John graciously opened the door so that Sarah could carefully push the cart into the classroom.

"You made it back. Good job!" commented their teacher. Sarah and John beamed. "What took you so long?" Sarah and John giggled as they handed out seventeen tiny cartons of chocolate milk and ten cartons of white milk, accompanied by lightly dusted peanut butter cookies. The kindergarten snack had once again been delivered in the trusty yellow cart, with the large, red wheels and the bright blue handle. This familiar cart can be seen twice a day careening down the hallways, driven by wild-eyed kindergarten students, imagining that they're behind the wheel of their first car.

Vignette # 2

Jimmy lumbered into the office, dropped down into one of the "waiting chairs," crossed his arms in a defiant stance and stared out the window. It was Thursday morning and this was the third time a teacher had sent Jimmy to the office this week. Jimmy was one of the bigger eighth graders, tall with broad shoulders. He was handsome and, therefore, quite popular with the middle school girls. Jimmy's smile and warm personality could win over the toughest critic. He often used his charming ways to try to extricate himself from the fairly consistent trouble in which he found himself. Jimmy's gift of gab also allowed him to slide through many difficult situations and come out rather unscathed. However, the truth was that Jimmy was a poor student, totally unmotivated to be in school, and distracting others in most of his classes. He rarely finished his work and was always behind. Jimmy had been identified with learning difficulties and he received extra help. However, he put forth little, if any, effort so even the extra help wasn't working. All of Jimmy's teachers loved him and, at the same time, were totally frustrated with his disruptive, clownish behaviors and lack of effort. He participated in class discussions but often called out, made fun of other student's answers and occasionally fell out of his chair. It seemed that most of Jimmy's out-of-control behaviors were, in fact, very controlling. He used his behavior issues to deflect attention from his difficulties in doing the work expected of eighth graders. His grades were mostly D's and F's, with an occasional C.

Shortly after Jimmy was sent to the office for disrupting a science lab, Marc stormed in the front door. He slammed the door, kicked a chair and pounded his fist on the table, all the while mumbling under his breath something about, "this is unfair." Marc sat at the table next to Jimmy, glared at him and said, "What are you looking at?" in a menacing tone and then turned his back to Jimmy. Marc was in third grade and he, too, was a frequent visitor to the principal's office. Marc was a very angry boy who threatened and picked on other kids and never backed down from challenges that he was the toughest guy in third grade. He hit other students at recess, threatened to beat them up after school and used profane language to fend off people and situations he didn't want to deal with at school. Despite the very rough edginess and explosive nature of Marc's personality, he could be as charming as Jimmy. Marc had learned at an early age what to say to adults to get what he wanted or to get out of trouble. He lied a lot and made up elaborate stories to cover the reasons for his misdeeds. Marc also possessed the gift of gab and he could talk himself out of many difficult situations. In many ways, Marc was more street savvy than Jimmy who was five years older. If Marc spent half as much time and effort at his studies as he did at his "image making," he would be an average student. As it was, Marc was failing, chose to disrupt rather than appropriately contribute to class discussions and projects and did whatever was necessary to focus on something other than his academic failures. He also received special education services but chose not to fully participate.

Jimmy and Marc didn't know each other before that fateful day when they both arrived at my office within a few minutes of each other. A casual observer, passing through the office, would have noticed the similarities in their body language. Both sat in a defiant position, arms crossed on their chests, bodies slouching in their chairs, smirks on their faces, and glaring stares that challenged the passer-by to say something. Where Jimmy was tall and solidly built with broad shoulders, Marc was short, wiry and agile. Even though they didn't look alike, Marc's body posture could have been a younger clone of Jimmy.

Marc and Jimmy actually had something else in common. They both had Mrs. Emerson as their third grade teacher. It was Mrs. Emerson who had just sent Marc to the office for arguing with her. Mrs. Emerson was a tough teacher who demanded respect from her students and would accept nothing less. She had a loud voice that could easily gain students attention when she needed them to listen. I noticed that Mrs. Emerson particularly liked to work with the "underdog" student who was either a behavior challenge or not making the academic grade. She defended her kids and stood up for them. If they deserved punishment, Mrs. Emerson would see to it. She was fierce when another teacher or student treated one of her students in a way that she felt was unfair or disrespectful. It wasn't a good idea to cross Mrs. Emerson. She was like a fierce lioness, loving and protecting her young. However, she didn't cover for them if they were wrong. They paid the price for their indiscretions.

Marc was one of Mrs. Emerson's most difficult, and most favorite, students. She recognized the hurt and pain inside of Marc that drove him to act out. She also saw the quick mind, ability to deal with multiple people and challenging life situations and his loving heart that was buried so deeply beneath the protective layers. Jimmy had also been in Mrs. Emerson's third grade class several years ago. He, too, had been one of her favorites. In fact, he still was one of her favorites and she talked to him whenever she ran into him around the campus. So, that Thursday morning, when Mrs. Emerson walked into the office to see if Marc had reported to the secretary, she saw two of her favorite students sitting like identical bookends, waiting to see me for their punishment.

"Well, well, well. What a pretty picture!" said Mrs. Emerson, smiling at both boys. "I know why Marc's here but what about you, Jimmy?"

"Mr. Johnson made me stand up in front of everyone to give an answer that he knew I didn't know so I rocked in my chair and fell over. Everyone laughed and he got mad and sent me to the office. It's his fault. I didn't really do anything so bad."

"Yeah, yeah, yeah, I've heard that one before," replied Mrs. Emerson.

Mrs. Emerson looked at Marc who had laughed when Jimmy related his classroom experience. "What are you laughing at? You're not here for being an upstanding student," she said in a loud, strident voice. "What a perfect pair!" Mrs. Emerson said as she walked out of the office. On her way back to the classroom, she thought about Marc and Jimmy and had an idea. Despite his poor grades and behavior infractions, Jimmy was one of the most popular students in the middle school. The younger students who knew him thought he was cool and they liked to hang out with him because he was a good basketball and football player. He was also big and strong which impressed smaller, weaker boys. Mrs. Emerson thought that maybe Jimmy and Marc and some of the other boys in her classroom could help each other out and do better in school at the same time. She put together a plan to take to the middle school meeting the following week.

"I know Jimmy well and also notice that he's constantly in trouble," said Mrs. Emerson to the middle school teachers, when she met with them the following week. "I have a student in my class who reminds me very much of Jimmy when he was in third grade. I also have several rough and tumble boys who are border line with their grades and behavior. So, I was thinking that maybe Jimmy could become a big brother to the boys in my class. We could set certain parameters about Jimmy maintaining his workload and behaving appropriately and maybe he'd do better. He seems to have such low self-esteem. Maybe this would help him and the younger boys. What do you think?"

"Well, Jimmy just can't afford to lose any more class time," said Mr. Thompson. "He's already so far behind."

"We don't want it to look like we're rewarding him by giving him extra privileges," commented Ms. Trailer. "He always takes advantage of anything good you try to do for him."

"I think it's a good idea," said Mr. Roberts, Jimmy's homeroom teacher. "Jimmy's not successful now and not even trying to get average grades. Maybe this would motivate him and empower him to feel good about himself. He sees himself as a failure and that's how he performs." The middle school teachers and Mrs. Emerson discussed the situation a little further and decided to start out with a trial period to see how it would work. It was decided that Jimmy would be a "big brother" to Mrs. Emerson's boys during recess. She hoped that instead of her boys running wildly around the playground bothering people, they would hang out with Jimmy. Mrs. Emerson and his homeroom teacher, Mr. Roberts, met with Jimmy the next day.

"Jimmy, the younger boys in my class really look up to you. They think you're cool," said Mrs. Emerson. Jimmy's warm and charming smile spread across his face. "I have a plan," said Mrs. Emerson. "I'd like you to be a big brother to my boys at recess time. You can play tag football or basketball or any other acceptable game to keep them involved and out of trouble. What do you think?"

"Yeah, that would be cool," Jimmy said nonchalantly, trying not to show his excitement.

"There's another issue here," chimed in Mr. Roberts. "You may only do this if your work gets turned in and your behavior improves. We don't want a poor role model working with these young students. Do you think you could get all your work finished?"

"I don't know," said Jimmy, hanging his head in defeat. "Some of it is just too hard for me." Jimmy didn't usually admit he couldn't do something. "I want to help Mrs. Emerson and her boys, so I will try to get my work finished."

"Jimmy, both Mr. Roberts and I will try to give you extra help when you need it," said Mrs. Emerson. "However, you're the one who has to put forth the effort. It wouldn't be fair if other middle school students saw you working with my boys and they knew you weren't getting the work finished."

"I want to do it," said Jimmy. "I'll try."

The following Monday Jimmy began his mentoring role with Mrs. Emerson's third grade boys. She met with all of them to discuss what was acceptable on the playground and what wasn't. Mrs. Emerson closely supervised this program during the first week and kept an eye on it afterward, checking with the recess duty teachers to see how things were going. Jimmy could be seen every morning at 11:45 quickly striding, sometimes running, toward the primary playground. He rarely missed a day. It was fun to watch Jimmy with the third grade boys. They huddled around him as if he were a notable celebrity. Many fourth grade boys also joined the group. Jimmy was in his element. He was firm but kind, trying to make sure everyone was involved. He was particularly sensitive to those students who didn't think they could play a particular game very well. Jimmy stood tall and confident when directing and monitoring these younger boys. He was serious but fun. He settled arguments before they got out of hand and he encouraged the boys to try their best. He was always high-fiving them and telling them what a great job they were doing. He knew the importance of saying something positive even to the most unlikely basketball player.

Jimmy's grades didn't miraculously improve nor did all his work get turned in on time. However, he was putting forth more effort, staying out of trouble and feeling positive about himself. Mrs. Emerson began meeting with Jimmy a few days a week after school to help him with his work. She knew this big brother role should continue because it was empowering both Jimmy and her current students. This partnership seemed to work for Marc because Jimmy took him on as something of an assistant in setting up and managing the games. Marc was a natural organizer and the kids listened to him. He didn't bully them but gave clear and concise directions and help. Marc's behavior improved and he began to finish more of his work than normal. He clearly looked up to Jimmy. Although the arrangement wasn't perfect, it did seem to help all involved and it continued throughout the school year. The recess duty teachers reported fewer behavior problems on the playground once this program began.

Neither Marc nor Jimmy ended the school year with greatly improved grades but they improved enough to pass. They still occasionally ended up in my office for behavior issues but those occurrences were greatly reduced. There were two noticeable changes to the boys that anyone who knew them could see. First, they appeared to be happier. They smiled instead of glaring, they were friendly and conversational instead of whiny and surly and they didn't swagger as much. Their former bravado was replaced with a deeper self-confidence because they both realized and saw that they had successfully worked together to help Mrs. Emerson's boys. They were looked up to and respected by other students. Teachers acknowledged them for their efforts. This level of positive feedback and recognition was a new and satisfying experience for both of them.

Jimmy moved on to high school the following year. High school was a rocky road for him. He was in and out of trouble and failing a few classes. Mrs. Emerson heard about this and got involved once more. She arranged for Jimmy to come over to her classroom and continue to work with third graders, as long as he worked to keep up his grades. She even drove to the high school on her break to pick Jimmy up. He managed to get through high school, although it was never easy, and now has a good job in the local community. Jimmy is thinking of entering the military to continue his education and get his life on the right track. Marc didn't fair as well. He stayed at our school through sixth grade. His grades were up and down and his behavior was always a little better when someone mentored him and helped him have positive experiences. Marc moved to a neighboring community for middle school. I was quite sad one day, several months later, to read in the paper that Marc had been arrested and expelled for bringing a gun to school to scare another student. Students will find personal empowerment in either positive or negative ways. Parents, teachers and principals must make sure that all of our students feel positively empowered through experiencing personal success in both academic and social areas in their lives on a regular basis each year that they're in school. There are thousands of Jimmys and Marcs passing through our classrooms every day. They cry out to be noticed.

....

Empowerment

Definition: *make someone stronger and more confident in controlling their life and claiming their rights*

Empowerment leads us to feel personally powerful, secure in who we are, confident in our abilities, and embraced through our relationships. Empowerment is the ultimate validation for our purpose on the earth at this time and in this place. It's a basic, gut level knowing that we are here for a specific purpose. Fulfilling that purpose is a coming home to self through discovering all of the inner strengths that we're courageous enough to bring forward into the light of day. Becoming empowered requires that we are risk-takers, willing to break through walls that hinder our progress. The journey to personal power is not an easy road. It requires steadfast tenacity and the ability to look inward, constantly redefining self in relationship to other people and specific situations. Empowerment comes with validation. Discovering personal strengths, vision and goals leads us to clarity about our direction in life that provides invaluable information for further growth. This is a life-long process of trying out new things, in relationship to what we know about ourselves, and making adjustments as we find out what supports our journey and what sidetracks our steps.

Empowering children begins at a very early age as parents and family members interact with youngsters to begin the process of helping them identify interests, define self in relation to other's reactions, and practice different activities to discover skill areas. This process matures as children grow older and enter school. The entire school experience is about empowering each student to become a fully functioning and successful member of society who feels self-confident and passionate about her work and life's path and possesses the necessary skills to fulfill these dreams. This is neither simple nor easy. It requires a consistent structure in which students may experiment in order to learn more about themselves. A safe environment, filled with supportive and honest people, provides the backdrop for this journey. Skills must be taught that allow each individual opportunities for academic growth and mastery. Each year's school experience is important in this development of fully functioning and self-fulfilled individuals. There are no years that can be wasted or set aside. This is one of the reasons that teaching is such a challenging and rewarding profession. Teachers have the power to make each student's path toward self a wondrous journey or one fraught with uncertainty, self-doubt and failure. This is a huge responsibility on our teachers and principals, which requires that they operate from their own empowered state.

The empowerment of adults is as arduous a journey as the empowerment of students. Most adults do not reach adulthood as fully empowered individuals. There really is no stopping place in our personal growth when we can say, "I've made it. My personal growth is finished." This is a lifelong journey that reaches plateaus where we alight for awhile but there is always another level to reach. Sometimes we choose to reach for that level, other times we stay where we are because it's comfortable and we feel content. Teachers, just like their students, are always learning more about themselves and their skills and interests as they relate to their occupation of teaching. Principals support teachers in their forward movement toward a greater sense of self, much like teachers assist their students. The process of teaching is one in which teachers constantly face themselves and their actions and ask the hard questions about their effectiveness in working with students. If great teaching is to occur in every classroom in this country, every teacher must become personally empowered in her work and in her personal life. Teachers will feel empowered when they have discovered their strengths and are living their passion because that is where they will contribute most successfully and powerfully. Principals play a significant role in assisting and supporting teachers to reach the highest levels of personal and professional contribution that is possible. When students, teachers and principals are operating from their fully empowered selves, schools will be vibrant, personally safe, supportive, and successful centers for learning and growth.

Schools filled with empowered students and teachers are wonderful places to learn and work. Pettiness is reduced when people feel powerful in their own right. There is no need for gossip, jealousy or criticism of another's successes. Just the opposite occurs. People are recognized and admired for their contributions and skills. Personal support among teachers and between teachers and administrators is the norm. It is expected, accepted, and appreciated. When school environments are free of rivalry and pettiness, more effective teaching and learning occurs. Teachers are happier, more motivated and willing to engage in new challenges. Students are involved in their learning and feel successful with their accomplishments and efforts. An empowered school is a powerful place where anything is possible when every avenue for excellence is pursued. The attitude is "can do" and "will do." There is little hesitation or uncertainty. It is this positive belief system that leads to a school culture that expects the best from every member in its community. Empowered teachers, students and principals empower others who, in turn, positively affect others.

Initially, empowerment is an internal, positive feeling and belief system embraced by an individual when she receives external feedback from her environment. Eventually, each individual must create and reinforce her own internal feelings of personal power. I cannot make someone feel empowered. Each person must develop and build her own belief system that leads to her knowing she is good, capable, talented and has something of importance to add to the organization. Empowerment is built through mental attitudes and concrete actions. If I believe I have something useful to contribute and I bring it forward into an action step, I'm demonstrating my power. Empowered individuals don't feel disenfranchised or maligned for their ideas. Teachers feel more empowered when they are listened to and their ideas are validated and adopted. Empowerment is a mental attitude that must be nurtured and supported for it to grow into action. The school leader clearly sets the tone, in a school, for inviting teacher's participation through shared leadership, or disenfranchising staff through practicing authoritarian rule. Totalitarian styles of leadership don't support the development of empowered staff members. Principals either encourage and support staff in becoming strong leaders in their own right, or discourage them and don't allow them to have a voice.

It's not enough for a principal to decide that teachers will have a say about curriculum and best teaching practices but not about management issues regarding the running of the school. Shared leadership should be present in all areas of school governance. By giving staff members a voice, principals ensure that there will be conflicts and disagreements that arise in the decision making process. An empowered teacher is more likely to express her opinion than a teacher who is hesitant about causing a problem or getting into trouble. Strong and bold teachers will not sit back quietly if they see something occurring that is detrimental to the students or the school. A principal who encourages staff to become fully involved should expect some lively staff discussions. This is healthy. Encouraging people to speak up and express their opinion will make the school a much stronger organization in the long run. It is only when all teachers become involved in the running of their school that the greatest amount of talent and power is available to help the organization realize its vision and attain its goals.

Teachers empower their students every day through helping them discover areas of skill and talent, developing these strengths, and then bringing them forward in ways that impact both the students and others surrounding them. Students feel powerful when their teachers trust them and assign responsibilities based on this trust. They soon develop the belief that they are strong, adaptable and can work through any situation. Empowered students are risk-takers who are less likely to give up when learning becomes difficult because they have a deeper level of confidence in themselves. They accept failures as learning experiences, rather than as dead ends. Empowerment breeds self-confidence and the belief that I am capable, skilled and important.

Empowering an individual reaches to the very depths of who she is as a person. Teachers work closely with students to develop this solid inner foundation of belief in self and one's abilities. This positive belief system is strengthened through the daily actions and accomplishments of the individual student. There is also the deeper reality that each student is uniquely and inherently powerful, in his own right, as a human being. It shouldn't be necessary to accomplish something to show that you are a powerful human being. Personal empowerment is a birth right we all possess. However, the existence of inherent goodness and natural ability is most often demonstrated through concrete actions or specific accomplishments.

Teachers approach their students from the belief that students have the right to be who they are in the fullest sense of feeling good about themselves as they realize their strengths and develop their skills. Teachers don't start a new year thinking, "I wonder which student or students I can empower through her successes." Rather, the teacher knows that each student brings a different level of possibility to the learning picture. Every student is helped to feel powerful about who she is as a person, regardless of her level of performance. This framework for empowerment is more strongly crafted when there are concrete examples, demonstrating this personal power to the student. Bad grades and repeated failures do not help in the development of empowered students. It's critical for a teacher to work with each student at the student's skill level and diligently try to raise that level. A student won't feel successful until she is successful. Teachers have a huge job to do in this area, especially with students who are below level academically. In order to develop feelings of personal power, it is necessary to assist each student in meeting with success in her learning. The challenge for teachers is great. The outcome must be personal success for every student. Confidence feeds success and success restores confidence.

We know that most teachers try to empower their students on a daily basis. But what does it look like when a principal empowers her staff? Why is it so important? The first part of the empowerment definition talks about making someone stronger. These strengths are demonstrated in both professional and personal work. In education, professional strength comes through staff development, course work, and teaching experience. Teachers mature in their craft when they participate in professional learning and growth opportunities. The building principal is responsible not only for scheduling and supporting staff development activities, but for encouraging teachers to constantly improve their skills. The principal must then follow-up on the training to ensure that it is being applied in the classroom setting. Specific feedback, from principal to teacher, is a critical step in enhancing staff development work. The principal reinforces the new or advanced skills that have been taught through her observing and responding to the teacher's efforts to incorporate this new learning in her work. A teacher's professional strength is developed through on-going learning experiences, application of new teaching techniques and receiving informed feedback.

In addition to professional power, that makes a teacher feel more confident about herself, there is the personal focus that is essential to feeling empowered. Principals empower teachers, in the personal arena, by showing trust and confidence in them as teachers and human beings. Of course, a large portion of this trust and confidence is based on the classroom performance of the teacher. However, principals should develop personal relationships with all members of their staff in order to help each teacher feel personally empowered, as a significant contributor, within the organization. Administrators and staff members form friendships and bonds of loyalty that ultimately become the foundation for further empowerment. Principals who know their staffs well see all possibility for the school within the talent pool of that staff. Relationship building is the key to empowering staff on a personal level. At the same time that the principal is leading the professional development initiative for the staff, she is building the personal relationships that serve as the foundation for each teacher's full empowerment. Principals help to make teachers stronger through sponsoring training, providing specific feedback, forming friendships, bestowing trust, and recognizing accomplishments and efforts.

The second part of the empowerment definition calls for helping someone feel more confident. This, too, has both a professional and personal component. The professional component comes forward when the principal spends time with the teacher, frequently observers her teaching, provides specific and timely feedback, reinforces areas of strength, and asks her to assume a leadership role based on her skills, talents, and interests. Teachers are also instrumental in providing feedback to their peers on a daily basis. In fact, the feedback that teachers provide to one another is often more specific and more meaningful because it's coming from an active teacher practitioner. Teachers often feel more comfortable asking their peers for feedback. Principals should encourage and reinforce teachers supporting one another. School environments that encourage professional dialogue and support will become places where teachers feel confident in what they have to offer their students and the organization.

Personal feelings of confidence are built on proven results. We see the successful end results of actions we take and these make us feel confident in our abilities. Self-confidence and positive self-esteem are tenuous and often fragile. No matter how strong a view we hold of our abilities, criticism, failure, or blame can easily knock down all the good we've created. Many people show a very strong, self-confident outer side but are much more fragile on the inside. Teachers see this fragility with their students. One cross or misguided word can send a student into retreat with feelings of failure. We must be so careful with both the words we use and the intent of our comments. Teachers, too, are quite sensitive to criticism, put-downs, lack of support, or inadequate attention given to what they do and how they do it. Administrators must be cautious with the words that are used when providing feedback. Words can build or tear down and teachers who appear to be self-confident can easily be devastated by ill-advised comments or disparaging attitudes. Principals who work to build close personal relationships with staff members should take care not to harm this trusting relationship that has been formed. When individuals permit themselves to be more vulnerable through forming close personal and professional relationships, they also expose themselves to the possibility of deep hurt. There is a huge responsibility on the part of both teachers and principals to ensure that the language they use assists growth toward personal and professional empowerment.

People who feel empowered don't sit back and let life happen to them. They make it happen through a proactive approach. If you wish to become more empowered or help others feel more empowered, try some of the following strategies.

1. Create an empowerment cycle

2. Step back and let others share the spotlight

3. Find a measure of success in everything you do

4. Get to know yourself and listen to your intuition

....

Strategy # 1 - Create an Empowerment Cycle

Action Steps:

- make a "something I learned today" bulletin board

- list all the positive actions you've taken during the week to remind and reinforce yourself

- provide multiple opportunities for your students to practice new skills in an emotionally safe environment

- encourage and recognize your teachers who move outside their comfort zones to improve their skills

- develop a strong internal "power voice"

Ultimately, empowerment must be grounded in self-confidence and internal feelings of worth and accomplishment. However, external influences are very important, especially in the building stages, to create the mindset of having confidence in one's abilities and ways of contributing. A cycle of practices and responses drives the creation and maintenance of an empowered mindset. An empowerment cycle has the following four stages; learning, application through action, feedback, and self-evaluation. When the cycle is fully turning, one characteristic building upon and supporting the next, empowerment will grow and flourish in the individual. There is no beginning nor end in an empowerment cycle as each characteristic leads to the next and ultimately returns to itself to create deeper connections and more lasting belief systems. Therefore, each step in the cycle is equally useful and important.

Learning new things and identifying interests is a good place to begin discussing the empowerment cycle. These two actually go hand-in-hand. We start learning about those things that interest us while, at the same time, we develop interests around the things that we are learning in school or in the world. Learning is a key to self-fulfillment. The more we know about a topic the more likely we are to either embrace it or let it go. When we embrace a topic of interest, we usually place additional effort into learning about it. If it is a skill or knowledge base related to our professional or personal life, then we are gaining personal insight through learning about the topic or mastering new skills. When we know enough about a topic to share it with others and incorporate it into our lives in a way that makes us more successful, we feel empowered. Knowledge and application of skills lead to empowerment. Therefore, life-long learning is a key to allowing personal and professional empowerment to be present throughout a lifetime. This leads us to realize that education, for both adults and children, is both an instrumental and an essential component for the creation and on-going development of powerful individuals. Once the new knowledge and improved skills become our own, we emerge as strong and self-confident individuals who are ready to contribute to life in meaningful ways.

In schools, teachers must actively and meaningfully engage their students in the learning process. Children discover new interests as they encounter various topics within the classroom and learn what they love. Experiential learning activities provide further support in the development of young people who know who they are and what they want out of life. The system has failed a student who completes eight or twelve years of education with no ideas of where her interests lie and no feelings of empowerment. Teachers must give students opportunities to try new interests out in a safe and supportive environment so that they can more quickly find their areas of passion. Students also learn that everything doesn't always work out the way they expected. Personal power is often strengthened in those situations that don't work out because students learn how to continue even when they might feel discouraged or disappointed. Internal fortitude is built upon the foundation of those situations and experiences that didn't work out. It is honed through repeated attempts to rise above fears of inadequacy and judgment that surface during difficult times. Teachers and parents provide children with learning experiences in order to create a basis for more in-depth knowledge of self, which leads to expanded visions of personal possibility. Therefore, it is equally important that adults develop and maintain feelings of empowerment. In fact, it may be even more important because adults guide the growth of the children. Learning and applying our talents and skills, whether as a child or an adult, is essential for the empowerment cycle to keep turning.

Once the foundational step of learning is in place, the cycle turns to action or application. This step, in the cycle, gives the individual a chance to take what she's learned and put it out into the world. This often feels like a very personally risky step because it involves opening herself up to possible criticism or failure. Many people move into this step reluctantly, or completely avoid it. However, to ultimately attain feelings of empowerment, it is necessary to apply what we have learned and what we can do to real world situations. These are the proving grounds for development of self-beliefs, whether positive or negative. We feel most successful when we've reached out into the world in some significant way. Deep joy comes from successfully taking a meaningful action, discovering a dream, impacting another life, or realizing that personal power is limitless and recyclable. Success instills feelings of personal goodness and accomplishment that keep the empowerment cycle turning and deepening.

Classroom and home environments must be created that allow children to grow within their areas of interest and discard or build upon each one as they see fit. This means that we must provide multiple learning opportunities, taught through diverse methodologies, in safe and friendly spaces. Cooperation is on a higher plane than competition in such settings. Competition builds self-empowerment for the winner but not for the loser. How do we create empowered students in environments of fierce competition for grades and test scores? The truth is that we don't. Individual competitiveness, where a student seeks to improve herself, can be healthy and productive. Achieving personal best is a huge factor, positively contributing to feelings of empowerment. Teachers and schools play a major role in structuring the action phase of the empowerment cycle. Our twelve or more years in school are the action phase of the early stages of our learning about self-empowerment. School is the playground for students to learn about themselves and the world. It ought to be a safe area for exploration, trying on relationships, practicing new skills, exploring interests, sharing talents, and living as a unique individual. However, it often is a place of harassing judgments, quarreling friendships, meeting failure, giving up, feeling defeated, and deciding that it's not OK to be who you really are as a gifted human being. Both of these scenarios exist in our schools simultaneously. Who will be the lucky students who will move successfully and happily through the first scenario? How does a student fall into, or be relegated to, the second category that leads to adulthoods shadowed by self-doubt and fears? Our society can't afford to continue to finance the second scenario in our schools. It is morally, ethically, and financially unsound.

Principals take an active role in supporting teachers in this action phase of the empowerment cycle. Teachers are human beings continuously developing and strengthening their own feelings of self-empowerment just like their students. Teachers are a little further along in the game but they still experience periods of self-doubt and questioning of their path and their contributions. The principal is responsible for creating a parallel environment, within the school setting, to that which the teacher creates in the classroom. Teachers, too, are given opportunities to learn more, practice new skills and apply information, in settings free from judgment and criticism. Creating such a school-wide environment is as challenging as developing it in the classroom setting. It is essential for the principal to create an environment where she allows a creative "trying things out space" to exist throughout the school. This risk-free attitude must also be supported and practiced by teachers with one another on a consistent basis. There are, of course, guidelines to what this "trying things out space" would look like. It doesn't mean that there is ungrounded experimentation going on in an unsupervised and undisciplined way. It does mean that the principal supports and encourages her teachers engaging in learning new techniques and regularly applying them in their teaching. Support for teachers trying new grade levels, practicing new skills, improving the achievement of their students, and continuing to feel passionate about their roles as teachers, should be provided by the principal in a consistent and encouraging manner. This kind of supportive environment encourages educators to meet with one another to collaborate on ways that they can become more effective teachers and principals. They feel more and more empowered to bring their skills forward in the classroom and school, with the support of colleagues and administration. Empowered teachers are the leaders of successful education in our country. Without them, the educational system is a monolithic daycare center, both costly and ineffective. However, schools that create and support environments for the empowerment of students and teachers provide us with hope that there is a bright future not only for our educational system but also for future adults in our society.

The action/application phase of the empowerment cycle leads to the feedback phase. Internal and external feedback systems are the sources of nourishment for a growing empowerment belief system. Internal feedback comes in the form of our inner voice telling us what it thinks about what we're doing and if we're succeeding or failing. Unfortunately, this inner voice is often a harsh critic that puts us down and dismisses our efforts. The inner critic is a significant influence for most people at some time in our lives. This voice of self can build us up and reinforce our efforts or tear us down and dismiss all that we attempt to accomplish. In order to build and maintain an empowered attitude, it's necessary to become familiar with our inner voice and learn to moderate the messages that might be coming through at any given time. Recognizing the inner voice is the first step in gaining control over how it operates in our lives. Notice when the "voice in your head" starts talking to you. This happens repeatedly throughout each and very day. The voice says things like, "I can't believe I said that – how stupid! I look so fat in this outfit". The inner critic relishes its role as evaluator and judge. It takes great pride in sabotaging our efforts and ruining our dreams. This voice is based in fear and feelings of inadequacy. It digs deep within our psyches to find those areas where we feel the most self-doubt and then it pounces on them, hoping to magnify our fears and reinforce our doubts. The inner critic is very successful in fulfilling its role in most people's lives. It doesn't matter whether you're the CEO of a large company or a regular guy trying to get by. The voice will surface in your life and try to become your trusted friend. Don't let it! This inner critic becomes stronger when you grow weaker. During difficult and challenging times that produce self-doubt and worry, the voice booms forward ready to take advantage of your weakened state.

The first step in creating a balanced life where the inner critic is a quiet friend, rather than a boisterous bother, begins with alerting yourself when the voice begins to take over too strongly. When you hear the voice saying something negative, immediately think, "there's the critic." Once you're aware that she's starting to talk, stop her in her tracks. Simply stop the thought before it becomes complete. Awareness and stopping the thought in its process will break the cycle of this inner critic. However, be aware that the voice doesn't give up easily. It will come back repeatedly. Once the negative message is stopped, counteract it with a positive internal, or external, statement – "That was an unusual idea I had but I think I can make it work." Learn to turn the inner critic into a "power voice." A power voice acknowledges the good things you do, the every day efforts you make, and the fact that you are a unique and wonderful person. The power voice, when used consciously and consistently, will fill in the space that the inner critic likes to occupy. Positive statements about self become habitual and support growth and risk-taking – e.g. "That was a brilliant idea I had even if no one understands it yet." If you ask empowered people about their inner voices, they will tell you that the inner critic is present every day of their lives. However, she has been relegated to an observer's role and is only invited to speak when her opinion might prove helpful. The power voice is the primary source of internal feedback within the empowered individual.

It's interesting to observe children and their inner voices. Most children, especially the younger ones, have an external self-critic that has not yet fully become an internal voice. You'll often hear children's inner critic make public statements – "Nobody likes me because I'm stupid." The child then usually observes the reactions of those around her to see if the statement is validated or decried. Ultimately, the child's external voice becomes a secretive internal voice kept hidden from public view. There are some adults who will occasionally allow the inner critic to make an external appearance. In these instances, the adult is looking for verification or denial just as the child does in similar circumstances.

Teachers, parents and administrators have a significant role to play, especially in the early years, to help instill power voices in children and also to teach them how to work with the inner critic. It's important for adults not to serve as external critics toward children. When they do, it increases the likelihood that the inner critic will grow strong and dominant in the child. To ensure that individuals lead empowered lives, it's essential to still the inner critic and activate the power voice. This is a balance that must be constantly readjusted and maintained throughout our lives. Adults are responsible for their own lives and how they live them. Truly empowered individuals rely on their inner knowing as reinforcement to guide them through life's passage. Those who rely solely on external reinforcement will become pawns in the thoughts and opinions of other people.

Parents and educators are responsible for teaching children about inner feedback and how to most positively work with their feelings and inner voice. Positive external feedback given to kids is at the heart of creating healthy internal feedback systems. We teach our children to speak positively about themselves and their abilities by serving as role models and guides. Don't accept put-down language from children, especially if it's about themselves. Develop and nurture the power voice within children to promote healthy and positive self-esteem. The earlier we're able to impact children in this area, the more empowered they will be as adults. If you have an adult friend or colleague who repeatedly voices the internal critic to make herself a victim, call her on it. Tell her not to use put-down language in your presence. That will help to create an awareness that might help her shift her perspective. When every adult and child understands and uses their power voice, inviting the inner critic to sit quietly and observe, we'll all ultimately benefit because there will be more empowered individuals in our world. The education system will certainly benefit because students will become more fearless in their learning, leading them to achieve greater levels of success.

Internal feedback is the most important factor in nurturing, growing and maintaining an empowered attitude throughout life. However, external feedback is also critically important in the formation of one's power voice that leads to feeling and acting empowered on a daily basis. While we don't want to live our lives based on other people's opinions of us, and suggestions as to how we should act, we do want to pay attention to feedback coming from reliable and honest sources. Receiving feedback is the way we measure what impact our words or actions are having on other people or situations. It's a barometer providing us with insight. The problem with external feedback arises when we accept it as the absolute truth rather than as an opinion that may or may not be useful to us. Discernment is critical when listening to feedback from other people. We'll know if the feedback resonates for us or if it's a suggestion that we pass on. Unfortunately, there is great pressure for individuals to "fit in." If we follow these ideas of what we should look like, act like, etc., we'll end up with a very strong inner critic because there will be a huge discrepancy between who we really are and who we're trying to be, based on someone else's idea of what is acceptable. It certainly is a great challenge to listen to and accept feedback for our growth but not become so ruled by it that we lose all sense of self.

Parents and teachers act with caution when giving feedback to children because it significantly impacts each child's self-esteem and self-image. Children are often more sensitive to criticism than adults and they will internalize a comment that an adult might cast off. Teachers give feedback to students every day. It's an important part of the learning process. Some of the feedback is critical; some is supportive. Critical feedback usually tears down and can often destroy. Supportive feedback offers honest response to student's efforts that provides them with insight as to what worked and what didn't work in specific situations. Students need to hear honest feedback, emphasizing that every experience is a learning opportunity and all efforts deserve acknowledgment, because that is how they grow. They can handle negative feedback when delivered in supportive ways that show how to use the feedback to make improvements. Students

know when they don't understand or aren't doing well so these issues or circumstances shouldn't be glossed over. Feelings of personal
empowerment come from feeling good about who you are and what
you're doing even when you make mistakes. Knowing that you'll be
able to overcome any obstacle, often with help from others, expands
feelings of empowerment and confidence in meeting any challenges.
Students who feel confident and proud of what they're presently doing, as well as knowing they have the ability to meet any challenges in
the future, will be successful. Empowered students are self-confident
in their ability to learn and grow. They achieve more on a daily basis
and perform better on testing. Most importantly, they feel personally
successful and valuable as people.

The empowerment cycle begins with learning, moves to application through action, and is nourished by feedback, that leads to self-
evaluation. The self-evaluation phase of the cycle occurs when an
individual takes the feedback she's been given and decides what to
do with it. Sometimes it's embraced and used for change; other times
it's rejected. Some people will totally ignore feedback, not reacting to
it at all. Evaluating the feedback that we receive forces us to look at
what it is that we're doing and why we're doing it. If the feedback was
positive and we agree with it, it will most likely increase our sense of
empowerment. When others acknowledge our strengths, successes or
efforts, it reinforces our positive belief system about ourselves. Even
if we're individuals who work diligently to ignore outside opinions,
we can't help but be influenced by the feedback that is given to us.
Critical feedback, if delivered in a supportive and non-judgmental
way, has the ability to either make us feel worse and become more
self-critical or prompt us to make some changes in order to become
more successful. The choice is ours. The inner critic feeds on external
criticism while the power voice thrives on positive feedback. The self-
evaluation part of the empowerment cycle takes us back to the first
step of learning and the cycle continues to turn all the time leading
the individual to greater depths of knowing self.

Strategy # 2 - Step Back and Let Others Share the Spotlight

Action Steps:

- showcase all students work in your classroom

- publicly recognize the individual and group accomplishments of teachers at your school

- act and speak in calm and centered ways when making important decisions

- include many voices in the decision-making process in your classroom and at your school

- make sure that each student is recognized regularly in ways that feel safe to that student

Empowered individuals are generous in sharing their power and themselves. They know that as long as they remain centered, focused, and free of fear, they will be able to handle any challenges that come forward. Integrity is an important characteristic, central to people who use their power in meaningful and appropriate ways, to contribute to others and the world at large. Power can be used or abused. Empowered people are magnanimous, willing to mentor others and use their power for good. Those who use their power appropriately are not ego-centered individuals. They don't need to be the center of attention to feel fulfilled.

One of the ways we can most quickly empower ourselves and build our self-esteem is through empowering others. Generosity of spirit is a mark of the person who feels good about herself. When we recognize the personal power and giftedness in another, we reinforce her positive sense of self. This positive sense of self then leads the individual to demonstrate more magnanimous acts leading to her and other's empowerment. It's a cycle that builds and reinforces itself and then spirals into greater depths of purpose and being. Deep and true power is a quiet force. It lies comfortably within our hearts and minds, coming forward to build and create when the time is right. This quiet side of power is the path we follow when we wish to help empower our students, colleagues, family members or friends. Working in the shadows, we bring light to the skills, talents and contributions of others in order to support their growth. By doing this, we are actually helping ourselves although that may not always be apparent. Since we are closely bound to anyone who comes within our life's sphere, especially family and friends, what we do to impact their lives affects ours. The power I share with another comes back to me in great abundance. Therefore, from a purely selfish standpoint, it makes sense for me to try to empower others. However, coming from a more altruistic place, I help to empower others because I know it is my responsibility and the right thing to do.

Children are empowered when teachers and parents share the spotlight with them. This means that we help children find their paths and practice their developing skills. Children who are given important responsibilities at home and school learn valuable lessons about themselves. They won't always succeed but "misses" as well as "hits" are important learning tools. Most children want to be loved and accepted for who they are both at home and at school. They like feeling important and valued. Some like the public adulation; others prefer private praise. It should be an easy task for adults to create situations that propel children into experiences of personal power where they use these experiences to build their positive self-image and growing sense of confidence. Unfortunately, this is not always the case. Many parents don't want to deal with the "messiness" of children learning who they are in life. This experimental process is not always orderly or comfortable. In fact, it's usually the opposite. Many adults believe that children should remain in a subjective role until they are young adults and then they can assume their adult power. It's often too late, at this point in time, to try to build self-esteem that has been kept behind closed doors, with no opportunities for growth through trial and error.

Adults have a duty to help every child feel powerful in her own right. This may be the most important role we'll have in our lifetime. Parents and teachers are not the only adults responsible for working with children to find their inner strength. All members of the community have a role to play whether directly or indirectly in educating our youth. Empowered children are not afraid to question some of the dictates of adults or ask for reasons behind their decisions. If we work to empower our children, we must be ready to hear their voices because they will come forward loudly and clearly. This will happen in both acceptable and unacceptable ways, but it will happen. That's why so many adults want to keep the lid on the depth of power that a child will discover or utilize. They might become too contrary and uncontrollable. We might lose our power over our children, which will make life more difficult to deal with. What we really should fear are the results of not giving children their right to develop and practice their power. For when they aren't given these opportunities, they grow into adults who are uncertain about themselves and their ability to contribute and be happy.

We do a great disservice to individuals and society when we allow children to reach adulthood with no sense of their goodness and positive personal power. The emphasis here is on positive personal power. Some children, when first assuming personal power, go to extremes with it. This is especially true when they haven't had the chance to experience power before. It's OK to swing to extremes as long as there is some guidance that helps the individual swing back into a balanced state. Many of our youth, when first given power, will use it forcefully and inappropriately. This gives the adults the chance to say, "See, I told you she couldn't handle this power," and they immediately shut it down. We all can relate many examples of times that we've done a poor job of handling our personal power. Some of these instances were hurtful to others and damaging to ourselves. Nevertheless, they were valuable learning experiences. Adults must not squelch children's varied learning experiences just because they might cause problems or result in failure. Some experiences might never lead to success. However, the development of personal power may be firmly built from the remains of failing situations. Sharing the spotlight with children should be an easy task for adults since there are so many ways in which to create meaningful situations where youth will feel successful and self-empowered. We must step outside of our ego and assist our students in becoming personally powerful at a very young age. It is our duty. It is our joy. It is our future.

Many teachers have difficulty standing back and allowing colleagues to shine. We can and should feel good when others are successful and feeling positive about themselves. Why is it that we so often feel defensive when someone else succeeds? Why do we often feel like failures if someone else takes center stage? Perhaps we have not yet reached a fully empowered stage in our own growth, if we can't bear to see others reach the top. The sign of a truly empowered person is that she is able to move through life accomplishing her goals and contributing to others in ways that don't require her to be a hero because she's taking these actions. There may be times when she's center stage and receives accolades for her efforts. However, more often than not, she moves through life doing the job that needs to be done without fanfare. Personal empowerment is strength whispered through gentle words. It's experiencing a personal satisfaction while standing in the shadows. Mostly, it's a knowing that every human being is inherently wonderful and capable of contributing to the whole. The spotlight is big enough to shine on us all, at one time or another. In order to be in the spotlight ourselves, we must share the stage. It's that simple.

Strategy #3 - Find a Measure of Success in Everything You Do

Action Steps:

- take a few minutes each day to pat yourself on the back for the accomplishments you've made and the obstacles you've overcome that day

- use your inner power voice to reinforce your outer actions

- strive to keep your focus in the present

- acknowledge and accept yourself as a talented and powerful person

- teach your students to recognize examples of success even amidst failure

Humans are inherently good people who do good things in life. That is the norm. Why then do so many people feel inadequate? Why do teachers and parents struggle with raising and educating their children? Why do so many children feel like failures at home and in school? How can we turn the tide of self-loathing and lack of self-confidence? There is a simple habit we can adopt that will assist us in fighting the self-doubts that arise on a daily basis. This is a habit we can instill in our children when they are very young. It will assist them in developing their sense of themselves as wonderful and capable individuals. Finding a measure of success in everything you do is simple and powerful. Here's how it works.

Begin by paying attention and being aware in the present moment. This means that you're focused on what's going on and what you're doing right now in this instance. When we pay attention to our life in the moment, we see and experience wonderful things about the world and about ourselves. Our self-esteem and feelings of empowerment are mostly built upon small, daily accomplishments. Most of us won't be famous and well known. We are regular people living our lives routinely every day. However, even within what seems like our often boring routine, there are magical moments to be identified and savored. We only notice these magical moments if we're paying attention and remaining open to the possibility of them occurring on a daily basis. Awareness, focus and acceptance are the keys to opening the gifts to be found in all the present moments of our lives. Every action we take in life has a successful component even if it's quite minute. However, we rarely make a conscious effort to notice these small successes or acknowledge ourselves for achieving them. Step one is awareness. Pay attention to your life! Take a moment on your way back from the grocery store to mentally review any successes or positive things that happened during that time – e.g. "I sure saved a lot of money by using coupons this time! I feel good about being calm when everyone in my line was complaining about the slow line. I'm a good mother and do the best I can for my kids." This mental review takes about two minutes but helps to build a sense of empowerment and positive self-view by reinforcing your role as a mother. Other instances will reinforce your roles as a wife, a teacher, a friend, and an overall good person. Awareness becomes habitual as we learn to pay attention as a regular part of our lives. It's very much like stepping aside and being an objective observer to the actions of our life. Our inner voice becomes an encourager and promoter rather than a critic when we consciously embrace living life through personal awareness.

Once we begin to practice awareness, we must then concentrate on focusing our thoughts toward remaining in the present. This means that we don't lose ourselves in thinking about the past or concentrating on the future. Life is lived in the here and now. So much of our loss of power comes when we blame ourselves or feel sadness about the failures or losses of the past or when we focus on our fears of the future. We don't support our personal empowerment when we live in the past or future. Life is here and now in this moment. When we discover our minds wandering away from the present, we must refocus. This, too, much like awareness, becomes habitual. Find yourself slipping into fear or guilt, return to the now. Upon returning to the now, focus on what successes you are experiencing in the moment. "That was a great way to solve this problem! I'm really getting a lot of work finished today." The inner voice plays an active role in helping you to stay in a present focus. Utilize it as an aid by asking it to reinforce the positive things about you and your actions that exist in the now. Besides you, your inner voice is the only other "person" who is constantly with you, paying attention to all that you do. Make it a power voice to support your present time actions.

To feel more empowered by discovering our individual strengths in each moment, we must become aware, focus on our actions and pay attention to our thoughts. Most people serve as their own worst critic. How many of us are able to fully accept and love ourselves for who we are in every moment of our lives? Self-criticism and thoughts of personal inadequacy haunt our lives and are, at times, difficult for even the most self-confident person to overcome. Reaching a personally empowered state is like climbing a steep, rocky mountain. It's a slow-going, one-step-at-a-time process often fraught with difficulties and doubt. The climbing becomes easier when we believe in self and feel confident about whom we are as human beings. The path presents challenges and creates doubts but we'll have better tools with which to make the climb when we accept that we are valuable and capable people. If we don't accept ourselves, with all our strengths and weaknesses, how do we expect others to accept us?

Parents and teachers, who practice finding some success in each moment and action of their lives, can easily teach this habit to children. Begin by giving feedback to your children at a very early age. Point out all the wonderful things they do. Young kids don't know they're doing wonderful things unless you show them and tell them. Teachers should be consistently pointing out small successes and accomplishments to their students throughout the school day. If educators rely only on testing to reinforce students, they are missing the most valuable way in which to build empowered students. We must train our children to astutely look at what they are doing and find a measure of success in every action they take. There is even success to be identified in situations that appear to be negative or misguided. Often the success comes from how a student learns to react to a situation that was initially viewed as negative or a failure. Realizing that every situation is a valuable learning experience and that we are all life-long learners helps to alleviate feelings of failure that come when situations don't work out for us. Each of us brings a bit of giftedness to everything we do. Personal empowerment is built upon a foundation of self-monitoring the observable actions we take. Therefore, to be aware in each moment allows us to focus on our actions and words in the present, leading to personal empowerment.

Strategy #4 - Get to Know Yourself and Listen to Your Intuition

Action Steps:

- practice using your intuition by being aware of and following your hunches

- ask your students why they take certain actions and how they make decisions to give them practice in listening to self

- spend quiet time in reading, journaling or reflection to gain insight about yourself and your life

- monitor and record daily intuition hits, over a two week period, to become more self-aware

- overcome fearful situations or decisions by becoming calm and quiet in order to become clear and decisive

People who feel powerful know themselves. They recognize their strengths, can identify their weaknesses, and realize that both of these areas are always evolving. When you know your inner self, you can better identify the fears that stop you as well as the skills that promote your growth. Since empowerment is created from inside yourself rather than from an outside source, it is crucial to listen to your inner knowing, identify how you feel about situations and people and follow these inner guidelines.

Friends, family and colleagues assist us in building our feelings of empowerment by providing valuable feedback to us. However, it is up to each one of us to find a way to be in touch with who we are at the deepest levels, identifying our giftedness and bringing this internal power forward into our lives in actionable ways. We all come into this world inherently knowing who we are and what we have to give. This knowledge is not always obvious or even available to us.

Most people spend a significant portion of their lives trying to figure out why they're here and what their purpose might be in this world. These answers are not to be found externally. They reside in the inner sanctum of our hearts and are revealed through our inner knowing, our intuition. Therefore, in order to become the best self-guides for our lives that we can be, it is necessary to have a relationship with our intuition, our inner knowing.

Intuition is not an abstract or New Age term that is only available to those who meditate or live alternative life styles. Everyone has an inner knowing that reveals who they are and what they're about. If we all have this knowing, why don't we all use it? How do we come in touch with it? Are children intuitive? If so, why would it be important for children to use their intuition? Our intuition often comes forward most strongly and usefully in areas of relationship. We often have a "sense" about a person whom we meet. We know if we like them, fear them or feel uncertain about them. We sense if they're angry, disturbed or happy. There is an inner registering of subtle clues, about this person, that is taking place within us. We are very often not even aware that this process is occurring as we interact with other people. Once we start paying attention to these "feelings" about situations and people, we become more adept at recognizing them. We also become more proficient in using this knowing to help us work and live with other people. It is often said that we have stronger intuitive connections with those with whom we are the closest (e.g. mother and child).

In addition to using our intuition to learn more about other people, we use it to guide us in making decisions about ourselves and planning our lives. The more we use our intuition, the more confident we become in using it. When we see concrete results, we believe more in our abilities of inner sight and deep knowing. This creates a personal internal/external feedback loop that helps us feel personally empowered. This sounds rather simple yet it is often difficult for individuals to utilize this full measure of personal power. Why? Doubt and fear step into the picture and often block forward movement. We may have a strong feeling about how we should respond or act in a given situation but we often doubt our knowing and fear what others will think about what we do or say. Most people don't regularly use and trust their intuition. We like to receive validation of the decisions we make. That doesn't always happen when we follow our inner knowing. This is especially true when the intuitive act flies in the face of what others are doing or expecting. Utilizing your intuition can often feel lonely. This sounds strange but standing up for what is best for yourself is often difficult and there won't necessarily always be support for what you choose to do. We become more empowered as we are able to follow our inner guide and make outer choices that reflect this belief in self. Trusting ourselves is an important step in becoming an empowered individual who is able to follow her own path and contribute in significant ways. Intuition leads us to self, which opens us to service and purpose. Whether we are consciously paying attention to our intuition or unknowingly using it, it guides us through each situation and every day of our lives.

Children are particularly intuitive, especially when it comes to sensing their levels of comfort or dislike when they're around other people. Unfortunately, this inherent self-knowing is often buried as the child grows up influenced by the expectations of the adults in her life. Many adults spend years trying to regain the natural knowing that is so much a part of our childhood. Teachers play an important role in assisting children to acknowledge and follow their inner knowing. Part of growing up is trying out different things to really find out what it is we like to do. Teachers are instrumental in providing opportunities for children to find their passion. It is often an astute teacher who first recognizes a child's interest and gifts in a certain area. Parents and teachers who pay attention to what children say and do will be able to act as mentors and guides in the process of developing self-confidence.

Intuition is a valuable learning tool for students. Successful students pay attention to hunches and thoughts about how to respond, what choices to make or who to trust. We won't tap into a child's intuitive self if we're always telling her what she should do and how she should do it. Choice is essential to learning. Children discover who they are and what they love through self-exploration and experimentation. Parents and teachers are responsible for providing children with these choices and new experiences, which reinforce those areas where students show their greatest gifts, talents, and interests. When students are listened to and acknowledged for their ideas and interests by their teachers, they develop strong beliefs in themselves and the ability to know what to do. Teachers who encourage students to use their knowing as a guide in their lives are building strong foundations for future use of personal intuition. Students who feel that they are capable of finding answers, knowing what to do, and working through challenges grow into empowered individuals. They need the help of parents and teachers to develop this positive sense of self. Intuition is a word that is not often used in schools. However, it is a tool that is regularly used by teachers and administrators in all their dealings with children and their parents. Teachers naturally follow their inner knowing or hunches about their students. They don't just rely on what testing data shows them. Instead, they get to know the whole child and make decisions based on that information. Administrators operate in much the same way with teachers. A good principal will encourage her teachers to use their intuition in assisting students to be as successful as possible. You will often hear a principal ask a teacher, "What does your gut tell you about this situation?" This is intuition at work. Intuition operates in conjunction with facts. The more information we have about a situation or a person the stronger and more accurate our intuition will be in making decisions or guiding us. Intuition is the key that unlocks the doors on our life pathway. There will be new doorways all along this path. We'll need the self-exploratory tool of intuition to continue to find ways through the many different shaped doorways. Empowered individuals don't allow closed doors to stop their forward progress.

Our schools will be most successful in educating all students when principals and teachers are empowered to be the best they can be and contribute to their classrooms and the school in meaningful ways. Talented teachers produce good results. They know how to most effectively work with the whole child to find hidden talents and bring them into the light through self-expression. Teachers, who look inward to discover their personal strengths, and build upon them, understand how to direct this same process in their student's learning. Empowering students is the main work of teachers. Finding out about their interests and learning more about the world and their place in it, is the main work of students. When principals, teachers and students come together in an environment that supports their individual talents and strengths, anything is possible. Personal interest and passion drive the learning process. Expanding our knowledge helps us discover our interests. Empowering every member of the school community is a win-win proposition. It is through attaining personal empowerment that we find our way in the world and feel successful through the many ways in which we contribute. Every person is on this earth to contribute in a special way. Teachers and principals have the honor of guiding our youth in this self-discovery process through their interactions with academic content and mastery of specific skills that will enable them to lead successful and fulfilled lives.

4. ENVIRONMENT

"Middle School Blues and the Walkout"

I MOVED FROM Pennsylvania to Arizona to become principal of a K-8 school. In my previous teaching and administrative career I worked with K-6th graders. I had no previous experience with middle school students before coming to Arizona. This lack of knowledge of middle school students probably was a good thing because if I knew what I was getting into, I might not have accepted the job offer! I had some inkling, when I said yes to the job, that there were some "issues" with the middle school section of the campus. I had no idea how many issues there were and how much energy and effort I would contribute toward handling them.

I arrived in Arizona two days before school began so there wasn't much opportunity to get a head start on planning or meeting with the teachers and learning about the students. The previous administration had left the office and school unprepared for the opening of school. Class and special area schedules and class lists were not in place. Textbooks and other teaching materials hadn't been ordered. Summer repairs had not been completed. I scrambled to get things ready for the opening of school. I remember the first day the students arrived. The middle school students looked so big. They also swaggered and acted tough. A few of the middle school teachers contacted me, prior to the first day, and told me that they needed help. The middle school was out of control. When I asked them what they meant by out of control, they said many of the students had poor attitudes, were disrespectful, harassed one another, didn't complete their work, were often disruptive in class and had been empowered in these ways because the previous administration hadn't backed up the teachers, when they tried to correct these problems. The defiant students overshadowed the students who were doing what they were supposed to do. After hearing these comments, I asked myself, "What are you doing here?" I was to ask that question over and over again during the next few months!

I decided to take a proactive approach with the middle school students and personally speak to each class the first day of school. I began with the eighth graders since they had been part of the middle school the previous year. Upon entering each class, I welcomed them back, gave them a little of my background, told them I was excited to be their principal and clearly outlined some basic behavior rules. After I outlined a few basic rules, a hand shot up.

"What if we break a rule? What are you going to do to us?" challenged one student.

"It depends on what you do," I replied. "You might receive a lunch or after-school detention. I might call your parents or invite them in for a meeting. You might get suspended from school."

"Suspended!" he said indignantly. "The old principal never suspended anyone. You can't suspend us just because we might break a stupid rule!"

Several other heads nodded in agreement. Most of the students sat watching, waiting to see what would happen. I stood facing the challenger, staring into his eyes, giving him the best "don't try it" look I could muster. I held my ground as I replied to his outburst. It felt like the showdown at the OK Corral.

I took a deep breath, scanned the classroom, making eye contact with every student and then focused my principal's laser-vision on the student who fired the first salvo. With a calm smile on my face, I asked, "What's your name?"

"Erik," he replied.

"Well, Erik," I said. "I really don't want to suspend you or anyone else but if I have to, I'll have no problem doing so."

Several students laughed and called out comments. Not wanting the situation to get totally out of hand or have Erik feel he was being singled out, I quickly sent out my best withering stare at those who had commented. Its harsh intensity pinned them in their seats, putting them on notice that any further challenge would be met with an immediate and punitive response.

"I consider calling out and answering back to be disrespectful behavior. I can't stand disrespectful behavior and I'll suspend a student for that more quickly than anything else. However, I'm sure that won't be a problem with any of you." I said in my most authoritative, yet friendly tone. "Please remember to follow the rules and we'll get along fine. However, I won't hesitate to suspend someone the first day of school if necessary. Don't let that be you. Are there any other questions?" The students were silent.

There was one other issue I needed to address, with the middle school students that first day. Several teachers, the custodians, the secretary and just about everyone else on campus had told me about the awful middle school lunch period. The students had been permitted the previous year to take their food outside and eat. There was no designated outside eating area with tables and proper facilities. Middle school students, who chose to eat outside, wandered the campus (ten buildings), sat wherever they wanted to, harassed the younger students and left trash all over the place. Of course, with so many wandering around, there was no supervision either. Several students would apparently sneak out into the surrounding forest area for a mid-day smoke. When I heard all of this, I decided that there would be no eating lunch outside unless it were a supervised, planned activity. When I met with the classes that first morning, I told them that there would be no eating outside. I listed the main reasons as lack of supervision, trashing of the campus, and unacceptable behavior, not to mention setting a bad example for all the younger students who were watching them. Needless to say, there were some unhappy and indignant students after I made that announcement! I could hardly wait for lunch to come on that first day.

I tried to say a few positive things about all the great activities they would get to do this school year and then I left the classroom. I was emotionally exhausted. I still had five middle school rooms to visit! "What am I doing here?" The other eighth grade classes went much the same way with one or two students setting forth the challenge. The seventh graders were a little more polite and subdued as they were new to the middle school experience. I had spent a huge chunk of the first morning in the middle school and I still had five other classroom buildings to visit, lunch duty to serve, schedules to finish, etc. I was quite overwhelmed on that first day. I came to learn how to function in an overwhelmed state, as that is where I remained for the next few months.

I felt somewhat discouraged with the hard-line approach I had to take with the students that first morning of the new school year. I'm not a punitive administrator and I don't necessarily think that suspending students is a good idea. In my previous ten years as a K-6th grade principal, I had suspended about two students per year. It was not my disciplinary method of choice. However, it felt necessary, in these circumstances to take a firm stand right up front. Little did I know how often and strongly it would be challenged. I've always believed that educators should take a positive and respectful approach toward working with students, acknowledging them for their efforts and accomplishments. I've found that being punitive creates resentment, hostility and often the continuation of the poor behavior. That first week of school, I immediately began to try to institute positive programs to reinforce the behaviors and efforts we wanted to see. The first year, working with the middle school, was a constant struggle for me, trying to balance the negative (which seemed necessary to gain control) and the positive, which was the desired approach. It was a delicate balancing act. I knew that the balance must swing to the positive approach, in the long run, if we were to create a safe and supportive school environment. No one wanted to deal with a bunch of thugs every day and most students didn't really want to act like a bunch of thugs.

It was with great anxiety that I dragged myself into the cafeteria during the middle school lunch those first few weeks of school. I had assigned a couple of teachers to be on duty with me, but I knew we would be challenged. It was difficult not yet knowing all the students because it's much easier to work effectively with students when you know them and their issues. The cafeteria was chaos those first few days with kids shouting across the room, walking around, trying to sneak outside with food and attempting to show that they had the run of the place. They did during those first few days! The first direct challenge to the rules came on the second day of school when two middle school students got into a food fight in the cafeteria. Ketchup flew out of plastic bottles and splattered on innocent bystanders. Chips were smashed and strewn across the top of and under the table. Soda cans were shaken and the content used as liquid weapons, hitting not only its mark, but also anyone who was unfortunate enough to be in the path. Students, in the immediate area, ducked and shouted. When a teacher went over to stop this activity, both students were mouthy and defiant. "He squirted the ketchup on me first. He deserved what he got. He's an idiot! I'm not going to pick this up. He should do it!" "You better watch what you say or you'll have more ketchup on you! You clean it up because you started it, fool."

I had come up behind them and heard their unacceptable tone of voice. They were extremely rude and disrespectful to the teacher. "Please clean up the food and go wait for me at the office," I said to them.

One boy started to clean up the mess. The other student brushed the crushed chips from his hands, wiped the ketchup off his shirt, blotted the soda from his face, and backed away from the messy table. Looking at me as he folded his arms across his chest and squared his shoulders the student said, "He started it. I'm not going to pick this stuff up. You can't make me."

"That's right," I said. "I can't make you pick it up. However, you're going to be suspended for one day for talking back to your teacher. Do you want to add to that for being defiant with me?"

"You can't suspend me. My dad will be really mad at you," he retorted. Apparently, the middle school students who acted up liked to threaten that their parents would "take care" of the teacher or the principal who disciplined them so unfairly.

"I'm sure your dad and I will have a very good talk. Now, please help pick up this mess and go wait for me at the office."

He complied with my request, all the time mumbling to himself. Since other students had been near-by overhearing all of this, it didn't take long for word to spread throughout the middle school that two students were being suspended. Would the other students get the message? Since I was worried about kids protesting these suspensions and causing trouble in the classrooms that afternoon, I went to each class and briefly said that two students had been suspended for disrespectful behavior toward a teacher and for having a food fight. I wanted the students to be clear on what had happened and to know what the consequences would be. I made it a practice those first few months of school to go to the middle school classrooms and give the reasons for suspensions when they happened. I never announced the names of the students, although the word always got out anyway. By keeping the students informed, they didn't develop outrage through misinformation. They could clearly see that specific consequences followed certain behaviors. Once we began emphasizing and rewarding positive life skills, poor behavior was reduced.

As a whole, great kids filled the middle school. There was a vocal minority who caused the majority of the disruptions and who were responsible for most of the poor behavior. The teachers and I met formally once a week to try to institute student-centered programs that would help us do a more effective job in creating a positive and safe environment. I spent a few hours every day in informal conversation with middle school teachers, trying to support their efforts in the classrooms to rein in these out-of-control kids. I thought my job was difficult. However, the teachers' challenges were much greater, and more frequent, than mine. I tried to support their efforts as consistently and fairly as I could. Our goals were to create a safe and supportive academic environment in which all students would meet with success. These goals were all reachable, but it would take us many months and hours-upon-hours of hard work to accomplish them.

No one fought in the middle school. They just called each other names and challenged their teachers' authority. By the end of the third week of school, I had already suspended nine students, mostly for disrespectful behaviors. I hated this! I felt like a judge and jailer. This was not how I wanted to run my school. In addition to creating many negative results, suspensions are a lot of work. First, there is the time spent interviewing all participants and documenting what they say. Then I'd speak to the teacher who was present during the incident. Once the suspension was given, parents were contacted. The superintendent and school board also had to be notified of all suspensions and the reasons for them. The student's teachers were notified of the suspensions so that they could prepare class work for the student. Finally, a report was placed in the student's file and the school discipline file. If the suspension was an in-school suspension, work must be gathered for the student to do during that time. When the student returned to school, I met with him or her and discussed how to handle re-entry and future behavior. Since there was no assistant principal that first year, I was responsible for the entire process. I was quickly getting a reputation, as a hard-liner, both at school and throughout the small community in which we lived. This was not the reputation I wanted to develop, but it did seem to create a feeling of confidence, among teachers and parents that someone was in control and was trying to turn around a difficult situation.

The turning point in the battle of who would control the school came at the end of the third full week of school. Friday had arrived, much to my joy! For some strange reason that I never really figured out, Thursdays were horrible days for the middle school most of that year. It seemed that chaos and serious behavior issues exploded on Thursdays. The teachers and I came to marvel at how different a calm Wednesday could be from a wild Thursday. By Friday, we were all exhausted and ready for the weekend. On this particular Friday, ten middle school students disagreed with something one of their teachers asked them to do. Rather than waiting until break time or lunch, when they could have spoken to the teacher or to me, they decided to stage a walk out! I received a phone call, from their teacher, saying that ten students were on their way up to the office, without his permission. They had been rude and defiant, challenging the teacher and then walking out of his class. I looked out my window, which faced the classroom area, and saw ten students forcefully striding toward the office. Great! Their body language revealed quite an attitude of self-empowerment and open defiance.

A loud burst of raw energy soon entered the outer office and flowed into my office, which was right next to the front door. The indignant outrage that poured forth amazed me. The students crowded into my office without knocking or checking to see if I was busy. They loudly began condemning the teacher and what he had asked them to do (I don't remember the specifics of his request but it didn't seem out of line at the time) and asked me to fire him! I think I sat there with my mouth open, stunned by the boldness and disrespect of these students. Many voices were speaking at once so I asked them to get quiet, which they did.

"Your teacher called me and said you left class without his permission," I said. "That's unacceptable behavior at this school. You must go back to class and try to work out your disagreements, with the teacher, in an appropriate way."

"But he won't listen to us!"

"He can't make us do that assignment!"

"I'm not going back to his classroom!"

"Can we tell you what he's trying to get us to do?"

"I'll be happy to meet with you at your break time, during lunch or after school," I replied. "I won't talk to you about it now because you just can't mouth off to the teacher and walk out of class if you feel like doing so. This isn't the way to handle a problem."

"You're just as bad as he is! Why won't you listen to our side?" asked the apparent spokesperson.

"I told you that I would be happy to meet with you at an appropriate time. I want to hear what you have to say, but not now under these circumstances."

There was a lot of grumbling and comments of, "not fair," "can't make us," "tell my parents," etc. The ten students were still very agitated. Several paced around the office. Others mumbled to each other. A righteous air of indignity filled the room. At the time all of this is going on, other students, parents and teachers were coming and going from the office, trying to get around the milling mob. It felt like a sit-in from the 60s!

"Everyone listen carefully to what I'm going to say," I told them. The office was finally quiet. "I will be happy to listen to your complaints, but at the designated times and in appropriate ways. You cannot walk out of a class no matter how unfairly you feel the teacher is acting. You definitely may not speak disrespectfully to your teacher. You may not storm the office and rudely interrupt my work or the secretaries' work. Now, I want you all to go back to class and quietly sit in your seats and do your work. I will meet with each one of you at lunch today to hear your complaints. There will be some consequence for walking out of class and speaking to your teacher the way you did." I planned to walk back to class with them to ensure that they returned quietly and politely.

"We're not going back to that class and you can't make us," said one of the students.

"Yea! You can't make us!" shouted several students.

"Make that teacher leave! Yea!" said a chorus of students.

Everyone watched to see how I would react. "What am I doing here?" The now familiar mantra echoed in my head once again! What a great way to spend a Friday afternoon.

"You all have five minutes to make a decision. You either go back to class quietly and politely or you'll be suspended from school."

"What?! You're kidding. It's not us! You should get rid of that teacher," said the ringleader. Several students shook their heads in agreement.

They were still feeling very empowered by their walk out. I tried to remain calm and balanced although I was seething inside with anger. How dare they? Would this defiance and battle for control never cease?

"Each of you should make your own decision," I told them. "You have two minutes left. I suggest you go back to class and we'll get this issue settled."

Two students, out of the ten, walked out the front door and headed back to class. I was furious but tried to remain calm. It was only an hour until dismissal and I had eight, uptight, defiant teenagers spread throughout the office. I had originally hoped to leave school by 5:00 this Friday but I knew that would now be impossible. I had learned, early in my administrative career, that it's best not to leave problems unsettled over the weekends because they tend to gain momentum and become a full-fledged crisis by Monday morning. I knew these kids would need to be dealt with immediately. I got them as quieted down as I could and began calling parents to come in and meet with me. I felt that the student's actions were a direct and serious challenge to the authority and rules of the school and needed to be fairly, and quickly, dealt with that Friday.

A series of parent-student meetings were set up over the next four hours. I asked each parent to meet with me, and their child, to discuss the incident, the student's attitude and actions, and how we could all more successfully work together in the future. I was quite nervous about meeting with these parents. Would they support my position or would they back the actions of their children? I had heard that the parents in this community often supported and enabled their children's negative behaviors. I had only been here for three weeks and I was suspending eight students in one day! What would people think? When would I ever get to be the educational leader of this school rather than the hammer?

The meetings with the parents and students went quite well overall. Every single parent supported the school's position and was apologetic about how their son or daughter had acted. Several students came into our meeting with a defiant attitude, which their parents quickly put an end to. Much to my surprise, almost every parent thanked me for taking a hard line stance on this and said it was about time this student unrest, which had been so prevalent, stopped. I felt totally supported and thanked by the parents. They weren't happy about the two day, out-of-school suspension their children received, but they agreed that it was fair. There were students, in this group, for whom this was their first, and last, suspension ever at school. They had been sucked up in the rhetoric of the few leaders who were out to disrupt whenever they could. The two students who returned to class also met with their parents and me. They received an in-school suspension for their participation in the walk out. I finally left school that Friday about 9:00 pm, exhausted and feeling fairly defeated. I was a principal who believed in building upon and reinforcing the positive and I had just suspended eight students. My stomach was in knots. I had a throbbing headache. The paperwork I had planned to finish after school still sat on my desk. It was dark outside and I sat in my office all alone and miserable, trying to muster enough energy to drive home.

The majority of the students, who were in this group, were not usually disrespectful and belligerent. In fact, several of them became very positive school leaders by the end of their eighth-grade year. They just needed positive activities in which to place their energy and enthusiasm. That Friday, in early September, was a turning point in the middle school for the remainder of that year. It sent a strong message to the students about being responsible and respectful. The other students, as a whole, actually seemed to be more relaxed and relieved after this incident. The majority of students was positive and respectful and had been overshadowed by the "mighty few." Their teachers also felt more confident after this mass suspension because they knew they would be supported as long as they were doing their job. Word spread quickly that weekend, throughout the community, that the crackdown was intensifying. I stayed away from the grocery and drug store, not wanting to run into parents and kids. I didn't feel good about what had happened, but I knew it was necessary.

The remainder of the year continued to be challenging with the middle school students. However, as the year progressed, I handed out fewer suspensions. As we added positive programs and emphasized and acknowledged appropriate behaviors, the negative school climate began to shift. It ultimately took us a couple of years to create the positive community that now exists at the school. Today the middle school is filled with great students who apply themselves, collaborate, and contribute to an overall positive school environment. Our middle school students win many awards, both locally and at the state and national level. They mostly behave honorably although sometimes their teenage characteristics over-rule common sense! These students aren't better kids than the group who filled the middle school my first year. The difference is that the school environment has changed from one of fear and division, which supported their negative attitudes, to one of positive support and mutual respect. The teachers, parents and I sang the Middle School Blues for weeks on end that first year. It was a struggle to get our kids back. Luckily, we won and so did they! I no longer asked, "What am I doing here?" I now knew.

......

Environment

Definition: *the surroundings or conditions in which a person, animal or plant lives or operates*

Our children spend almost a third of their day at school. These hours spent at school may be the most intentional, focused and supportive part of a child's day. Students face intense interactions with others and learn more about themselves during this time away from home. Academic and behavioral expectations will, at some time, challenge most students. The majority of children begin the school year with an optimistic and hopeful attitude. They want to enjoy learning, feel successful and make friends. The school community of students, teachers, the principal, parents and other volunteers, form the away-from-home family for students. This core of peer and adult support helps create the educational and social experiences for each student in a particular school. The strengths or weaknesses, in the school environment, form the backdrop that supports a student's academic achievement and personal growth. Therefore, it's essential that a student-centered and highly supportive school climate is established and reinforced throughout the year. School environment becomes tangible when you see it through actions, hear it through words and feel it emotionally. A student knows immediately if a teacher or a peer likes and accepts him. Parents can see that a school has adequate materials for both students and teachers to do their work. The language used between students at lunch or on the playground provides clues to the levels of respect that are encouraged. The physical condition of a school also makes a loud statement about how that community supports education.

The classroom and school-wide environments, in which students participate every day, significantly impact their success or failure both academically and socially. The fullness and excellence of the learning environment, created to support the educational goals of the school, plays a major role in the realization of those goals. If you're a teacher, principal or parent, who wishes to make positive improvements in your school, look to the school's environment for guidance. As you look around, ask some questions. How does our school environment support our academic and social goals? How do people interact in our school? Are teachers and students excited most days about coming to school? What mechanisms are in place to insure that all students and teachers feel safe, valued and part of the community? How are teachers supported in doing their job? Do parents feel welcomed and enjoy being here? Through examining all facets of a school's environment, including academic learning and social interactions, we are better able to identify those areas that need to be strengthened. The environmental conditions in a school significantly contribute to the success or failure of the students and teachers in that school.

School environment contains a physical, emotional, relational, and academic focus. Educators and parents must focus on all four areas to create and maintain an over-all positive school environment. The first component, the physical environment, is rather obvious and includes the actual building/s on the campus as well as the equipment, furniture and materials necessary to support the system. The condition of the classrooms and the school building itself is critically important in the education of our students. Seven hours is a long time to spend in one or two rooms. Think how it would be for you to spend that much time in one location. The condition of the space in which students work sends a message to them about how valued their educational process is to the adults in their world. Spending significant portions of time in decaying, dirty and colorless classrooms can be debilitating to students. Entering a colorful, warm and nurturing environment each morning sets a positive and supportive tone for students, telling them that they and the learning process are valued at this school. Unfortunately, a large number of students in our country enter schools every day that are dark and in disrepair, leading to despair and inequality. An important first step to improving the educational system in our country would be to send every student into a clean, colorful and physically supportive school environment each and every day. That action alone would change the picture of education in the United States.

Learning materials, including furniture, textbooks, computers, equipment, instruments, and other supplies, are a part of the physical component of the school. Doctors don't perform surgery without specialized equipment. Musicians don't play symphonies without the correct instruments. Teachers should not be expected to teach without the proper tools and materials. Unfortunately, many schools lack the basic supplies needed for the daily educational process. Under-funded schools have had to resort to asking students to bring in their own supplies. Some schools even ask students to bring in items like paper towels and toilet paper to support the shrinking school supply budget. Students in many schools share textbooks in class. This becomes a problem when a book needs to be taken home for additional study. In many schools, teachers who purchase supplies aren't reimbursed for their expenses. They put out their own money because they know that certain materials are essential to them in the teaching process. Huge inequalities exist in our schools when we look at the physical environments. It makes sense that some of the best educational experiences will occur in those physical school settings that are most suited to the needs of the educational processes of teaching and learning. Sub-standard schools, lacking adequate materials and teaching tools, send a negative message to teachers and students. The message is one of lack of support and low priority for the educational process and those people integrally involved in it.

Equally as important as the physical environment of a school is the emotional environment of support that is created in the school setting. This second component, the emotional climate of a school, impacts student success. Learning is best accomplished in a setting that encourages risk-taking and exploration. It requires the learner to move outside of his comfort zone and discover new things about himself and his world. Students show their vulnerability every day by raising their hands to answer, standing up in front of the classroom to present, or just showing up and being who they truly are in life. Students must be willing to fail in order to succeed. Teachers must be willing to be ineffective at times in order to find the most effective ways in which to reach all learners. This level of vulnerability and risk-taking doesn't occur in school environments that are hostile, threatening or judgmental. Rather, the best setting for risk-taking and exploring the vast unknown is found in school environments that are emotionally strong and supportive of students and teachers emotional selves. Students and teachers must feel both physically and emotionally safe when they go to school each day. Emotional safety occurs in flexible and open environments, accepting of diversity. In fact, in such supportive environments, diversity is honored rather than just accepted. Emotionally safe schools allow students and teachers the freedom of being who they are and discovering what they can do the best. These schools model mutual respect and acknowledge that each student has inherent talents and gifts to discover and surface. Emotionally safe school environments don't demand that everyone be the same. A school, where students have to fit in and be just like everyone else, is not an emotionally safe learning space for them and robs them of their individuality.

Emotional safety for students means that they won't be teased and harassed because they might look different, learn in unique ways, or feel unsure about themselves. Teachers, parents, and administrators must work diligently to eradicate teasing and harassment from our classrooms and schools. These devastating factors exist in every school. They are one of the greatest hindrances to learning because the students who are being teased or harassed constantly dwell in a state of stress, worry and fear. They become reluctant to take chances for fear of being teased. Fearful students live in a state of tension, always waiting for someone to say or do something to them. This effectively takes their focus off learning. Often students will choose to skip school in order to avoid the harassment. They can't learn if they're not present. However, just being present doesn't guarantee that learning will occur. Being present in environments where harassment occurs may be more harmful than being absent. Environments devoid of emotional support stunt the learning process.

Another facet of emotional support occurs in schools when the teachers utilize a wide-variety of teaching strategies with their students. A teacher who teaches to all his students' various learning styles creates a safe emotional space because he acknowledges that differences exist and says that it's OK to be different from other students. Emotional safety means we can be who we are and learn through the modalities that are best suited for us. Good teachers recognize the importance of, and honor the differences in, the learning styles that exist among their students. Classrooms, where all students are expected to fit into a particular learning style, become harmful to some of those students because they don't fit the mold. They receive a message of personal failure and defeat, which damages a child's sense of self and causes confusion and despair. Students can only feel safe in classroom settings with teachers who acknowledge each child as a whole and wonderful person with many skills and positive attributes to contribute. Teachers are responsible for creating emotionally safe classroom environments for their students. This requires consistency, understanding, hard work, intuitive knowing, caring and focus from the teacher. Emotionally safe classrooms are rich centers for learning and personal growth.

Emotional safety is often difficult to achieve in a school setting. Small schools lend themselves more readily to the creation of emotionally supportive environments because every student has the opportunity to have meaningful relationships with teachers. Students are viewed as individuals in these settings rather than numbers. The knack to forming emotionally safe environments is to ensure that everyone is treated as a valuable individual with different strengths to contribute. With that belief in place, structure is then established within the school setting that eliminates harassment and increases recognition for student's uniqueness. Teachers who know their students well are better able to assist those students in their learning and to come fully into who they are as creative individuals. Interactive opportunities provide the vehicle for teachers and students to get to know one another. Teachers who know and understand their students discover how they can best challenge and help each student move through his fears and celebrate his successes. A student who trusts that his teacher knows him and is interested in helping him will be willing to try just about anything his teacher asks him to do. The bond of trust between student and teacher forms a foundation from which the student can explore new arenas and find out more about himself.

Schools must be emotionally safe for teachers, as well as for students. One might think that teachers should be able to handle and work in any environment since they are adults. However, adults are no less vulnerable than students when it comes to risk-taking and moving outside their comfort zone. In fact, many teachers become very set in their way of doing things and completely resist change. An emotionally safe environment for teachers is one in which they are supported and encouraged, by the administration, to stretch themselves and tap into all of their gifts and talents in order to be the best teachers they possibly can be. If teachers are all expected to fit into the same pattern of teaching in the same way, creativity and passion will be lost. We do a great disservice to our students when we ask all teachers to teach in the same way and run their classrooms in a rote manner. This squashes individual talents and strengths that each teacher has to share and reduces teaching to a sameness that can be harmful to all who engage in the educational process. Principals ought to spend a significant amount of their time supervising, providing feedback and meeting with their teachers because they are the key component in delivering good education in the classrooms. Principals must come to know and understand their teachers as teachers do their students. Good administrators who know their staff will figure out how they can best work with individual teachers to make certain that every teacher receives support in doing a great job in the classroom. Teachers who feel happy and safe in their work setting will be up to the challenges that present themselves each year with a new class and with the additional demands placed upon them. Teachers who work in environments that don't feel safe retreat and protect themselves, reluctant to move outside the box and less likely to expect that of their students.

An emotionally safe school environment creates a setting of joy. Teachers and students enjoy coming to school every day when they know they'll be treated with respect and appreciated for who they are as individuals. We can walk on a school campus and get a good sense of the environment fairly quickly. It will be evident in the way people interact, the physical appearance of the school, the body language of the students and teachers and the level of engagement in the learning process. Listen for laughter. Watch for friendly and respectful interactions. Feel the space. Ask questions. Notice how focused students and teachers are on their work. Pay attention to how you feel. What does your gut tell you? If you are a parent, teacher or principal trying to choose a school, spend time at the school, watching and listening. You will learn a lot. Emotional safety must be present for effective learning to occur in schools.

In addition to the physical and emotional components of the environment, every school environment has a third factor, a relational component. This is actually one of the most critical components necessary for a school to function well and meet the needs of all who work there. Relational interactions fill each school day. Students and teachers don't operate in isolation. The act of learning itself is relational in that the learner interacts with the subject matter. As we build relationships with others, we find out more about ourselves. The social aspect of the school experience provides a wonderful learning opportunity for students and teachers alike. It is through our interactions in the outside world, that we get important feedback about our actions and way of being. We try out new personas and vary our activities to test new ideas and find out what really works best for us. Relationships are the playground where we learn more about ourselves, and our world. Humans need frequent personal contact and meaningful relationships to feel complete. Some of our closest bonds form in school settings.

Students have the opportunity in school to form meaningful connections with other students and adults. As children are learning subject matter, they are also learning how to interact with others to be a friend or a partner or a critic. The classroom is a center for trying out new things and this includes new ways of acting with other students. It's a testing ground to see what works and what doesn't work; what is appropriate or inappropriate; who is trustworthy or who will betray. These relational interactions must be monitored by an adult, usually the teacher or principal. Children need the guidance of a firm, yet gentle, hand to steer them through the labyrinth of relationship building that can become so confusing at times. Students move through their school years experiencing the ups and downs of relationship building. They mature into young adults who are capable of developing and maintaining significant adult relationships. Socialization is an important component of their learning and occurs most effectively in schools that build upon and honor relationships among all members in the school community. Successful students actively engage in their learning through connecting with other students, teachers and the subject matter at hand. Schools that promote students working totally independently or in isolation from others do a disservice to those students. They are missing an important socialization component. If it's not found in the schools, it must be cultivated elsewhere for the student. Most of us spend our days interacting with other people. Therefore, relationship building is an important skill to possess in order to be successful in life.

A solid relational environment is particularly important to teachers and teaching. Teachers, who work together and grow in their skills together, usually make the entire school setting a supportive and fun place to be each day. Teaching is a very difficult and challenging job that can often be isolating. Teachers sometimes find that they are bereft of adult conversation and interaction because they spend all day engaged with children. They also find it difficult to schedule time to interact with other teachers to discuss teaching and learning. Teachers spend much of their school day moving from one challenging situation to another, often dealing with these issues by themselves. When this happens, teaching can be a difficult and lonely path to follow. School environments that encourage and support teachers working together are usually great centers of learning for both students and teachers. There must be a conscious effort on the part of the administration to create a system-wide support mechanism to allow teachers the time to plan and work together. Creating time for teachers to work together is cost effective in the long run. Teachers are the expert practitioners who are working in the classrooms every day. They are the best source of help and guidance for each other. However, there must be openness, on the part of the teachers, to work together. Often school administrators will create time for planning and interaction but the teachers won't use it. It is up to the principal and the leadership team to encourage, develop and support teachers working together in schools. The teachers must make this work meaningful and significant as it relates to teaching, student learning and achievement.

In schools where teachers work together, they will find creative solutions for the diverse challenges that come forward. There are likely to be more creative school-wide projects, teacher-led committees and innovative learning programs because teachers creatively feed off of one another. Most teachers are life-long learners who love pursuing knowledge and developing new skills. They are anxious to create opportunities for their own growth and that of their students. Their contagious enthusiasm often brings less enthusiastic teachers into the climate of excitement about growth and change opportunities. A principal who wishes to bring change to his school must carefully cultivate and support a strong relational environment in which teachers are encouraged and rewarded for working together. The change process will proceed much more quickly in a relational environment than in one where people work in isolation.

The fourth component of school environment is academic focus. Good schools have a strong academic focus that promotes a serious environment for teaching and learning. Since student achievement is the major goal of schools, resources and efforts must be directed in that way. When all members of the school community emphasize the importance of academics, a support system forms within the school that creates an environment of high expectations for students learning and teachers teaching. A strong, academically focused school climate promotes both excitement and seriousness in learning. High expectations for student achievement must come from parents, teachers and the students themselves. Creating a climate of high expectations and promoting the importance of education to our students most effectively develops a school-wide attitude that supports academic achievement.

Schools that have a strong academic focus spend significant time and resources building and supporting this focus. Curricular materials, aligned with the standards and the school's educational goals, provide support to academic programs. Teachers are given opportunities to participate in regular staff development activities in order to continuously hone their skills. Administration emphasizes the importance of instruction by providing teachers with frequent monitoring and feedback. As these other essential components are provided and begin to work together, an environment of respect for learning grows within the school. If each teacher takes teaching and learning seriously, so will his students. When students are recognized for their academic efforts and teachers for their instruction, the message is sent loudly and clearly that teaching and learning are valued at that school. Support builds momentum. Soon, there are high expectations on a school-wide basis. Students, entering the lower grades, quickly learn that school is not only fun but mainly about learning. Since they have no other models than what they experience, when they begin school, they easily internalize a focus of learning and doing well. As students grow older and move through successive grades, this academic focus becomes a normal expectation and way of being in school. Positive efforts and achievement become the norm for students. Creative teaching becomes the standard for teachers. Providing an exciting, challenging and successful learning environment becomes the goal for schools. Once these standards are established in a school, they grow and mature as each passing grade of students moves to the next level, building the mass of students who know only one way to be in school. As a result, the academically focused school environment, with proper support from all members of the school community, establishes itself as the norm.

Teachers and parents play an instrumental role in developing a school environment that both supports and encourages a strong academic focus. Parents are the initial trainers of children and they help their kids develop attitudes about school and education well before they set foot in a classroom. It is essential that parents instill, in their children, serious values about school and its importance. Parents must also be clear about what they hope children will achieve and how they will help their kids meet success in school. Once children are in school, parents continue to play an important role in helping them maintain positive attitudes about their schoolwork. Students who accomplish the most have parents and other adults standing behind them for support and encouragement. Parents and teachers must work together on behalf of each student.

The teacher's daily focus on teaching and his time spent with students makes him the primary source for developing a child's view of education, learning and achievement. Students watch their teachers, listening and observing how the teacher interacts with the students and the curriculum. Teachers who model a love for learning and an active and inquiring approach to topics become positive role models for children. Most students respect and love their teachers and become very attached to them. Teachers bear the responsibility of leading students through the labyrinth of learning on a daily basis, providing motivational and appropriate learning opportunities. If a teacher minimizes a topic or project, students receive a negative message about learning from that experience. Teachers play a significant role in developing their student's attitudes about learning and personal success.

We want our classrooms to be safe and motivating environments where students realize that learning is their primary work. It's an important and serious job, but it can be fun and personally rewarding. When individual classrooms promote this attitude, the school becomes a united front, dedicated to teaching all students to be successful. Schools that promote an academic focus offer support for the classroom activities through a myriad of additional programs, clubs, and other enhancement experiences, creating a unified picture of high expectations for school-wide excellence. Success becomes a self-fulfilling prophecy. Schools in which students are learning, achieving and relationally growing, are labeled excellent schools and their reputation spreads in the community. This attention then causes the members of the school community to work even harder to support the school's positive growth. As a society, we must do all we can to make certain that every school in America has the support it needs to create academically and socially successful school environments. These efforts will breed more growth and success for the future of each school and for the educational system in general.

The following strategies will help to create a more supportive school environment.

1. Provide a safe and appealing physical environment.

2. Promote responsible actions and positive talk.

3. Create a balance between academic and social learning experiences.

4. Emphasize efforts and accomplishments.

5. Pay attention to the small things and notice the daily miracles.

....

Strategy # 1 - Provide a Safe and Appealing Physical Environment

Action Steps:

- create a colorful, interesting and welcoming classroom environment for your students

- invite parents and community members to support projects that improve the school's environment

- work with other teachers and your principal to co-create school-wide programs that promote life skills

- involve students in mural projects, anti-liter campaigns and other school improvement projects

- institutionalize a no-harassment policy and strictly enforce it

School buildings don't need to be new to be safe and appealing. Classrooms don't need to have all of the latest materials and equipment to be interesting places for learning. There are many ways to work with the facilities, resources and classroom space at hand in order to improve the physical component of your school. Most teachers set up their classroom environment based on the style in which they teach most comfortably. This classroom space will usually reflect the way they organize their personal space. If a teacher's style is orderly, allowing for few distractions, his room will mostly likely have desks in rows or groups and be neat and tidy. If a teacher favors exploring and trying out new things, his room will probably be full of centers, students grouped in teams, with materials and equipment littering the room. The law of averages would suggest that a student going through twelve years of school would hit his style of learning in a few classes along the way. Classroom experiences should provide students with many different ways to learn, to arrange themselves, and to interact with the content and each other. A safe classroom environment is created when a student has choices and variety in his learning experience. Providing choice and variety often means that the teacher must move out of his comfort zone and try new techniques or ways of arranging space to meet the individual needs of students. The principal plays a key role both in encouraging and supporting teachers in this effort. Classrooms should have space for both individual and communal learning experiences. There must be quiet space for thoughtfulness and noisy space for exploration and celebration.

A classroom is appealing when it has color, order, interesting materials on display, examples of student work hung up, and a feeling of friendliness and safety. The classroom should have a fresh coat of paint, appropriate furniture in good repair, balanced lighting, and comfortable places for students to sit while exploring and interacting. When students spend the most significant part of the day in one, often crowded, room, it should be a wonderful place that supports their happiness and growth. A room in disrepair, with poor lighting or inadequate ventilation, sends a negative message about the value of education. Visit classrooms and ask yourself these questions. Does this room support various learning styles? Are the furniture and other materials adequate? Is there too little, or too much, stimulation in this setting? Does the teacher have all the materials and supplies he needs to teach? Does this room feel comfortable, welcoming and supportive? What could I do or contribute to help the teacher make this classroom a great learning environment?

We can also get a good feeling for the attitude, regarding the school environment, of the students and teachers at a school by walking the campus and noticing the amount of litter lying around. Schools that have positive climates, where everyone buys into the concept that they're all responsible for creating the school atmosphere, have clean campuses. If we see litter and trash all around the school, that's a warning sign. There may be a lack of pride within that school. Schools that promote pride among their students and teachers have programs to teach life skills and appropriate behavior. Students, who are practicing the life skills and behaving appropriately, are consistently recognized.

A school "wears" the level of pride that the students and staff possess toward their school. Even older facilities can shine and feel healthy. School board members and superintendents are responsible for making sufficient funds available to maintain school buildings and keep the grounds in good shape. This task is becoming increasingly difficult with the cuts in school funding. The scarce funding is primarily going toward salaries and teaching materials. However, the classroom and school environment is just as important a factor in student learning and achievement, as are the textbooks or other teaching materials. They actually might be more important because they create the context and setting for learning and self-exploration to occur. There is a great disparity in our country between wealthy and poor communities and the condition of their schools. This is a national shame. You can support your local schools financially by passing bond initiatives and finding other ways in which to provide more funds to the schools.

Beyond being appealing, schools must be safe. Following the spate of school violence over the past several years, teachers, parents and administrators have begun to place a major emphasis on creating physically safe schools. To do this, principals have met with local law enforcement and safety personnel to develop comprehensive plans for school lockdowns and evacuations in case of emergency. Reducing on-campus violence has also been a critical component of creating safe schools. Principals have instituted more one-on-one interactions between adults and high-risk students. Harsher punishments are now meted out for student misbehavior of a serious nature. Counselors provide services to those students who are in crisis. Teachers and administrators know the signs to look for that might lead students to participate in violent activities. Principals, teachers and students should work together to establish classroom and school rules. Students need to clearly understand the rules and the consequences for breaking the rules. Teachers and administrators must act swiftly and fairly to mete out punishment, when rules are broken. Inconsistency causes the system to break down and leads to increased numbers of rule violations. Schools that focus all of their efforts on punishment and don't encourage positive behaviors actually increase the number of negative behavior incidents.

In order to provide safe learning environments, teachers and principals must establish and maintain a balanced approach between prevention programs and punitive actions. Students must understand that there are school rules to be obeyed for everyone's safety. When these rules are broken, they must pay the consequences. However, a proactive and positive approach toward behavior issues is preferable to a punitive approach. Does your school have a program to develop life skills that teaches students appropriate ways to behave in differing situations? Are students taught how to behave and communicate in ways that are not threatening or abusive? Life skills programs should be introduced at the pre-school and kindergarten level and taught and reinforced every year as the student progresses through school. The life skills will obviously be covered in greater layers of depth and sophistication as the students advance through the grades. Students who learn a variety of life skills, and are recognized for following them, are more likely to develop consistently good patterns of behavior and control any negative impulses to react. Life skills are quite easily woven into the curriculum and in fact, the curriculum is filled with examples of fictional and real people living lives that embody many essential life skills. Schools that teach and reinforce life skill guided behaviors to their students have fewer incidents of school violence.

Strategy # 2 - Promote Responsible Actions and Positive Talk

Action Steps:

- provide opportunities in class for students to speak positively about themselves

- use words that encourage others and take actions that help

- give students specific positive feedback on a regular basis

- remember that your proactive attitude may significantly influence your peers

- walk away from conversations in which colleagues are criticizing others

An emphasis on personal responsibility is required of all members of the school community in order to create an environment in which excellence will flourish. Any weak links will negatively impact the entire system. The old saying that actions speak louder than words is certainly true. Teachers and administrators serve as key role models for students. Children are particularly cognizant of how adults are acting and they know immediately when the words don't match the actions. The actions and words of the adults set the tone for a respectful and responsible school environment. Educators can positively and proactively influence children's lives by leading daily lives, filled with optimism and action. Every member of the teaching staff, at a school, bears responsibility for every child at that school. When this belief system prevails, students know that their teachers and principal are looking out for them and expecting the best from them. Students will ultimately feel valued as individuals when teachers pay attention to them and befriend them. All teachers should expect that every student with whom they come into contact will act in responsible ways. This attitude is then reinforced with the students through repeated contacts with various teachers and the principal throughout the school.

If you're a teacher, show up each day with a positive attitude and firm belief that, under your direction, your students will try their best and do well. Share this belief with them and help them design their day in such a way that it does become a successful and fulfilling time well spent. Teachers must model optimism and enthusiasm for teaching, learning and social interactions. If you're in a bad mood, don't make your students suffer because of that. Put aside your personal issues and focus on your professional responsibilities. Students quickly pick up a teacher's sadness or upset. They can be negatively influenced by a teacher's emotional state and lose focus on what it is they are supposed to do. Try to maintain a balanced and poised approach with your students even if you don't feel like being in the classroom that day.

Students pay attention to how adults solve problems and interact with one another. Model only respectful communication and interaction with other educators and parents. Disagreements and dissatisfaction should not be aired in front of students. Parents have the same responsibility in their interaction with teachers. If you're a parent who disagrees with a teacher or who wants to complain about something, don't do it in front of your kids. Don't talk negatively about your child's teacher in front of your child. Criticizing teachers in front of children damages the learning process in the classroom. There are many avenues for teachers and parents to voice disagreements or complaints in appropriate ways and places. When students attend school every day and observe the adults acting in positive and responsible ways, they learn to do the same with their peers and their teachers. Not only are the school rules clear about the necessity of respectful interactions, that is what the children see over and over again between the adults. Students pick up on nuances and will notice subtle or deceptive interactions. Therefore, model only respectful connections. A school environment that fosters responsible communication among all members of the school community provides a healthy place in which to teach and learn. A climate of responsibility toward and respect for each person helps to alleviate some of the pervasive harassment issues found in schools today. Students who become involved in school clubs, teams, and other activities are more likely to stay out of trouble and do well academically. They are focused on positive interactions, which ultimately impact their entire day, both academically and behaviorally. "Walk Your Talk" is a good motto to teach to and model for students. They'll get it. They'll internalize it if it's the primary expectation in every classroom. Walk through an excellent school and notice the interactions between people. They are positive, respectful and supportive.

In addition to promoting responsible actions, we ought also to engage in positive talk. This is not just for the purpose of being nice or making someone feel good. Scientific research in the area of neuroscience shows us that words are extremely powerful tools to be used for good or ill intent. Our words become our physiology. The words we use and the emotion tied to those words triggers the release of chemicals throughout our bodies. These chemicals attach to and influence our cells, which, in turn, influence our behaviors and actions. If a learner constantly receives positive feedback from the adults and peers in his life, neural networks are formed that reinforce this view of him as a successful person. Actions will follow to support this belief, which, in turn, reinforces the concept of success. Students, who believe they are capable learners and supported in this belief by their teachers and parents, are usually successful. Their successful actions reinforce and further build their belief system. It's a circular effect that grows stronger and deeper as it expands. The same is true when negative words are used to criticize or judge a person and his actions. Negative words promote negative belief systems and lead to actions that often self-sabotage. Put downs and criticism wound the human spirit and one's belief in self. Teachers know that their verbal interactions with students are pivotal in each child's success. One carelessly spoken criticism can shut down a student for months or years to come. Teachers hold a great deal of power in their hands to mold a child's belief system. They reinforce a student's positive or negative sense of self through the types of leaning experiences that they design for kids. The young psyche is a fragile organism that requires tenderness and support during both successful and unsuccessful times.

Teachers, too, need to hear positive talk from their peers and principals. Reinforcement contributes to successful human interactions. Principals who focus on the good things that are occurring in the classroom and school provide teachers with encouragement to continue to improve and try out new techniques. Trusting relationships form when teachers and principals respect one another. Principals strengthen respectful relationships when they acknowledge successes and discuss failures and challenges in non-judgmental ways, using language that supports rather than attacks. Walk around your children's school. What kind of verbal interactions do you hear? Are people complimenting one another? Providing feedback? Using supportive language? Being respectful even in disagreement? How do the students speak to one another? A school climate that promotes responsible actions and positive verbal interactions is a place of deep learning and continuous personal growth.

Self-talk is one of the most important characteristics for achieving personal success. Self-talk is that voice that operates inside of our head, making comments about everything we do. These comments are often very self-critical. Most of us are more critical of ourselves than others are of us. The inner critic can be quite ruthless at times, treating us unmercifully. Many adults struggle to shift the inner critic to an inner cheerleader who acknowledges our efforts and successes rather than focusing on our failures. Younger children often verbally express their inner critic by saying things like, "Nobody likes me because I'm stupid." Children are much less guarded in exposing their self-critic. However, as they grow older, students tend to stuff the criticism inside and the inner critic grows in stature. Teachers, parents and principals are instrumental in assisting students to develop strong and positive self-talk and banish the voice of the inner critic. This is no easy task as the inner critic is well established by the teen years. If we start assisting our very young children to engage in positive self-talk, we have a chance at significantly influencing their success in school and in life. This is a big challenge. Positive talk must be modeled by adults and peers. A school environment that supports positive self-talk through positive interactions and honest feedback is a place where students will thrive as they learn to acknowledge themselves for all the good they do and for who they are as people. Belief in self and our abilities is a significant gift we can bestow upon our children. A positive self-image will be more instrumental in future success than just about any other human quality. It should be a major focus in our schools.

Strategy # 3 - Create a Balance Between Academic and Social Learning Experiences

Action Steps:

- make a list of the various ways you address the multiple intelligences in your classroom, making sure there is a balanced approach

- teach your students how to appropriately interact both inside and outside the classroom

- attempt to incorporate a social experience within each learning opportunity

- acknowledge students for both their academic efforts and appropriate social encounters

- model a balance between your work and social life

All learning experiences are not formal lessons taught in the classroom. As much learning, if not more, occurs through informal activities and social interactions. Parents, teachers and principals are responsible for providing a balanced education for our children. Students are first and foremost social beings. Even the shyest students desire friendships and interactions with peers. Schools are great social environments, providing constant opportunities for shared interactions of both a positive and negative nature. Students attend school to learn content, develop thinking skills and meet the academic requirements. They also come to learn about friendship, communication and other life skills that contribute to being both happy and successful in life. The most academic learning experience has a social component to it and many social encounters are wonderful learning experiences. Middle school students, working collaboratively on a scientific problem-solving project, experience the excitement of learning something new and the fun of working with peer support. A school that focuses solely on the academic is missing the boat. It is also creating an atmosphere that is not conducive to students learning in the most effective ways. We must be careful that we don't lose sight of the importance of the social even in the midst of attempting to focus on the mental.

Balance is a state of being we seek throughout our lifetime. Adults are constantly trying to find a balance in their lives, usually between the personal and professional arenas. Children are less likely to consciously think about balance. They seem to gravitate to it through being out of it. Most kids swing too far in one direction, then too far in another before they find the middle ground. Education is a path to follow to find out who we are and what we like to do. Balance is a key component in that pursuit. We don't often think of balance in the context of kids and schools, but educators and parents must be aware of its importance to their children. Schools are responsible for providing a balanced program for students that educates the whole child. Classroom and school environments that provide balanced academic and social activities and experiences are settings where students discover themselves. Students need to have experiences that demonstrate learning is about more than just memorizing material or working math problems. It's about self-discovery and finding out what wonders of the world drive our passion and fill our thoughts. Education leads individuals to self and place. This requires a broad and balanced approach that recognizes the importance of every aspect of the life experience.

Our students who have the most difficulty in learning and behaving tend to be out of balance. They don't have a view of themselves as complex people who are capable of many wonderful things. They often only see themselves from one limited viewpoint. This viewpoint is often negative and therefore, their work and behavior reflect this one-sided picture of self. The student who spends more time in the principals office than in his classes forms his self-view based on this "bad guy" image which is reinforced every time he's sent to the office. Educators often try to help these students, using punitive means for poor behavior and providing remedial work in the academic areas. Neither of these approaches will give the student a positive or balanced viewpoint. Rather, they will reinforce the negative picture of self that the student holds. How can anyone see himself as successful when his learning experiences have only produced failed attempts and poor grades? Teachers and principals must help students expand their field of vision so that they see beyond the failing persona and begin to identify those areas of success that are found within their personality. Educators facilitate this happening when they provide students with a variety of learning experiences through which they see themselves more expansively and clearly and begin to develop positive self-images. This is a huge challenge with those students who have been so defeated that they not only don't believe in themselves but they are often hostile and angry. Many educators are feeling alarmed at the direction that the focus on teaching to the test is sending schools when it comes to their most at-risk students. Schools are taking away the very opportunities and experiences that allow students an expanded self-view, showing that there is life beyond the purely academic. We will continue to lose more and more students if we don't address this issue of balance in their view of themselves and the world. This will best be accomplished by providing supportive and experiential activities that develop a true sense of self. Some of these activities might include:

- ask each student to name two personal strengths and share how he uses them

- have the student's peers identify two more of his strengths and tell how these strengths are helpful

- encourage students to write their life story and share it

- allow students to give short presentations on their areas of interest

It's fairly obvious where and how the academic experiences take place in schools. Since there is ever increasing pressure put on teachers to make sure that all their students meet the standards and pass state testing, the focus in education has shifted to the purely academic. Tutoring companies sprout up like weeds. Test analysis firms, that can provide disaggregated information, vie for school contracts. Arts, sports and "extra programs" are being cut back or eliminated because they take up too much precious time and dilute the academic focus. Parents are questioning school boards and PTA's asking why field trips are being approved when the focus should be on learning. The pendulum is swinging far a field in education and our students will pay the price for our folly in creating this unbalanced state in our schools.

Our teachers are already paying for this imbalance. It's alarming to see so many senior teachers becoming disheartened with this loss of a reasonable focus regarding teaching and learning. For many of them, the current rigid approach to instruction is removing the joy from teaching which has become rote and monotonous. Young teachers, too, are turning away from teaching because it's not what they thought it would be and they don't feel passionate about the work, as they were sure they would when they chose this profession. Schools are becoming uptight places, tightly wired like a guitar string, ready to pop under any additional stress. Is it necessary for our schools to be environments of fear and stress and joyless academic pursuit? Is there a way for the academic achievement to be accomplished in a balanced and personally supportive environment? It's not only possible, but the very best way in which to realize good test scores and high levels of achievement. A sane and balanced approach is certainly the best way in which to assist students in their learning and keep good teachers from leaving.

Creating a balanced educational approach means providing a variety of learning experiences through different teaching techniques. Schools whose focus is to educate the whole child are rich in their programming, offering many clubs, organizations and teams that students may join. Plays, art shows and science fairs are among the many multiple and diverse opportunities provided for students to explore content in various interactive ways. These well-rounded schools have strong academic programs that provide a major focus for student's time and attention. Learning to write occurs in the formal classroom setting as well as while working on the yearbook. Problem solving expands well-beyond math class and is enhanced through exploring other creative projects. While students are bumping into other aspects of themselves, in these various projects and learning opportunities, their view of self grows and matures. This expanded, and hopefully positive self-view, facilitates the success of the purely academic program upon which so much importance is currently placed. A student with a limited self-view will perform in limited ways. A student who has discovered an expanded view of who he is and what he can do will surge forward in his achievement and personal growth. We can't afford to graduate only students who have shown great academic achievement, but might not be well-rounded individuals. Our complex world needs people skilled well beyond just the purely academic. Finding a balance between the academic and the social learning experiences is one of our greatest, and most important, challenges in education. Some students will learn more effectively in one modality than the other. Both must be available to all learners or we'll lose many more students and teachers than we're currently losing. School environments that encourage and teach a balanced approach, for both students and teachers, are the most successful places for learning to occur. We must embrace them for the sake of our children, our teachers and our future.

Strategy # 4 - Emphasize Efforts and Accomplishments

Action Steps:

- make at least one positive, fact or action-based comment to each of your students every day

- praise colleagues and students for their efforts even if they don't succeed

- teach your students how to acknowledge each other's efforts and achievements

- give frequent feedback to your teachers

- help students see the learning that comes from failed efforts

Schools ought to be centers of learning and growth for students and teachers alike. This occurs when the structure and tools for learning and teaching are in place. Where good teaching is the norm, you'll notice that teachers encourage students to do their personal best at all times. They reinforce this concept of personal best by recognizing the efforts and the accomplishments, no matter how small, of each student on a daily basis. A student's personal sense of self grows minute upon minute, day after day. Students are in a phase of their life where they are interacting with their environment and testing out what works and doesn't work for them. As educators, we want to encourage students to constantly explore, risk, try again, problem solve, learn from failure and meet success. We assist this expansive learning process when we give kids feedback on the things that they are doing at school and home.

If you're a teacher, try to stay in the present moment as you move through each school day, noticing the little things that students do. Watch their social interactions and comment upon their willingness to embrace all types of learning and move through their fears. Comment when a disheveled student shows up looking organized. Encourage a shy student who takes a risk by standing up to respond to the class. Praise an advanced learner who has gone above and beyond the norm on an assignment. Point out to a student how adeptly he works with younger children. If every child, in every classroom, received positive feedback for their ordinary actions during the school day, they would become extraordinary students with full self-esteem. All humans want to be successful and receive praise and acknowledgement from other people. We thrive when our proactive actions and personal risks are noticed and commented upon. It doesn't take much for a teacher to notice the efforts and advances a student makes. It does take some work to make sure that student knows you notice what's going on. Students, who have teachers that recognize and praise their efforts and accomplishments, work harder. They are more enthusiastic and highly motivated to succeed. When you take a risk, it feels good to have someone notice and say "good job". We repeat actions that feel good because we need to feel good. The more the environment supports positive feedback, the more successful the students will become.

Teachers require validation for their efforts and accomplishments as well. Principals who wish to make significant forward progress in improving a school's climate need only to begin to notice a teacher's daily work and provide specific and frequent feedback regarding the successful practices and actions they observe. This is called "Doing the Dailies." Take time to spend a few minutes with teachers to give them feedback about something they were doing that you observed. Notice small actions that make a difference and comment on them. Write thank you notes that show appreciation and recognition for effort and accomplishment. This is the quickest way to build loyalty and a school-wide ethic of doing whatever needs to be done to get the job accomplished. Teachers who feel appreciated and validated by the principal work diligently and tirelessly for their school. They will go beyond all normal expectations to co-create dynamic school environments where everyone is growing, succeeding and feeling good about it. A formal teacher observation, given once or twice a year, is not enough reinforcement for all that teachers do. Passing back student's test scores is not enough reinforcement. Feedback must be frequent, focus on daily efforts and accomplishments, specific, honest, and consistent. Teachers and principals hold the power to create classrooms and school environments that are dynamic learning centers where students and teachers are focused on their work, feeling happy and self-fulfilled, and achieving their goals. Focusing feedback on the daily routines of life, in the school setting, is one of the quickest ways in which to begin to change school culture. "Doing the Dailies" is a powerful method for change and should be applied by both teachers and principals.

Strategy # 5 - Pay Attention to the Small Things and Notice the Daily Miracles

Action Steps:

- make an inspiration wall where you and your students place pictures or thoughts about what inspires you

- point out, to your students, examples of inspiring daily actions that occur at school

- take your students on class trips to diverse places, pointing out the many people and things that offer inspiration

- spend time outside with your students and ask them to identify environmental characteristics that inspire them

- schedule ten minutes at the end of each day, or each block, for you and your students to review the day and mention people, events or actions that were memorable

An essential component for a healthy school environment is inspiration. There are many things that inspire us on a daily basis. These might include other people, nature, good deeds, heroism, a book or movie, small or large successes, and courageous actions. Inspiration moves us out of ourselves. It places our focus outward to observe a person, an event or a sight. If we connect emotionally with that person, event or sight, we may be moved by it. Inspiration is a powerful force in our lives because it is a connection that we make at the heart level. This is the most basic and human level upon which we can deeply connect with another person, event or object. When we feel inspired, we're more likely to move to a higher level of performance or excellence because we feel a drive to rise to the level of what has touched us. Being inspired or inspiring others fills our heart and nurtures our soul. School environments that provide daily emotional connections for their students and teachers become centers of excellence in which everyone is trying to reach higher levels of personal achievement. If you work in an inspirational environment, you know how motivating it can be to show up every day for work. This same motivation exists for students attending school. Inspiring people and events move us out of our mundane existence and provide us with hope, insight and vision for the future.

We must assist students to recognize inspirational actions, events, or natural occurrences. Point out a beautiful flower, acknowledge a student who performed a kind action, discuss a heroic rescue, study about someone who overcame great odds. There are literally hundreds of events occurring on a daily basis that have the power to inspire us to be better people. We must take time to see them and recognize their power to touch our lives. They don't have to be huge events. It's important for all of us to become adept at recognizing the small examples of inspiring acts that bombard our world each and every day. Did you see the fiery sunset last night? How about the bus driver who comforted the crying child? Isn't it wonderful that Jimmy has learned to read so well? Pay attention and notice the world around you. Most adults don't take time to do this. If we're going to teach our children to recognize and be aware of the inspirations in their lives, we must be aware of them ourselves. Once again, teachers have a serious responsibility in this arena since they spend so much time with their students. If every teacher in America decided to point out five inspirations a day to his students, the environment of the classroom would grow in a very positive way. An important part of seeing inspirational people or actions is acknowledging them. If you see someone perform a kind act, thank him for doing it. Live an aware life by seeing, listening and responding. Inspiration is all around us. It bombards our senses, trying to get us to notice. Open your eyes. Open your hearts. Receive all the magic that is offered to you on a daily basis and then give some of it back to the world.

Excellent schools have inspirational environments where students and teachers are recognized for the heartfelt actions they take. As this recognition occurs and grows, people become more cognizant of life around them. They begin to notice every day gifts. This makes life richer and more fulfilling. Inspired students and teachers reach higher than those who are uninspired. They achieve more and contribute more. It is imperative that schools develop a climate that points out, recognizes, and encourages our connections with people and actions that touch us. It will raise the entire school community to a new level of performance and contribution because we all seek purpose in life. Inspirational schools are fun, exciting, high-achieving and safe communities in which to belong.

An achievement-oriented, healthy, personally supportive and safe school environment serves as the foundation for realizing all the dreams and goals of the students, teachers, principals and parents in a school community. A healthy environment will embrace everyone positively with high expectations for personal success and contribution. Building and maintaining a positive school climate is a full-time job for all members of the school community. It requires skill in the areas of communication and relationship building. Principals must take the lead in demonstrating that both students and teachers will be supported in their teaching and learning roles. Teachers work diligently every day creating student-friendly environments that provide exciting, challenging and successful learning opportunities for each child. An intentional and supportive school is a dynamic force for creating excellent educational programming and responsive participation from all members of the school community.

5. OPTIMISM

....

"The Gift"

"THIS IS MY present," said Charice, dragging the large, odd shaped box from beneath the Christmas tree in the school lobby. "This is my ice cream maker."

Charice dressed in bright red pants that were mismatched with her over-sized orange top smiled joyously as she removed the box from its tucked away position. The petite and energized five-year-old kindergarten student struggled to pull the brightly decorated package across the worn carpeting in the school lobby. A flood of rushing students, just off the school bus, moved around Charice on their way to their classrooms. No one stopped to see what she was doing. Charice, oblivious to the stream of children flowing around her, began to tear at the wrapping paper.

"Charice, this present belongs under the Christmas tree," I said, gently taking the box out of her hands. "Let's put it back under the tree. It isn't Christmas yet. Presents can't be opened until Christmas."

"But it's still my present, isn't it?" asked Charice, following me, as I carried the bulky package to the Christmas tree.

"Well, I'm not sure if it's your present. It might be for someone else. We'll have to wait until Christmas comes," I told her.

"I know it's my ice cream maker," she replied confidently.

"Charice, walk down to your classroom now. Mrs. Jackson will be wondering if you're here today."

"I'll open my present on Christmas," she said. "When is Christmas?"

Charice put her thumb in her mouth and stared at me with her huge, brown eyes, not moving an inch, waiting for my answer.

"Christmas is coming in two weeks," I said. I placed my arms on Charice's shoulders and gave her a gentle push. "Get going to your classroom, Charice, you're going to be late."

"How long is two weeks?" she asked, determinedly.

"Charice, go to your classroom now," I said. "Two weeks will be here very soon."

"OK" she replied, as she ran down the hallway.

Charice and her two older sisters, Janessa and Chloe, had been in the school since before Thanksgiving. The older girls were quiet and unobtrusive. Charice was outspoken and full of energy. The girls had moved into the new Red Cross homeless shelter with their mother. The family had been living in an old, black station wagon for the two months prior to moving into the shelter. The girls had been in and out of schools, mostly out.

Charice's sisters had the cautious, mistrusting, evaluating look in their eyes that comes to children who have experienced uncertainty, loss and homelessness. Charice was young enough not to yet have been jaded by the disappointments of life. She was happy, fiery, sweet, and totally optimistic. Charice loved her kindergarten class and was always lively and positive. She had not yet noticed that life can be painful and people will often let you down. Her mother and sisters knew this but Charice still held on to her innocence. Charice lived joyfully. How long would this gift of innocence remain?

"Charice is here to see you with a note from her teacher," said my secretary a few days later.

Charice came into my office, right thumb stuck in her mouth. She leaned on the arm of my chair and handed me a note. She stood quietly as I opened it and read, "Charice says she's hungry."

"Did you have anything to eat this morning, Charice?"

She shook her head back and forth, indicating "no," with her thumb still firmly in place.

"OK, let's go to the cafeteria and find out if they have something for you."

I took Charice by the hand and we walked to the cafeteria, which was located directly across from the Christmas tree in the lobby.

As we passed by the tree, Charice paused, took her thumb out of her mouth, pointed to the package and said exclaimed joyfully, "That big present is mine! It's my ice cream maker." She looked at me with a radiant smile.

"We'll see about that at Christmas time. Let's find something to eat."

Charice hungrily gobbled down a bowl of cereal and drank two cartons of milk. She then sat stirring the leftover milk in her bowl, not particularly worried about missing anything in class. Charice finally had to be sent from the cafeteria because she was running around the tables!

I often wondered how Charice acted at the homeless shelter. She had so much energy and was always in motion. There wasn't much room at the shelter for running around. There were two large rooms at the shelter. One of the rooms was the "sleeping area" where seventy-five cots were lined up in rows, quite close to each other. Students who lived there often told me that it was too noisy at night and they couldn't sleep. No wonder they were so often tired and lethargic.

The second large room was a cafeteria / social area, filled with long tables. Meals were served, cafeteria style, in this area at specific times. If a resident missed the serving time, she missed the meal. Food was not allowed in any other area of the shelter. I wondered what life would be like when you couldn't have a snack or rummage in the refrigerator at night. What if you were hungry an hour before dinner or wanted a snack before going to bed? When the students, from the shelter, first began attending my school, I noticed that they snuck food at lunch and hid it in their backpacks. At first, I didn't know why they were doing this since they were receiving plenty of food. One of the older students filled me in, saying they took the food so they could have something to snack on at night. From then on, we made sure that all the homeless students had plenty of food at school and we didn't interfere with their need to take it home with them. The shelter cafeteria was used for many different purposes. Before and after dinner, the kids were permitted to work on their homework at long tables. This multi-use area was also the place all the kids came when it rained and they couldn't go outside. There were board games and art supplies for their use. Charice lived as if life were a game. Luckily, she had not yet been affected by the hopelessness of homelessness.

Since a small breakfast was served to the kids at the shelter at 6:00am, these students were often hungry when they came to school at 8:15am. Therefore, we provided them with cereal, doughnuts or toast, milk, juice and fruit. This was a new procedure at our school since there was no breakfast program in place. The older students usually chose not to participate in breakfast. This puzzled me at first because I assumed they would be hungry also. When I asked if they were hungry, they said "yes." When I asked if they wanted to come in to the cafeteria and get something to eat, they said, "no." Finally, I asked a couple of the older students why they didn't want to eat breakfast at school. They said that they didn't want their classmates to know that they lived at the shelter. If they went into the cafeteria for breakfast, it would be obvious and they would be "marked" as homeless kids. I hadn't fully realized the depth of the stigma attached to being a homeless student until that time.

One morning, as I was walking down the hallway, as the students came into the building, I heard shouting coming from the cafeteria.

"I want the prize!" I immediately recognized Charice's voice. When I walked into the cafeteria, I saw her struggling with another student, each pulling at one end of a cereal box.

"No, it's my turn," yelled Jonathan, yanking the box out of Charice's hands.

"Give it to me!" Charice wailed, grabbing the open box, as Cheerios flew through the air.

"Stop the fighting! What's going on in here? Pick up those Cheerios!"

"I want the prize in the box!" said Charice, folding her arms across her chest and plopping her thumb in her mouth.

"It's my turn to have the prize," said Jonathan. "Charice got the prize yesterday."

"No, it's my turn!" Charice shouted.

"Both of you come over here right now and stop arguing with each other," I said in my firmest principal tone. "Pick up all the Cheerios that are on the floor and the table. Then sit quietly."

Breakfast in the cafeteria had become a battleground for the younger students with the winner realizing victory if he or she could claim the prize from the cereal box. I discovered that the cereal was not being eaten but the boxes were being pillaged for the prize bounty. It became clear that a tiny, junky, plastic prize was important to five year olds who didn't have many toys or possessions. I ended up buying an assortment of tiny, plastic "prizes" and giving them out each day with breakfast. It did seem to stop the fighting.

"Let Jonathan have the prize today. There'll be other prizes for you to have, Charice," I said, taking the prize from her and handing it to Jonathan.

"Thank you," he said.

Charice glared at me.

"Finish your cereal, Charice, and go to your classroom."

"I don't want anymore," replied Charice, slamming her spoon on the table. She picked up a doughnut, took one bite, and set it back on the tray. Charice then got up, pushed her chair into the table and marched out of the cafeteria.

Whew! What a bundle of energy! This little lady knew how to make a statement and she wasn't afraid to do so!

Charice and Jonathan actively participated in their classroom activities. However, many of the older students, from the shelter, often kept to themselves, only talking to or hanging out with other homeless students. Some of them became reclusive and sullen, others angry and antagonistic. Many just sat quietly in class, doing their work but not interacting unless they had to. The haunting mistrust in their eyes, the defeated slump to their shoulders, and the struggle to adjust to another new school set them apart. The fact that other students talked about their houses, clothes, vacations and toys they owned created huge gaps that couldn't be bridged, no matter how hard other students tried to be friendly and kind. Why form a friendship when you might be leaving next week? Why endure more pain when you can create a protective wall that keeps the pain, and other people, at arms length? There was a lingering sadness and hopelessness that hung around the shoulders of most of the students from the shelter. This was especially true of the older students who had lived this way longer and understood what a homeless lifestyle brought with it. Most of the younger students were still optimistic about life, especially Charice!

It was six days before Christmas and the weather had turned bitter cold. Hats and gloves had been handed out to all of the homeless students as well as to other students who needed them.

"Charice, what are you doing?" I called out, hurrying down the hall one morning. Charice had crawled under the Christmas tree, which was leaning slightly to one side, and managed to find "her package" at the back where I had tried to hide it, hoping she would forget about it.

I'm opening my ice cream maker," she replied, beaming a somewhat toothless smile. Charice continued to tear at the wrapping paper.

Since the box didn't contain her ice cream maker or any other present, I knew Charice would be terribly disappointed if she succeeded in opening the package.

"Charice, it's not Christmas yet. There are six more days to wait. Do you think you can wait?"

Charice shook her head "no" and continued ripping the paper. I took her hands away from the box and scooted her out from under the tree.

"I know it's hard to wait, Charice, but just a few more days," I said, giving her a hug. "Do you think you can wait a few more days?"

Charice stuck her thumb in her mouth, nodding "yes."

This experience was causing me to question our placing a Christmas tree and presents in the lobby. It had apparently been a tradition at this school for many years. However, this was the first Christmas we had homeless students in our school. Were we creating even more longing and pain for these students? What of the other students who might not have a tree with presents under it? We'd definitely have to rethink this practice. It wasn't our intention to make any students feel bad or different but I think that was exactly what we were doing.

What was I to do about Charice and the big, empty box? She was convinced that her long dreamed of ice cream maker was in that red and green box under the tree. Charice stopped and looked at it every day when she entered school. She pointed to it each day as she was leaving, telling anyone who would listen that it was her ice cream maker.

I decided that I would buy Charice an ice cream maker for Christmas. How could she not find one to open after seeing it at school every day? What had I done by placing those fake presents under the tree? That evening I went to a local toy store and investigated the current line of kid's ice cream makers. I decided to buy the machine and ingredients because I knew they wouldn't be available at the shelter. I chose a cute, pink and blue model. I was excited because I knew that Charice would fall in love with it. I thought about how much fun she would have making ice cream for her friends. As I walked to the checkout, thinking about what other supplies to purchase, I suddenly stopped when I realized that Charice couldn't have an ice cream maker at the shelter! There was no place to store the machine or the ingredients. There was no place to make the ice cream since the kitchen area was off-limits to the residents. There was no place to eat ice cream since the cafeteria could only be used for eating during meal hours and no outside food was allowed. I was stunned as I stood, in the crowded isle, holding Charice's ice cream maker. I put it back on the self and left the store feeling totally dejected.

I cried on the long drive home for Charice and her dream that wouldn't be realized this Christmas. I cried for the needy kids, who attended my school, and for all the kids in our country who have been robbed of the chance to be kids and grow up with the simple pleasures of life. I cried when I thought of a Christmas spent at the shelter. I cried with feelings of total hopelessness and helplessness.

The last day of school, before Christmas vacation, had arrived. The students excitedly streamed into the building, carrying gifts for their teachers and food for their parties. Two more days until Christmas and everyone was excited! Once again, I found Charice pulling her present from under the tree.

"It's almost Christmas. I'm taking my present home with me today," she said.

"Well, Charice, you don't have to take your present home with you. It's too big and heavy to carry," I said. "Santa's helpers will come to school tonight to pick up all of the presents and Santa will deliver them on Christmas. So, you may leave your present under the tree. I'll tell Santa's helpers that it's for you."

Charice seemed satisfied by this explanation. She pushed the present back under the tree, stood up and gave me a big hug.

"I love you!" she said enthusiastically, turning and skipping down the hallway toward her classroom.

My heart broke.

As I sat with my family on Christmas Day, opening presents and enjoying good food and a comforting fire, I thought of Charice. What was her Christmas like at the shelter? Did she find and open the large box I had secretly delivered that was wrapped identically to the one that she had claimed at school? Was she disappointed that the box didn't contain an ice cream maker? Did she like the stuffed animals and other toys that I had packed in the box, hoping they would make up for not receiving the ice cream maker?

I wondered if this Christmas would be the beginning of Charice losing the gift of her innocence and joy for living. I hoped that her naturally optimistic spirit wouldn't be crushed too soon. I never found out if Charice was disappointed that Christmas morning. When school resumed, after vacation, the Wilson children didn't come in on the bus. I was notified that they had moved, destination unknown. I never saw Charice again but I think of her now and then, especially at Christmastime.

....

Optimism

Definition: *Hopefulness and confidence about the future or the successful outcome of something*

The attitude and feeling of optimism tangibly affects our daily lives, driving the decisions we make and influencing our beliefs about ourselves, others and life events. Optimism leads to personal happiness and professional success. It is an approach toward living that assists us in choosing the actions we take in order to accomplish goals and get what we need. Optimism is both strong and fragile. Holding an optimistic view can powerfully lead us to new and significant heights of accomplishment and achievement. On the other hand, one negative turn of events or loss of hope can squash an optimistic perspective, leading to pessimism and failure. Optimism may seem to be an unusual building block for a successful school. As it turns, out, optimism is a trait that, when consistently applied, helps to create success in many arenas. The mental attitude of optimism is a belief in the inherent good to be found in other people and in our individual worlds and in the world at large. Optimism is alive and well in the classrooms in our schools. Educators practice this trait in the simple act of showing up for work each day, knowing that the ever increasing challenges that face them can be met with determination and grace. Is it important for teachers to be optimistic? Should they teach optimism?

Optimism is an essential characteristic that should be possessed by every teacher. We feel energetic around people who practice an optimistic viewpoint. They find solutions to problems and view every mountain as climbable. Teachers who are optimistic believe that they can reach every child with whom they work no matter how great the challenges. Optimistic people have difficult days but don't give up in the face of hardship or failure. They find another way, open another door, seek another solution. They don't settle for a dead-end result. People with an optimistic viewpoint love life with all of its ups and downs. This proactive attitude is contagious. Optimists are our leaders, our role models, and our most effective teachers because they see the inherent good and the hidden giftedness in their students. Recall your most memorable teachers. How many of them would you classify as optimistic people? Probably most of them were optimistic. They believed in themselves and their innate abilities and giftedness and they encouraged and supported their student's success.

Optimistic people aren't necessarily all "warm and fuzzy." Some of our greatest military leaders and strongest political leaders combined toughness with a "can-do" attitude. Optimism also doesn't connote having an unrealistic, Pollyanna attitude about life. Optimism stands upon a very specific belief system, trusting that life is good and that we are in the world to live happily and contribute to the whole. Optimists don't get bogged down in negative victim roles that lead nowhere. They face difficult situations in their lives and find ways to work through them without being defeated. As the challenges to education and educators continue to multiply and intensify, optimism as a strategy becomes even more important. The teacher who shows up each day with an optimistic view of what he'll be able to accomplish with his students is the teacher who will succeed. He will find ways in which to more positively impact student's lives. It is easy to fall into a pessimistic place when looking at the condition of the world and the educational challenges that we face. However, pessimism will not take us where we want to go in our lives. It will not create the climate of collaboration and achievement that we desire in our schools. Pessimism leads to defeat and hopelessness. Optimism creates success and belief in self and purpose.

What would an optimistic school climate look like? Why is it important? Belief in self and one's abilities is at the core of success in the educational arena. Students who believe in themselves will be willing and able to take risks in their learning. Risk-takers learn the most because they face their fears and move through them. An optimistic school climate supports the building of positive self-esteem among students. When students receive the message, from every staff member, that they are valued and capable, they begin to believe it, and eventually, to live it. An optimistic school climate sets the tone for learning and exploration in an environment that says, "Go for it. You can accomplish whatever you put your mind to." Humans are beset with constant self-doubt and self-questioning. Students fit into this category and, in fact, may be even more prone to self-doubt than adults. It only takes one comment from an adult to make a child feel defeated or pessimistic. Teasing or bullying, from peers, will also set the tone of fear and pessimism on a school campus.

A school with an optimistic climate believes in all learners innate ability to succeed. It emphasizes the fact that there are many ways in which to succeed and that we're all different in how we bring out gifts forward into reality. Optimism, practiced by teachers and parents, creates a happy and confident environment in which the whole child is recognized and taught. Optimism is a mental attitude, but a heart feeling. When we teach children to be optimistic, we're leading them to their hearts and their ultimate passion for life. We must educate more than the minds of our students. We must also touch their hearts and souls if we expect them to reach out and ultimately impact the world in which they live. An optimistic teacher helps a student move through the difficult times, realizing that things don't always work out the way we want them to. Students experience failure all the time; failure of others to recognize their potential; failure to meet the standards set by someone else; failure to measure up socially with other students; failure to be heard; failure to accomplish what they wish to do; failure to feel that they are successful and significant. If we don't teach students that failure can be met with optimism, we take away the hope that they'll need to work through the difficult situations in their lives. Some schools are places of hopelessness for students because they experience failure and see no way out of that pattern. Our teachers and principals must create environments that prove to be bastions of optimism even under the most difficult circumstances.

Optimism is not only critical for our students. It is an absolutely essential attitude for our teachers and administrators to possess and practice. The art of teaching continues to evolve and circle through different stages and shifting techniques. The basic act of a teacher interacting with a group of students each day in meaningful ways has not changed all that much in the history of education. Teachers are still at the core of the process of assisting all students to recognize and bring their gifts forward into the world. The bond formed between student and teacher is one of the most important and significant relationships that exist in our society. A deep level of trust forms between student and teacher. This trust then opens the door for vulnerability on the part of both the student and the teacher. Vulnerability, in turn, leads to true growth and learning more about self. How devastating it must be for a child to place all his trust in the hands of a teacher who turns out to be a pessimist. When this happens, the child's self-esteem is usually damaged. Those people with whom we spend the most time influence us most significantly. Educators influence children's lives and ultimately their belief systems. Parents must establish a practice of expressing and living optimism in the home so that schools reinforce and build upon this base.

What must educators and parents do to create optimistic youth?

1. Create home and school environments that demonstrate optimism is real.

2. Help children realize their power in holding optimistic views.

3. Demonstrate how our belief system helps to structure our reality.

4. Build intentional communities that support children.

....

Strategy #1 - Create Home and School Environments That Demonstrate Optimism is Real

Action Steps:

- share your positive view of daily life events with your students

- talk to your students about negative situations that impact them such as the death of a friend, school or world violence, etc. and try to alleviate their fears

- demonstrate that you believe in your student's ability to succeed by giving specific feedback about all they do well or the efforts they make

- find ways to show your students that their personal world has many wonderful people and events in it

- be a positive role model to your teachers, demonstrating the power of an optimistic approach when working with other people

Children require safe and stable environments in which to grow and thrive. These places of support and nurturance must exist on a consistent basis in the lives of children. It's hard to hold an optimistic view of the world when your experience of it is negative and unsupported. It's not good enough to tell kids that everything is going to be OK in their lives. They must actually live and experience the fact that life is most often positive. Unfortunately, for many children, this isn't the case. Many home situations are quite negative for children. That makes the school experience even more critical in impacting the lives of students both in the present and for their future development.

Teachers work diligently to help students succeed. When students succeed and recognize their own gifts, they experience optimism. Therefore, it is essential that each student, in our schools, experience personal success and academic achievement. Optimism is built upon reality over a period of time and in a steady manner. Students who attend a school where teachers hold and practice a positive view toward them are more likely to be successful and develop a belief in their ability to succeed. Year upon year of meeting success leads to a solid foundation for optimism to exist and grow. Belief in self is perhaps the most important outcome of helping students develop an optimistic attitude. Strong belief in self allows the student to grow into a successful adult capable of facing the many ups and downs in life with an attitude of confidence and a strong belief system. When optimism is built over a period of time and becomes deeply instilled in student's psyches, they will weather difficult times as adults and not lose their belief in the goodness that exists in their lives.

Students love to spend time in an optimistic classroom because it supports and encourages them. It recognizes that they are much more than their grades. They are beautiful, talented, limitless individuals who have much to contribute to the world. Our world will be a much safer and more positive place if we focused on teaching and reinforcing optimism in our schools, homes and churches during the growing up years. Unfortunately, many adults have lost their hopeful viewpoint and are, therefore, unable to share this gift with children. As adults we must be careful not to impose our jaded view of the world onto the children. Our lives are not their lives and they will have their own opportunities to create and live a life of hope and trust – or not. Our task, as significant adults in their lives, is to offer them hope and teach them skills with which they will be able to deal with the many challenges, both positive and negative, that life will present.

Student and teacher levels of optimism greatly impact the cycle of teaching and learning. Classroom teachers know that their students learn best when they feel good about their own abilities, trust that they can be risk-takers and not be criticized, and experience multiple methods of instruction. Depressed and disheartened students aren't lively, engaged learners. In fact, they are quite the opposite, turning off and out to the teaching in the classroom. Teachers know that they must first pay attention to the student's readiness to learn before they can successfully teach them anything. Assisting a student in being ready to learn includes helping that learner to develop and maintain a positive view about himself and his ability to contribute and be successful.

Parents serve as partners in this journey of helping children create a belief in self and a confidence that the world, although flawed, is a good place with unlimited possibilities for self-expression, happiness, and hope. The home situation exposes many children to more emotional ups and downs than they experience at school. They see their parents argue or express discouragement when there isn't enough money, work is too stressful, jobs are lost, relationships cause problems, and children aren't performing as expected. The stressful situations that arise in family life become important sources of learning for children. Parents should be open about discussing frustrations and discouragements with children old enough to understand. However, parents may also use these opportunities to express their belief that things will work out and the world will "return to normal." Children need these assurances. We do our children a disservice if we teach them that the world is perfect and everything is great. The first time they experience the opposite of that belief they will think that the adults have lied to them and that they can't be trusted. To show that optimism is real, parents must actually demonstrate and point out to children the good that returns after difficult times have passed. Children don't necessarily see that or focus on that without having it pointed out to them.

Optimism is to the soul like breath is to the body. Humans won't experience success and fulfillment in their lives without possessing resiliency. It's not enough to teach a student to read or multiply or dissect an animal. We must also teach him that reading and math and science will all contribute in some way to his future happiness and success in the world. Despair kills dreams. Optimism opens worlds of opportunity and possibility in which we envision what we want and know that there is a very good chance we can bring our dreams into reality. Every human wants to be special and significant to others in their lifetime and leave an indelible mark that says, "I've been here." Optimism drives that desire and creates the scenarios for it to be realized.

School administrators, working purposefully with teachers, have similar roles to teachers who teach optimism to students in the classroom. Classroom teachers can certainly teach optimism and work from a hopeful perspective in schools that don't have an over-all optimistic environment. However, that becomes a lonely uphill battle often mired in discouragement and despair. For energized classroom environments to exist, teachers themselves must experience a belief in and support of optimism from their peers and administration. Effective school leaders are, first and foremost optimistic people who communicate and live this belief. They are realists as well as dreamers, finding many different answers for every question and multiple solutions to every problem. These administrators share the basic attitude that everything is possible and problems are manageable. Optimistic leaders do become discouraged and disheartened at times, but they quickly rise from that low spot and move toward the doable and the possible. Teachers look to their leaders for this positive approach and attitude when they feel discouraged and disillusioned. If our respected and effective leader believes that there is a way out of this quagmire, there must be one. Leaders who consistently demonstrate that practicing can do view will really lead to solutions, powerfully influence the lives of others. Principals who inspire teachers and create vital school environments, become the role models for teachers who, in turn, inspire their students. Optimism is circular in its movement in that it turns back on itself and continues to pick up speed and grow in power. Small circles of optimism grow as they link with other circles. Schools are places where many pockets of optimistic people interact with and influence other circles of people who then impact others. Pessimism works in much the same way. Would we rather spread circles of hope or pessimism? The choice is ours. However, as a society we really have no choice, if we want to create successful, well-educated citizens who will contribute their gifts to the world. Optimism is not an option. It's a necessity.

Imagine a world in which positive people surround our children, in their homes, in their schools, and in their communities. When government officials, educators, parents, and community members decide that our greatest priority is the growth and development of our children, positive and optimistic citizens will arise in the world. Optimism spreads when practiced. One "carrier" with an optimistic viewpoint can have unlimited positive influence on all those people with whom he comes in contact. As adults, we must commit to becoming carriers of optimism. Most of our children begin their lives as optimists. However, some are quickly turned into disbelievers because their experience and the adults in their lives tell them otherwise. As a society, we have an obligation to ensure that optimism is practiced in our homes, taught in our schools, and alive in our communities. Nothing less than this will prepare our children to deal with the growing complexities found in their lives.

Strategy # 2 - Help Children Realize Their Power in Holding Optimistic Views

Action Steps:

- point out the different choices that your students can make in any given situation – be specific

- teach your students that an optimistic attitude will help them develop more friendships than a pessimistic approach

- show children what optimism means by trying to develop a positive approach to working with a challenging situation – be specific and show them your choices

- model the belief that a challenge can be worked out rather than just giving up

- read stories to and with children that show characters who have overcome obstacles and met with success through a positive, can-do attitude

The power of choice may be the greatest advantage that human beings possess. At any given moment, we have the ability to choose our reactions, our emotional responses, and the actions we'll take in any situation. This is the ultimate personal power that allows our own decision making to play the key role in any choice that we make. The best way in which to empower our children is to teach them that they have the power over their own reactions. Children actually learn at an early age that their reactions cause different consequences to events in their lives. Young children throw tantrums or react in other similarly strong ways to get what they want or need. Older children become more sophisticated in trying out different ways to utilize their power over other people. Teaching children that they have choice in their decision making is not the same as teaching them to be manipulative. Rather, it is showing them that despite being under the control of parents and teachers, they ultimately have the final say based on the decisions they make.

Personal choice is a gift given at birth and it is with us until the day we die. No one can take it away from us. Optimism and pessimism are both choices. The events of our lives dictate the choices we make, choosing to be either an optimist or a pessimist. Certainly people who have very difficult, and often tragic, lives may lean more toward a pessimistic view of the world. This would be a natural result of their negative life experiences. However, many people who have overcome the greatest odds and raised themselves from the depths of pessimism have found stunning success. It's very difficult, if not impossible, to be successful if you're always pessimistic. You'll not only fail with this negative viewpoint, but most people will want to stay away from you because of your attitude.

Students who are pessimists soon discover that they have very few friends. They usually don't know why that's the case. They just know that others avoid them. They tend to whine or complain a lot which makes them undesirable as friends. Teachers should talk about optimism in the classroom and create scenarios where students can role-play both a pessimistic and an optimistic attitude and see the different results that occur. Children naturally take on an optimistic or pessimistic view of the world based on their parent's worldview. However, schools play a significant role in influencing, and changing, that worldview. Therefore, it's necessary for teachers to both practice optimism and to teach it. Teaching optimism occurs by showing students that they have choice and that there is a positive side to almost any situation, despite outward appearances to the contrary. For example, students may be initially upset about a cancelled class trip to the Science Museum and express a pessimistic attitude. The teacher can demonstrate an optimistic response to this situation by creating a fun and motivating alternate activity. Students are often not sophisticated enough to see that a failure may have been a wonderful learning opportunity and helped them in the long run. They must be taught that success and growth occur in many ways and often through failure.

Many children grow up in desperate home situations and develop a negative worldview long before they enter school. Teachers play a significant role in shifting children's negative worldviews. They do this through empowering their students, helping them meet with success and giving them the tools they need to lead positive and productive lives. If a student enters kindergarten with a pessimistic view of life and his ability to succeed, and he graduates feeling the same way, then we've failed him. A large part of the learning experience leads students in finding out about themselves and what they're capable of doing. Personal growth and academic success pave the way for our students to grow up thinking that the world is an OK place and that they'll be able to find their way in the world once they leave school. Many children live in troubled family situations, including abuse, poverty, and lack of attention and love, without basic material needs. This should not condemn them to lives of desperate failure, following in their parent's footsteps. Teachers and schools make a huge difference in the lives of children when they show their students how to change and grow through making different choices in life in order to realize different outcomes.

Students learn optimism through experiencing success. Teachers who set up and deliver learning experiences, through which their students succeed, teach optimism and belief in self. The quickest way for a teacher to try to counteract a student's negative view of life is to assist that student in reaching successful outcomes. It is also important for the teacher or parent to point out specifically what the child did to create that successful outcome. Teachers and parents who use words like, "You chose to put in extra time on this project and that helped you do a great job," help students see that their decisions led to success. The linkage between making positive or negative choices and the end result must be demonstrated over and over again to children.

It is imperative for teachers to teach their students about the power of personal choice. Another child kicks you in the leg at recess. What do you do? There is choice here that will influence the results and set up the consequences. Children must be shown that their reactions impact the consequences that, in turn, deliver certain results. If a child chooses to punch the student who kicked him, that creates a different set of results than if the victim walked away from the incident. Individuals have great personal power. However, many children and adults don't realize that they possess this power of choice, which will significantly impact their lives.

Children and adults also have the power of choice over their feelings. Most children and many adults don't recognize this either. Those students and adults who constantly act victimized often don't understand that they have a choice in how to react when something bad happens to them or influences their life. Every person has the ability to change his mindset in any given moment. If Bobby wouldn't play with me on the playground that could mean that he hates me or maybe he already started a game with someone else and didn't think about me. A student's choice of how he'll react to that scenario sets up whether he becomes a victim and displays a pessimistic worldview ("nobody likes me") or whether he chooses to move on and not be victimized by the experience. We all make the choice, at times, to feel like victims. However, it's the child or adult who constantly believes that he's a victim, who displays a pessimistic view, which, in turn, contributes negativity to his life. Students who lack hope and optimism won't ultimately succeed. Their failures will contribute to more feelings of hopelessness and pessimism. Teachers and principals must set up learning environments in which students experience personal and academic success and, in the process, learn how they contributed to that success. Teachers should constantly point out to their students how the student's decisions and choices impact the outcome of their learning and their forming friendships. The power of personal choice is one of the most important concepts we can teach our children. It's a practical strategy that will empower them to take control over their own lives and create the future they hope to achieve. Everyone possesses it but everyone doesn't use it. Help your students grow in their optimistic worldviews through showing them that they hold the key to their own future success. Optimism is a powerful attitude.

We live in a time when it's easy to become a pessimist. Look around. War, poverty, hunger, despair, natural disasters and daily events that dampen our optimistic viewpoint fill the world in which we live. These desperate world conditions make it even more imperative that we teach our children, who will ultimately play a role in solving these world problems, how to be optimistic, realistic and action oriented. Pessimism will not cure our societal problems. It will only sink us into further depths of despair. Educating a new generation of optimistic and practical thinkers and problems solvers will be one way in which to significantly impact the world. This process begins with the interaction between one student and his teacher. Optimism is a powerful tool for change.

Strategy # 3 – Demonstrate How Our Belief System Helps to Structure Our Reality.

Action Steps:

- teach your students how to select actions that will help them achieve their goals, whether a completed project or making a new friend or qualifying for the soccer team

- show your students how to look at results that they're unhappy with and link them to their original thoughts before they took actions that ended up failing

- share with your students specific examples of how you changed your teaching strategies when what you were doing didn't work

- work with students who frequently have behavior problems to show them that they always have choice in deciding how to react

- role play negative situations to demonstrate how a different approach and change of attitude might have led to a more satisfactory outcome

The power that lies in holding an optimistic viewpoint is tied to the end results of our beliefs through the actions that we ultimately take in any situation. If a student believes that he'll become the spelling champion of the school, does that belief automatically make him the champ? Of course it doesn't. There are action steps that he must begin to create the end result of achieving the championship. He must study, compete, and work hard to accomplish his goals. Our beliefs don't immediately create what we're thinking. However, beliefs do play a significant role in our successes and failures. If we hope to teach our children to become successful in life, we must teach them about the power of their belief system to positively or negatively impact their lives.

Utilizing beliefs to influence reality is a cyclical process. What we think or how we perceive people and situations influences the actions we take and the words we speak. Our actions and words, in turn, create certain results, positive, negative or neutral. If we like the results that we've created, we usually continue the belief system that created them. If we don't like the results, then we circle back to the beginning of the cycle and change our beliefs, which changes our actions and words, which changes the outcomes. This circular process can easily be studied and monitored. Think of something you've recently either succeeded or failed at achieving. What was your initial thought process regarding this situation? What actions did you take or what did you say about the situation, based on your beliefs about it? What results did your actions and words achieve? How could you have changed the end result based on changing your initial attitude? This step-by-step process is easy to track and can be successfully used with students in the classroom to help them see that their thoughts do ultimately impact their success. The power of personal choice plays a strong role in this process. Students and adults are empowered when they realize that there is a definitive connection between what they think and what they get. Think how powerful a learning experience it would be for students if the teacher led individual students or groups through this self-reflective process at the end of a project or lesson. It would be as simple as asking the students to do the following. Write down three things you thought about this project before you began – e.g. "I don't know anything about building pyramids. I'm lousy at figuring out the math. This will be hard." List three steps you took to accomplish the project and link them to your initial thinking – e.g. "I thought this project would be too hard so I didn't start it on time. I started it the night before it was due." Write one sentence telling the outcome of the project – e.g. "I received an unsatisfactory because I didn't finish the project." Let's think about changing your initial thoughts about the project and see how they influence the steps you take and the results you get. The circular process is then followed through so that students see the connection between their initial thoughts and the end results. If students were trained to look at their successes and failures with an emphasis on their thinking both at the beginning and during the process of accomplishing something, they would be more powerful in creating desired outcomes.

This same cyclical process, of relating beliefs to realized out-comes, is an important strategy for teachers and principals to use to determine why some things succeed and others fail. If we hope to have every student achieving, do we believe that's possible and what steps are we implementing to ensure those results? It is particularly useful to carefully examine our successes and failures to see how we reached them and how we might shift end results to other more de-sirable outcomes. An optimistic viewpoint usually allows us to cre-ate more interesting, successful and creative action steps. When we believe that just about anything is possible, we find creative ways to realize that truth. This often causes us to think outside the box and become more innovative than we might have otherwise shown. When we act hopeful and optimistic, we're less likely to give up when the situation becomes challenging or appears to be failing. We read about so many highly successful people who realized their successes after multiple failures where they never gave up, but always demonstrated an optimistic view of reaching their goals.

The school environment as a whole will be significantly impacted by the belief system of each individual in the school community. Therefore, it's critical that the principal work with teachers, students and parents to create an environment where all hold optimistic views for the success of students and the school as a whole. This positive approach will open more doors of possibility and allow for more creative problem solving to occur to counter the ever-increasing challenges that face educators. When principals work from an optimistic viewpoint to help all teachers succeed and teachers work from an optimistic viewpoint to ensure their student's success, schools have a real chance to make a positive difference in the lives of all children. It's often difficult to hold an optimistic viewpoint when we see that our world appears to be crashing down around us. That is precisely the time when we must operate from an optimistic perspective because the power of an optimistic viewpoint has the potential to turn even the most difficult situation around. If we can instill this idea in our students and teach them not to give up when the going gets tough, they will be more successful in school and in life. Working through challenging times, for students or adults, requires the ability to see what isn't working and take steps to correct the situation. Knowing the power of our personal belief system and the ability to choose our reactions at any moment, provides us with a greater sense of personal power in those times when we feel so powerless. Choice is a key that opens many doors, allowing us to decide which ones we want to go through. We actually do have some say and personal power in creating the lives that we desire to live.

Strategy # 4 - Build Intentional Communities That Support Children

Action Steps:

- gather the entire local school community together to determine how it can best support the work of building optimistic citizens in our schools

- create daily opportunities for your students to meet with success in both academic and social situations

- talk to your students about your doubts and share with them how you find solutions or ways to overcome those doubts

- point out to students when they use pessimistic or optimistic language because awareness is an important step in teaching self-monitoring

- spend time talking with your students so that they'll feel comfortable and safe going to you when they're worried or afraid.

Adults are responsible for creating a safe world in which children may grow up with hope, optimism and opportunity. Children form optimistic viewpoints when they have the material support they need, love from family and friends and a sense that things are OK and they feel safe. What can parents, educators and citizens do to create home and school situations that support the growth and happiness of our children? How do we help children feel optimistic in natural and consistent ways?

When we look to the federal government and its role in supporting our youth, we see failure in many areas. Unfortunately, national mandates fall short of providing the resources necessary to keep our children out of poverty, free from illness and achieving in academically sound and safe schools. Our country shamelessly places children low on the priority list for receiving support. Parents, educators and local citizens must become more vocal in their demands for fair and equal treatment for all of our children, providing them with the financial aid and human support they need to live happy lives and grow up safely. Children often feel the uncertainty, economic impact and fear that so often creeps into the world of the adults in their lives. How do we shelter children from the dangers of terrorism, school violence, poverty, illness and poor learning conditions? Where do we start when the picture is so big and our efforts seem so small? How do we establish optimistic environments when there often appears to be little hope for optimism? Can we truly serve our children if we feel pessimistic and lead lives of despair and fear? These are difficult questions, posed in challenging times.

Parents and educators must collaborate to form intentional communities at the local level that support all children. Intentional means people plan and live with purpose and specific focus. This means working together to create environments that demonstrate to children that optimism is real and that it holds a place in their lives and plays a significant role in their future happiness and success. In order to do this, parents, teachers and principals must serve as positive role models, showing through their actions that they believe the world is a good place and most people are also good. This doesn't mean that we deny danger and evil. However, it does mean that we focus on the ways in which we can teach our students how to successfully and happily find their way in the world. In addition to role modeling, they require constant support and coaching along the way in order to decipher what is real, what is safe and who can be trusted. We must reach out beyond our own families and schools to support the building of intentional communities for children throughout the world. It would be a mistake to focus only on our own small area of local influence. The future challenges that face our children will require that they're able to think clearly, creatively problem solve, and provide practical solutions. They will succeed more often in working through current and future challenges if they are hopeful people with optimistic approaches to life. Children learn optimism from adult role models and from living it each and every day in their lives.

Schools become important intentional communities that support students experiencing and practicing optimism. Teachers and principals influence their student's life experiences and worldviews in significant and lasting ways. Therefore, a school staff should carefully examine the strategies and attitudes of the learning environment they provide to students to determine if it practices and teaches optimism both in and out of the classrooms. What does practicing optimism mean in a school setting? It means that teachers and parents work with students to help them discover their gifts and talents and bring them successfully into the world, resulting in high self-esteem and the belief that they can succeed. The experience of optimism breeds more optimism. A teacher who believes in his student's ability and goodness and communicates this to the student provides that child with an experience of optimism. A student meeting with success in his learning reaches higher levels of belief in self and the goodness of life, which increases his optimistic viewpoint. This, in turn, fuels future success both in school and in her personal life. Adults can't expect children to be optimistic all on their own. They look to us for guidance in this area. They pay attention to our attitudes. They watch how we solve problems and work through disputes. Our attitudes, whether optimistic or pessimistic, shine through. When children always hear negativity from the adults in their lives, they develop negative attitudes themselves. Schools and school personnel play significant roles in helping all students to grow up as optimists. This is especially true for those students who come to the school setting having lived lives in pessimism and despair. School may be the only hope they have for changing their worldview from a self-defeating to a self-empowering attitude.

The classroom setting may be the perfect place for building intentional communities that support children and provide them with experiences that assist in the development of optimistic attitudes. Classrooms become like family units, only on a larger scale. They provide all the dynamics that exist among people. However, since classrooms are controlled environments, they become labs for dissecting human interactions to see what forms the basis for success in this area. If student's experiences in their classrooms significantly impact their ultimate view of the world and approach toward life, we ought to pay more attention to what occurs in our classrooms. The future of our world is at stake. It would seem reasonable that classroom communities, as development centers for future societal leaders, would receive our society's highest level of financial, mental and emotional support. Sadly, this isn't the case. Actually, quite the opposite is true. Fortunately, most classroom teachers and school principals forge ahead and create intentional communities that support children developing an optimistic view point, within their classrooms. They do so at great personal sacrifice, knowing that they really have no choice as our future is on the line. Parents, teachers, principals and citizens must constantly strive to develop intentional communities to support children at the local, national and international levels. This work is crucial to the future of society. We cannot rest. There is no time for lack of focus or weakness of intention. Our children need to live positive and optimistic lives that provide them with hope for their future and with useful strategies to apply in their lives in order to become successful adults.

6. ACCOUNTABILITY

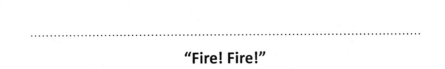

"Fire! Fire!"

THE SCHOOL PRINCIPAL is both a manager and a leader. Perhaps the most important leadership role, of the principal, is to supervise teachers. Teacher observations may be formal or informal. Formal observations are scheduled, pre-planned and officially written up. Informal observations are drop-in experiences, usually with verbal feedback given to the teacher. In some schools, principals view observations as chores to be completed as quickly and effortlessly as possible. However, observing teachers is an important way to measure accountability on a daily basis. Effective leaders will view supervision as providing opportunities to speak with their teachers about their skills, successes, and areas that need improvement. Observations are particularly important for beginning teachers who need frequent and specific feedback. Experienced teachers should also be regularly observed and recognized for their skills and accomplishments. Informal observations are quite useful for getting a clear sense, over time, of what a teacher does in his classroom and how the students respond. Frequent informal observations and drop-in visits to the classroom help to create an environment where the teacher feels comfortable with the principal in his classroom at any time.

Formal observations, although carefully preplanned by the teacher, do have a way of sometimes getting off track. Watching how a teacher handles a lesson gone astray provides important information for the observer. Part of the joy for me, in observing teachers teaching, was to see the many creative ways in which teachers ply their craft. It was always an honor to observe a teacher at his best. I felt that if I ever chose to go back into teaching, after serving as a principal, I would know so much more about good teaching, having spent so many hours watching incredible teachers.

I would like to share a few "observation vignettes" that occurred in my fifteen years, and hundreds of hours watching teachers teach.

Vignette # 1

It was late September. We had a new physical education teacher at our school. Pat had been transferred from her high school position to our K-6th grade elementary school because of retirements and a more senior PE teacher who bumped her out of her position. Pat was angry with this transfer and, I believe, quite worried because she had never worked with little kids before. I think she felt comfortable with the 4th-6th graders, but not the younger students. Prior to school opening, and during the first few weeks, I had spent a lot of time with Pat, giving her ideas and trying to help her get adjusted to the elementary level. After almost a month, she was still struggling. I decided that I needed to spend time with her every few days, suggesting ways that she might more successfully approach working with the younger students. After these drop-in supervisory sessions, I met with Pat and we discussed the lesson and the strategies she had used. One Thursday afternoon, I left a note in Pat's mailbox saying that I would come into her kindergarten class on Friday morning to unofficially observe and give her some pointers. This observation wouldn't "count" as one of her formal observations. Rather, it was for the purpose of providing useful feed-back to Pat. I hoped that she would become less angry if she met with more success and began to like the younger students.

I arrived to observe Pat about five minutes before the kindergar-teners showed up. Pat seemed nervous and I sensed that she wasn't too thrilled that I was sitting there. She glanced at my notepad with a scowl and sighed loudly. Pat turned toward the gym door when the sound of talking kids got closer. The kindergarten teacher walked in with her charges, all in a quiet, single-file line. She showed them where to sit down, encouraged them to work hard and left them alone with the PE teacher. Pat, a very large woman, rather menacingly hovered over these five-year-olds who sat quietly and attentively. "Shrilllllllllll!" Pat blew her whistle. It surprised everyone, including myself. We all jumped. The students began to giggle.

"Everyone stand up," Pat barked. The kids immediately stood up, anxious to get going and to please their teacher. "OK, get into your squads," Pat ordered. The kindergarteners regarded each other with confused looks and then piled into one big, jumbled group of squirm-ing bodies! Of course, the noise level greatly increased during this movement and confusion. Soon, twenty-five little bodies were run-ning around and purposely body bumping one another, laughing all the time. They seemed to be having a great time forming their squads! Pat looked stunned. "Shrillllllllllll!" The loud whistle blasted through-out the gym until every little body stopped in its tracks.

"Sit down right where you are and face me," Pat screeched, obvi-ously quite unnerved. This was a good strategy so I wrote it down. Pat went on to remind the students that she had formed little groups, in the last class, and they would start off in these groups at the beginning of each class. Pat quickly called out names and put the kids in their squads.

Time to speak up I decided. "If you give each group a color," I suggested, "then you can ask each color group to line up and they'll probably remember after doing it a few times." Pat glared at me, but followed my suggestion. The students now sat expectantly in their color-coded squads, waiting for directions. Class was half-over. These energetic kids still hadn't participated in any organized physical activities. The gym was marked off for basketball and other activities, which meant there was a large circle in the middle of the gym. This would become the next focus of the lesson.

"Shrilllllllllllll!" the whistle blew. Talking immediately stopped and all eyes were on Pat. At least they seemed to know now that when the whistle blew, they should get quiet and look at the teacher. "Stand up!" commanded Pat. "Everyone go and stand on the circle in the middle of the gym." Some students immediately began aimlessly running around while others stood in perplexed silence. Soon, there were five-year-olds swarming all over the gym like a family of ants at a picnic! They didn't know where the center of the gym was. What did center mean anyway? Many didn't yet know what a circle was, at least one that big. Besides, what does it mean to stand on a circle? Those who saw the circle and knew to go there weren't sure whether to stand on the line, outlining the circle, or in the circle itself so they did both. Pat stood in the middle of all this activity with a look of horror on her face. I had to work very hard not to double over with laughter. This was no laughing matter to Pat who was obviously quite disturbed.

"Shrilllllllllllll! It worked again. Everyone sat down and got quiet. The only problem was that kids were scattered all around the huge gym. Pat took a deep breath and pointed to a spot to her right. "Red squad, sit over here!" Five students ran to the designated area and within a few minutes everyone was in their squads. Well, that seemed to work. Write that down! Pat then showed the students where the circle was and brought two students forward to demonstrate how to stand on the line. "OK, when I blow the whistle, everyone run over and stand on the circle line," Pat said. "Shrilllllllllllll!" With precision and speed, the kindergarteners lined up on the circle. Success noted. There was now about five minutes of the thirty-minute class left and Pat looked exhausted. The kindergarteners appeared to be enjoying themselves and they had no idea the class wasn't progressing smoothly.

"We don't have much time left but we're going to do the hokey-pokey. Do you all know that one?" Pat asked. "Yea!" A huge cheer went up. I couldn't believe, with five minutes left, she was attempting the hokey pokey. Pat obviously wasn't yet understanding that five-year-olds require clear and simple directions with ample demonstrations all of which takes time. "Shrilllllllll! Here we go!" Pat turned on the music and the entire circle began gyrating. "Put your right arm in," Pat sang as arms, legs and butts entered the open circle. "Now your left arm," Pat called out before the music gave the command. Many of the students didn't yet know right from left or in and out so there was a lot of free flowing movement but everyone was obviously having a wonderful time! Soon the music stopped. "Shrilllllllll! Time is up. Line up by the door," Pat called out. There were four doors to the gym so you can imagine what happened next!

Vignette #2

I had scheduled a formal, early afternoon observation with Mrs. Dorsey, who was an exceptional second grade teacher. She was a no-nonsense teacher who was strict but loving with her students. Mrs. Dorsey's lessons were always well-planned and taught with precision. She liked her classroom to be orderly and her students organized, responsible and polite. Mrs. Dorsey's students loved her, as did their parents. I wouldn't characterize Mrs. Dorsey as rigid, but there was no doubt that she was in control and had a clear view of the way she wished things to progress. The written lesson plan she turned in, prior to the observation, was well written and clearly outlined the steps she wished to follow in teaching a Language Arts lesson.

When I entered Mrs. Dorsey's classroom, her students were quietly working in pairs on a science project. She asked them to put away their work and get ready for Language Arts. The students immediately, and quietly, complied and sat looking at their teacher. Mrs. Dorsey's class was always in control and attentive. How did she accomplish this? I had noticed on prior classroom visits that she had procedures and systems in place for accomplishing most classroom tasks. The students who were placed in her class were those students who thrived on orderliness and predictability, both of which abounded in Mrs. Dorsey's classroom.

Mrs. Dorsey began to introduce the lesson. "Today, we're going to learn about quotation marks," she told her students. "We see quotation marks in our reading books all the time. Today we'll find out why they're there and how they can help us become better writers. Look at these sentences I'm going to write on the board." Mrs. Dorsey began writing two sentences, one with quotation marks and one without, on the board. A hand at the back of the room shot up into the air while Mrs. Dorsey was writing. I could see that she caught sight of the hand, out of the corner of her eye. "Not now, Jenny," Mrs. Dorsey said, continuing to write. Jenny put her hand down.

"John, would you read this first sentence, which has no quotation marks?" asked Mrs. Dorsey. As John began to read, Jenny's hand flew up into the air again and began to wave. Mrs. Dorsey looked solemnly at Jenny and shook her head "no", while John continued reading the sentence. Jenny lowered her hand. Obviously, Mrs. Dorsey didn't want the flow of her lesson broken. "Very good reading, John," said Mrs. Dorsey when John had finished. "The sentence John just read is a sentence that gives us information so there are no quotation marks around it." Mrs. Dorsey told the class. "Let's look at this other sentence, that has quotation marks, and see if we can figure out the difference between the two. Beth, please read the next sentence on the board." Beth began to read and Jenny's hand flew up into the air one more time, waving wildly back and forth. Mrs. Dorsey looked at Jenny in a stern manner that said, "Don't interrupt in the middle of this process." When Beth had finished reading, Mrs. Dorsey said she would answer questions as soon as they had discussed this second sentence. She looked at Jenny as she said this and Jenny's hand, which was still waving, returned to her lap.

"This second sentence has quotation marks because this sentence tells us what someone is saying. We use quotation marks to show the words a person says. We see quotation marks in our stories because people are often talking to one another in the stories," said Mrs. Dorsey. Jenny's hand flew up into the air, waved wildly and now "oh-oh's" had been added to the action. All the students turned around to look at Jenny because her pleas for attention had become so vocal. Mrs. Dorsey looked at Jenny with a look of resignation and frustration that Jenny was taking this lesson off its planned course of action. Mrs. Dorsey had not yet asked the students any questions so Jenny couldn't be raising her hand to discuss the lesson. "For heaven's sake, Jenny," said Mrs. Dorsey. "What is the problem?"

"There's a big old cockroach climbing up the wall, behind your head," Jenny replied in a worried voice. "I thought it might jump on your clothes," she added. Mrs. Dorsey immediately turned around to face the wall behind her. Every student, who had been looking at Jenny, swiveled around to look at the wall behind Mrs. Dorsey. I turned to look at the wall. Sure enough, there was a huge black cockroach slowly making its way up the wall behind Mrs. Dorsey. "Oooooo! Yuck!!" shouted the students. "Kill it!" someone called out. "Don't let it get loose!" another student called out. Mrs. Dorsey grabbed a book and smashed the cockroach on the wall. "Oooooo! Cool!" shouted a few boys. "Gross!" said the girls.

"That's enough class. Thank you, Jenny," said Mrs. Dorsey. "Now let's get back to our lesson." She wrote the following sentence on the board, carefully placing quotation marks in the appropriate places.

"Mrs. Dorsey, there's a big old cockroach climbing up the wall behind your head," said Jenny. Another great teacher recognizing a teachable moment!

Vignette # 3

Mrs. Jackson was a teacher of gifted students at our school. Students at every grade level hoped to be in her class one day because she did such cool projects. Early in the fall, of this particular year, Mrs. Jackson began work on a Science project with her intermediate students. They studied rockets and jet propulsion, linking their studies with other subject areas such as math, history, reading and writing. The students typically worked on a project for a month or two, in order to fully explore the topic. They researched the topic, discussed it and debated pertinent issues, wrote about it and ended up with a thorough understanding of the subject gained from many vantage points. Since I dropped into classrooms on a regular basis, I had followed the progress of this exciting project from the beginning. Mrs. Jackson and her students were particularly excited about this project because it would culminate with the students assembling rockets and launching them.

One day Mrs. Jackson stopped me as I was walking across the campus. "I just wanted to let you know that the kids have finished their rockets and we're going to launch them on Friday over in the soccer field," she told me. "You're invited for the launch. Maybe you'd like to do an observation of the launch since you've seen our work from the beginning," she suggested. "I've also invited the intermediate classes to watch."

"I'll be there and I will do an observation. I can comment on all that I've observed over the past month and then use this event as the culmination of all that work," I replied. Principals are always looking for observation opportunities and this looked like a good one since I could show all the work that I had previously observed, building up to this event. "How far up will these rockets go? Where will they land? Do we have to worry about safety issues with this launch?" I asked Mrs. Jackson. I had never been involved with rocket launches before.

"They should go straight up and straight down, returning to the vicinity of the launch area. If it's a windy day, we'll have to reschedule the launch. I have parent volunteers who will rope off the viewing area and keep the kids far enough out of the way so there won't be any danger," she said. "We'll only launch one at a time so we can control the situation. Once a rocket lands back on the ground, the student who made it, may run over a retrieve it. We'll later study the residual effects on the rockets," Mrs. Jackson said. "No other students will be allowed near the launch area." The launch was to take place on the large soccer field across the street from the school where there was plenty of space to keep a large, clear area open for the launch and rocket retrieval.

Friday dawned clear, beautiful and calm. It would be a perfect day for the rocket launches. I saw Mrs. Jackson rushing toward her room. "Janice, are you ready?" I called out, as I approached her.

"Isn't this exciting?" she replied. "I hope everything goes OK."

"Did you invite the newspaper?" I asked her.

"No, since this is our first launch, I decided not to call them. Maybe next year."

Mrs. Jackson's rocket students spent the early morning assembling their rockets and reviewing the launch instructions. Mid-morning the intermediate classes walked out to the field and sat in the observation area. A few parent volunteers were assisting Mrs. Jackson and the students. The rocket scientists were all in the immediate launch area setting up their rockets. There was an air of excitement on the field. It felt like a carnival or a July 4th event. I decided to go to the far side of the launch area, where there were no students or parents, to do my observation. I would have a clear view but wouldn't be interrupted by anyone. I doubted that anyone would even notice I was out there. I had my clipboard with me as I walked over to the edge of the field and stood next to a drainage ditch.

Soon, Mrs. Jackson's voice boomed over the portable PA system. She welcomed all the students and parents and advised them of the procedures and safety rules. "Is everyone ready for the launch?" she called out. 'Yea!" responded the hundred or so students as they began to chant, "rocket!, rocket!, rocket!" The excitement was building as Mrs. Jackson announced the name of the student who would launch the first rocket. A huge roar arose from the crowd as the student walked into the launch area. The rocket scientist turned, smiled and waved to his fans. This was so much fun! I was quickly writing down impressions and recording events as they unfolded.

The first student readied his rocket, took the launching button in hand and moved about fifteen feet away from the rocket, standing next to Mrs. Jackson. There was an automatic hushed silence. Mrs. Jackson held the microphone near the student's mouth so he could begin the countdown. He shouted, "ten, nine, eight..." Soon, the entire crowd had joined in the countdown. Excitement shot through the air as the final numbers were chanted, "three, two, one, blast off!!" The student pushed the red button. There was a momentary pause. Would the rocket lift off or was it a dud? Suddenly, there was a loud "whoosh!" and the rocket slowly lifted off its launch pad. The crowd roared! The young rocket scientist jumped up and down, just like they do at NASA! The rocket shot up into the sky, then the nose cone separated from the bottom stage of the rocket. A tiny parachute popped out and the nose cone drifted back down to earth. It floated right back into the launch area and the student was able to catch it as it neared the ground. The bottom section of the rocket also fell back to earth. The victorious student raised his nose cone high into the air amidst the cheers and chanting, "rocket!, rocket!, rocket!' The next launcher was called forward. The crowd cheered him on. This procedure was followed for the next seven young scientists. Finally, there was only one more student to go. The crowd was still cheering and having a great time. This was going to be a great observation to write up!

Jack, the last student to launch his rocket, came into the launching arena. Some of the intermediate students and their teachers began to head back to class, since it was almost lunchtime. As Jack began his countdown, I noticed that the wind had come up a little. I felt a burst of wind that fluttered my papers. I looked around and noticed that a slight breeze was stirring the bushes. I remember thinking that it was a good thing this was the last launch. The rocket rose as had the others and separation was complete. However, both the nose cone and the base of the rocket were picked up by the wind and blown over in my direction. The nose cone drifted down at the edge of the field near where I stood. I saw Jack searching for the nose cone. I waved to him so he'd see where it had landed. As I watched Jack, I noticed something flashy out of the corner of my eye. I turned around and saw that the drainage ditch was on fire! Small flames rapidly spread horizontally through the deep ditch. A gust of wind whipped up the flames, which now shot up out of the ditch and onto the nearby hillside. Apparently, the bottom section of the rocket had landed in the ditch that was filled with dried brush, sparking a fire. "Fire! Fire! Fire! Fire!" I screamed, waving at the people across the field. Since they were cleaning up and heading back to class, no one noticed me! "Hey, there's a fire here! Fire!! Help! Fire!!" I screamed as loudly as I could while waving my arms back and forth. Nothing. Nada. Meanwhile, the fire was quickly spreading and I got a little panicky. One last time, I yelled, "Fireeeeeer! Over here, help!" There was still no response. What was wrong with all those people? Why didn't they see or hear me? What should I do? I looked at the growing fire one more time and decided to run to the office to call the fire department and get a fire extinguisher. The office wasn't close and I knew this would take valuable time. As I started running across the field, Jack was running toward me to get his nose cone. I didn't want him near the fire. I clearly remember thinking that Jack was twelve years old and could run a lot faster than I! Also, I thought someone needed to stay near-by to keep people away from the growing flames.

"Jack, there's a fire!" I shouted. "Run to the office and tell the secretary to call the fire department and then get a fire extinguisher to bring back. Hurry!" Jack took off. I'm not sure but I think he was on the track team, as evidenced by his speed in sprinting to the office! I couldn't believe that no one else had seen the fire yet. It was growing and gray smoke was beginning to climb skyward. I ran back over to the fire thinking I should try to put it out with dirt from the field. I found an old bucket in the ditch, scooped up some dirt, then ran and threw it on the flames. I did this several times before I realized that the fire continued to spread and my efforts weren't doing much good. I was becoming engulfed in smoke and decided that this was a stupid thing to do! I moved back from the fire and just watched it grow larger, as it fed on the weeds. By this time, some of the parents had seen the fire and run over to see if they could help. Apparently, someone driving past the school had seen the flames and called 911. We heard sirens off in the distance just as Jack and one of the custodians ran up with fire extinguishers. I grabbed the fire extinguisher from Jack and began spraying the fire. The custodian had a little trouble controlling his extinguisher and soon it was spraying me! "Hey, watch out!" I called as I tried to get out of his line of fire. He finally gained control and focused on the flames. We had most of the fire put out when the fire department arrived on the scene. Wow, what an observation this would be!! Where was my clipboard?

The fire chief later gave Mrs. Jackson and I a lecture on fire safety, when shooting off rockets, and offered to be on hand for future launchings. I was so grateful the local newspaper reporter had not been on the scene! I could envision that headline and see the bedraggled picture of me at one of my finest moments! Most of the students had missed the fire and were still talking about the launches. It was a glorious morning for them. I reeked of smoke and was covered with white fire retardant spray. I had to drive home to shower and change my clothes. Mrs. Jackson scheduled rocket launches in succeeding years, but she always called the fire chief and asked him to have a truck on hand. We never had another fire on launch day.

Accountability

Definition: *(of a person, organization or institution) required or expected to justify actions or decisions; responsible*

Accountability is a shared responsibility in the school setting, requiring a solid team effort to ensure that every student meets with success. It requires a clear understanding of the learning and teaching processes. Teachers and principals are held accountable every day for the outcomes of their interactions with students. This huge responsibility becomes increasingly difficult as more and more outside conditions influence our students and impact their learning environment. Teachers are responsible, every minute of the day, for what their students learn and how they perform and behave. This is a stressful, yet integral, part of the job of teaching. Accountability means that a teacher knows it's his job to find the ways in which to reach every one of his students. He may ask for help and other teachers may partner in the effort, but the primary teacher is responsible for pulling the support team together and for monitoring their work with individual students. It sometimes feels quite discouraging, and unfair, to have such a heavy burden placed upon your shoulders. The pressures on teachers to be accountable are greater now than every before. These are fair expectations when teachers receive adequate support in the job they have to do. The discrepancy between the high expectations, placed on educators, and the low levels of support given to them causes major problems. How much of a student's success is a teacher responsible for and what is fair to expect or unrealistic to realize?

At the very basic level, accountability means an individual shows up on the job and works tirelessly to focus everything within his control on his efforts to successfully complete the required work. It is an individual commitment first and foremost. However, it becomes a group commitment at the school level because it takes all members of the community to overcome the many obstacles that arise, in order to realize success in the end. Therefore, it's absolutely critical that every teacher, principal and parent assumes their individual responsibilities and contributes to the whole, beginning the first day a child enters school. Successfully passing the fifth grade end-of-year test is not only the responsibility of the fifth grade teacher. It's also the responsibility of the kindergarten through fourth grade teachers, the principal and the parents. When we place most of the blame, for failing students, on their current year teacher, we're acting unfairly and irresponsibly. Accountability requires educators to do all that they can do to develop their skills, teach effectively, create partnerships with home, and prevent students from becoming lost in the system. There are no young lives that we can afford to leave behind through ignoring or failing to meet their needs. Accountability requires teachers and principals to be exceptional educators every minute they're on the job. The pressures on them are great; the expectations high; the outcomes life changing.

The basic goal of our schools is to educate and graduate students who have mastered important skills and are able to think critically and globally. Every school must focus its vision and goals on this most basic premise of educating every student. There are many ways to hold educators accountable for their work, but the most recent emphasis is on making teachers and principals responsible for their student's yearly, standardized test scores. This is one measure of accountability, but it's not the only one nor should it be the only one upon which schools focus. Teachers and administrators are in charge of their own growth and skill development. Personal accountability is a way of being, an ethic for living, and a daily life practice. People who practice personal responsibility live lives of integrity. Responsibility is a deep knowing that guides us in right ways of action, whether someone else is watching or not and whether it "counts" or not.

Most teachers take accountability, for their work, quite seriously. They know that the lives they touch each day grow under their tutelage. Teachers realize the awesome responsibility that they assumed by entering the teaching profession. They know that the end result of their work is a changed life. Teachers constantly work and study to further develop and advance their skill level. Professional development should be on ongoing part of each teacher's professional life plan. Whether individual teachers, the school or the school district sponsors learning experiences, they must be ongoing. Students' success, in the classroom, lies heavily upon the shoulders of individual teachers. No matter how senior or well-trained the teacher, there is always more to be learned and ways to refine existing teaching strategies. Schools and school districts must support on-going professional growth activities for all staff members to grow and more successfully realize goals for student achievement. If we're going to hold teachers and principals accountable for their student's achievement, then we must hold the institutions accountable for providing growth opportunities for all staff members. School districts with focused and well-run staff development departments help to improve teaching and reinforce the practice of life-long professional growth.

Conducting regular staff development opportunities is challenging for most school districts because of budgetary issues and time constraints. These two reasons are often used to justify a weak or non-existent staff development program. It's not unusual to hear administrators saying, "We just don't have enough money to bring in a trainer and pay for subs." Or, if the work will be conducted outside of the school day, there isn't enough money to pay teachers for their time. Teachers will often respond to staff development opportunities, saying, "We need this day, without kids, to work in our classrooms. If you expect us to come after school or on Saturday, you'll have to pay us for our time. And, it's really a pain to have to leave lesson plans and be out of class if the training is on a school day." All of these excuses, whether from administrator or teacher, are valid. There isn't enough money. Time is always an issue and it's difficult to find a block of time that doesn't cause some problems for someone. However, teachers and principals really need to get beyond this level of nay-saying and together, find ways in which staff development may move forward supported at all levels.

The burden of making staff development opportunities and timelines work should not be thrust upon the teachers. Administration must find ways to provide quality time for the teachers to interact with one another to learn new ideas and techniques. This quality time must occur in appropriate and supportive environments that encourage personal and professional growth. Teachers ought to be adequately reimbursed for their work outside of the school day and paid for their extra work when preparing to be out of their classrooms for staff development. Most often, we don't make staff development a very attractive opportunity for teachers. Most professional training, conducted in the business world, is held in nice conference centers, well-appointed boardrooms or hotel facilities. Why are teachers squeezed into classrooms, small school libraries or inadequate meeting rooms for their training experiences? Most business training days include continental breakfast, snacks, beverages at break times and healthy lunches. Why do most teacher training days look so different than those in business? The training experience should be one of nurturing support for the hard work and thoughtful interactions that will take place during that time. Most often, teachers don't have a nurturing or appreciative environment supporting their professional growth. What could be positive growth experiences often become days of dread, rather than days of excitement. When staff development becomes one more burden, stacked upon all the others, it will lose much of its effectiveness, regardless of how good the presenter might be. If federal and state departments of education are serious about helping every child succeed through consistently training the best educators possible, they must put money behind the words and the mandates. It's fine to spew the rhetoric surrounding the issues of student mastery, but it will be only words without the backing to bring the desired changes forward. It's an unfair burden to tell a teacher he's responsible for specific results with his students, if he's not properly trained and prepared to do the work necessary to meet those requirements. The blame game needs to stop. Administration must find ways to create staff development programs that support teachers raising their skill level, which ultimately assists students in reaching their goals. The necessary level of commitment, to create viable staff development programs, requires sufficient funding, strategic planning and thorough implementation. Creating viable staff development programs in schools is not solely the responsibility of administration. Teachers must move beyond their complaining about staff development and take a proactive approach to co-creating programs for their professional growth. Personal responsibility for professional accountability is the name of the game.

Many schools are beginning to wake-up and realize that they have a huge pool of staff development resources among their own teaching staff. Every school in which I've ever worked has had a plethora of great teachers. These staff members form the in-house pool of experts. The principal is not usually the teaching or curriculum expert in a school. He may know about curriculum and teaching strategies but he's not teaching in the classroom. The teachers are in the classrooms doing the work and bearing the burden of responsibility for the outcome of their teaching. There are many advantages to using "local experts" for staff development opportunities within schools. First of all, they are usually very credible among their peers. They are more often listened to and respected, by other teachers, because their work is visible throughout the school community. These local experts are teachers who optimally know what's going on throughout the school so they also have a good sense of the various levels of expertise from which other teachers teach. An outside expert wouldn't possess this level of knowledge about the staff. Another reason to use local talent is that it doesn't go away when the training ends. Having a local expert on the school campus, and available to staff provides ongoing support. Many training programs prove to be ineffective because of lack of follow through and follow-up. The focus and energy of a project is often lost if there's not someone to spearhead its continuation. Teacher experts are on hand for consultation, problem solving, cheerleading, and further professional development around a particular initiative. Classroom teachers often feel more comfortable going to a peer to express their confusion, lack of understanding or inability to make something work than they would consulting an outsider. However, there is a note of caution here. It's easy for administrators to take advantage of "expert teachers" who come forward to work in staff development arenas. There is often a thought pattern that says, "I can save a lot of money by asking John to do this training and he'll be on hand to follow through with it." Administrators must ensure that teachers, who become involved in training and coaching their peers, receive compensation and support with prep time, materials, and administrative oversight and assistance.

Many teachers are exceptional leaders. Some feel content to focus their leadership abilities in their classrooms. Others naturally assume school-wide leadership roles that provide them with professional challenges and growth opportunities they might not have otherwise had. Teachers, who are excited about teaching their peers and who have good skills and knowledge to share, ought to be encouraged to step forward into these leadership roles. There is a certain status, in a school, that goes along with being chosen to lead staff development opportunities. This form of peer recognition is both meaningful and supportive for those teachers who provide leadership. Serving in a leadership role also provides the teacher with professional growth opportunities himself through preparing programs and presenting them to his peers. It's truly a win-win situation in a school. Schools often end up paying less when they utilize in-house talent so more training opportunities may be created through this strategy. Another advantage to showcasing in-house teaching talent is that it plays out well in the local community. Parents see that there are teachers, at the school, with great skills who can work well with their peers. This raises the credibility level of teachers and provides good public relations for the school. It also demonstrates that the school community works well together on behalf of the students. I've noticed that there appears to be a correlation between those teachers who are viewed as "teacher leaders" by peers, parents and administration, and parental requests for specific teachers. Parents more often request those teachers who are perceived to be the best because these teachers have chosen leadership roles. Teacher leaders provide inspiration and encouragement to their peers and principals on a daily basis in an unassuming way and often without extra pay. It's a natural part of who they are as human beings.

I don't want to suggest that in-house experts are the only way in which staff development should be delivered. Excellent and inspirational professional trainers abound. An outside voice often provides motivation and credibility. An essential key to effectively utilizing outside consultants and trainers is to build in some follow-up support to their work. This could be accomplished by having them return to the school for more time with teachers or they could train local teachers to carry on the work. One-shot training experiences can be effective in learning a new skill or hearing about a specific program. They also often provide an inspirational experience, which encourages teachers to pursue their interest in a particular topic or further develop new skills on their own. However, long-term growth and institutional change will be best supported in a professional development program that includes both local and outside experts. Administrators can more fully and fairly hold teachers accountable in the classroom when those teachers are consistently trained and well prepared. Teaching is a challenging job with significant consequences surrounding success or failure. We can't afford failures because we're working with human lives.

The principal is ultimately the person held accountable for everything that occurs at a school, both in and out of the classroom. He must be knowledgeable, visible, interactive, approachable, and an excellent communicator to fulfill this duty. Communication is a key tool used by the principal not only to hold teachers accountable for their teaching, but also to support them in achieving the successful end result upon which their skill levels will be measured. As a principal holding teachers responsible, I can read their student's test scores at the end of the school year to judge a teacher's performance, but that's not enough. A minimum level of daily supervision must be maintained. In order to know what teachers are doing, thinking, planning and worrying about, principals should be in classrooms frequently and practice regular communication. Knowing teacher's areas of frustration and failure are as important as recognizing successes and challenges that have been overcome. Monitoring accountability is not just walking in and out of classrooms on a daily basis. It also involves asking hard questions. "Why are you using this strategy? How do you plan to help your special needs students on this project? Why didn't Joe understand this concept?" It also means looking at short-term results and achievement measurements. Teachers collect reams of data, on each student, as the year progresses. This material should be studied, interpreted and utilized to adjust programs and techniques for individual students who might be falling behind or leaping ahead. Challenging each student to succeed at his own level is a huge job for teachers. It requires hard work on a consistent basis with each child. Teachers are so absorbed in this monitoring and adjusting of student programming, on a daily basis, that they sometimes get tunnel vision regarding a particular student or situation. The principal plays an important coaching role in assisting the teacher to think out of the box and see beyond the existing set of circumstances.

Accountability has become a dirty word for many teachers when it solely relates to test scores that will be broadcast so publicly across the front page of the local newspaper.

It is discouraging and unfair to reduce all of a teacher's professional growth efforts, their focused and intentional teaching and hours upon hours spent working closely with each student to a few end-of-year test scores. There are so many extenuating circumstances that affect each child's performance in school. It's impossible for the teacher to be responsible for every aspect of the student's life and persona that contributes to his end-of-the-year test scores. However, this fact doesn't negate the value of test scores as one measure of both student success and teacher accountability. Test scores paint a useful picture of student growth and achievement. When carefully studied and skillfully interpreted, they provide valuable data for teachers, parents, and administrators. However, a teacher should not be judged solely by his student's test scores. There are numerous ways that teachers and administrators are able to ascertain student progress and mastery during the school year. These daily and weekly efforts to measure and record student achievement are actually more useful tools for educators because they show areas of strength and vulnerability and provide teachers with a clear, and steady, picture of what is required for each student on a daily basis. A teacher's accountability is part of his every day life as a teacher. It's both a privilege and a burden. It's why he entered the teaching profession and why he thinks about leaving it.

Teacher accountability requires that teachers take a reflective look at their work, understand best practices and find ways in which to bring the two together. This requires that teachers meet with one another to discuss and share various strategies through which they create success for all students in their classrooms. It means taking a hard look at what's not working and why a particular student fails and figure out what to do to resolve the issue. Teacher accountability shows up each day with the teacher as he enters his classroom and it never quite leaves. Teachers often feel alone in dealing with the accountability challenge. It's critical that teachers and administration work together to support one another in their responsibility to ensure that all students succeed. One teacher can't do it alone. It's a joint effort of teachers, administrators and parents.

If teachers are to be held accountable for each of their student's academic performance and yearlong achievement, there must be a strong working bond between teachers and between teachers and administration. There must be shared responsibility, throughout the school community, for the education of our children. An environment, within the school, that allows for teachers to rely on one another and the principal for help in solving the unique and difficult learning challenges presented by many students is essential. Teachers who feel safe enough to admit they don't know what to do with a particular student will ask for help. It's OK not to have all the answers when working with a particular student. What isn't OK is if you don't know what to do, and you don't seek help.

Parents play an equally important role in the entire accountability picture. Schools will be most successful in raising levels of student achievement when parents are partners with teachers. Although it's the teacher working daily, in the classroom, with each student, parents also influence student achievement. Parent's attitudes toward education greatly influence their children's attitudes about school. Communicate to your children how much you value education and why it's essential. One of the most important ways for a parent to influence their child's school experience is instill a positive, can-do attitude and then support that by working with the child and teacher. Parent involvement is especially critical when working with students who have learning problems or behavior issues that interfere with their learning. Difficult cases require team effort to resolve the many issues that contribute to students not reaching their fullest potential. Educators should invite parents into the classrooms and the school, as welcome and important partners in the educational process. Parents actively participating in the classroom and school send two important messages to their children. The first is that they love their children and want to help them in any way possible. The second is that they think learning and mastery are important and they support the teacher and the school. Both of these messages are critical to impart to students. For those students who don't have supportive parents, the teacher and other school personnel must take on an assistive role. Schools with active volunteer programs are able to assign tutors and other personnel to serve as support people for those students who may be on the learning journey with no other assistance. There are many hurdles to overcome in the learning process. Some of these hurdles are personal issues and others are work or study related. The more help that both student and teacher are given in this journey they travel together, the more success they will each meet along the way.

Parents are a vital resource for teachers and schools to utilize in their efforts to maximize success with every student.

The principal certainly plays a significant role in the accountability arena, carrying the responsibility for all that occurs in the school. An important first step for the principal to take, in accepting responsibility for student achievement, is to intimately know each teacher's areas of skill and weakness and be familiar with what is occurring, on a daily basis, in their classrooms. This requires time, attention, focus and effective communication on the part of the principal. Not only is it important for the principal to known the teachers well, it's also necessary for him to know the students. It's impossible to work to meet the needs of each student if you don't know him or his needs. The principal who knows the students in his school will be better equipped to work with the teacher and parents to maximize student success. Principals must also take the time to meet with teachers and discuss student achievement and mastery as an on-going process, offering support where necessary. Sometimes a teacher needs support but is not sure what form that might take. The knowledgeable principal will be able to work closely with the teacher to resolve difficult dilemmas with individual students and suggest strategies that might work in any given situation. The principal partners with the teacher in educating students, serving as a resource person who provides material, professional and human support to the teachers. Much as a teacher works with the student who isn't achieving up to par, the principal works with the teacher who isn't succeeding with all his students. The principal also collaborates with those teachers who are successful in order to learn from them and to utilize their skills in helping others. Principals assume proactive roles in working with staff to ensure that everyone is held accountable for the job that has been assigned to them. Accountability is a shared responsibility.

While teachers are primarily held accountable for the success and mastery of their students, principals are accountable for the successful outcome of all operations throughout the school. There are innumerable systems, throughout the school, that must be in place to support the work of the teachers in insuring that all students are achieving. The principal cannot focus solely upon curriculum issues but must see that the entire organization is lined up in support of what occurs in each classroom. An efficiently run cafeteria contributes to student success. Buses that run on time, driven by bus drivers who are caring and compassionate affect a student's day. The environment in which students participate and interact with others greatly impacts their learning. Providing teachers with protection from "outside forces" so that they can focus on the job at hand is a critical action that supports student growth. The principal is accountable for overseeing every segment of the organization to make sure that all the pieces are in place to support both the teaching and learning processes. Strong leadership in a school is essential for individual and organizational success. Success is found within environments that are conducive to its growth and nurturance.

The recent trend in focusing teacher effort and school resources on test preparation and teaching to specific skills covered on standardized tests, at the exclusion of other important topics and skill sets, is somewhat alarming. Teachers, principals and parents must ask themselves some important questions as they search for the best balance of programming in their classrooms and school. If we focus only on specific testable skills, what do we eliminate from our curriculum? What is the range of different experiences that should be available to students in school? Is the teacher still passionate about teaching? How do we know that each student achieves mastery? Should we educate "the whole child" or just the academic side? What happens to "soft subjects" like art and music? How do effective teachers integrate various subjects so that students are exposed to many different learning experiences? Can we afford to shift our entire system toward teaching to the test? What comprises a good education? A great deal of discussion and soul searching is necessary to answer these important questions. School personnel must be very clear on what the educational goals, of the school, require of them. Once the staff and principal decide on what direction the school needs to head, they can more effectively build the support systems to buttress this pathway. If the staff disagree with one another and have differing goals, it will be difficult to reach the organizational harmony and support level so necessary to make progress. Therefore, it's critical that all members of the organization come to some level of agreement on the goals for which they are all being held accountable. There will be many different, yet appropriate, strategies through which to implement the agreed upon goals. The current focus on teaching to the test has caused teachers to take a closer look at best practices and their own teaching in order to become more effective. This has been a positive result of the fervor surrounding test scores. However, teaching to the test has also created paranoia in many schools and driven teachers from their center, in the name of accountability. A coalesced staff has the power and wherewithal to develop a viable framework through which individual teachers will be able to reach their teaching goals but not lose their love for teaching in the process. Constant dialogue and creative solutions are required. Leadership that is not afraid to stand up for what is best for teachers and students is imperative.

Teachers are accountable for their student's mastery of specific skills. Principals are responsible for creating and maintaining a support system that allows for student and teacher success. Parents are expected to participate in the dialogue around achievement and support the school in its efforts with their children. State and federal departments of education are accountable to financially support the mandates that they impose on schools. Local communities support their schools both financially and in spirit through volunteering, attending programs and partnering with the school to provide additional resources. All of the above people and organizations are responsible for the success of our children. Educators, parents, community members, and federal agencies must work together to find creative solutions instead of wasting so much energy in avoiding responsibility or placing it elsewhere. Accountability begins with each teacher, principal, parent and community member stating, "I am showing up today and each day, knowing that I am responsible to do all within my power to help these students succeed." This solemn intention must then be supported with real efforts, leading to lasting results.

The following four strategies will help to improve accountability in schools.

1. Know your work and prepare for your job responsibilities.

2. Reflect on your teaching to promote professional growth.

3. Develop and utilize ongoing and alternative methods to measure student mastery.

4. Create opportunities for meaningful parental involvement.

....

Strategy # 1 - Know Your Work and Prepare for Your Job Responsibilities

Action Steps:

- begin each school year with a personal plan for your professional development

- subscribe to newsletters, magazines, newspapers of journals that provide professional information

- make time to thoroughly plan your lessons

- state expectations clearly and specifically define goals

- improve areas of weakness rather than ignoring or minimizing them

It's difficult, if not impossible, to successfully teach students if you don't know your subject well, possess effective teaching skills and understand precisely what you will be held accountable for accomplishing. The importance of staff development has already been mentioned. However, it's important to reinforce the importance of teachers knowing their subject area and content material. It's imperative that school leaders see that well trained teachers receive frequent opportunities for professional growth. Just as important as knowing your subject area is preparing for your job responsibilities. Teaching on the fly can be effective, in the short term, with a very good teacher. However, teaching without specific intent, effective strategies and precise direction in mind will, ultimately, lead to unaccomplished goals. One of the best outcomes of the standards movement has been to refocus teachers on the importance of well-planned lessons that are linked to the standards. Precise focus on teaching goals draws teachers into a deeper exploration of their work and effectiveness. It takes time and reflection to successfully plan a lesson that helps students master a skill or reach a goal.

There are many ways in which you may increase your knowledge of the subject matter you teach. The most obvious way would seem to be through staff development. However, staff development more often focuses on teaching skills and strategies rather than specific content or subject matter. So, whereas professional development is important, it's probably not the most effective way to gain this additional knowledge. Spend time with your subject area to familiarize yourself with it and become one with it. Read and study. Play with the content. Explore linking various ideas or topics together to better see their interrelatedness. Talk to other people about what you teach. Describe what you know to be important about the topic or subject. Write notes about the key ideas to be covered for understanding to be present. We gain a clearer understanding of content and topic material when we're able to logically discuss and describe its characteristics or intelligently write about it in such a way that others understand.

Of course, one of the best ways to become knowledgeable about your subject area is to teach it over and over again. Through attempting to teach another person, you quickly learn what you know or don't yet fully understand. If you can't fully explain a topic, you don't really understand it. As you teach a subject or particular topic more often, you discover your own knowledge gaps. Teaching constantly changes and evolves, allowing teachers deeper understanding and mastery of their content area.

Teachers in middle and high school are required to be in-depth experts in their subject area because they most often teach only one or two subjects. In some ways, these teachers are able to remain more focused on developing a depth of knowledge because they have fewer subjects to master, although their level of mastery must be highly specific. Elementary teachers, on the other hand, are required to become knowledgeable about a variety of subject areas. They could be categorized more as generalists, rather than specialists. Being a generalist requires as much work as a specialist who is mastering one or two subjects in depth. However, it's a different type of work and study. Teachers who are generalists must not only become knowledgeable about several subjects, but they must also be able to smoothly link and blend the various subjects. This requires a depth of understanding and the ability to see and make connections. Whether you teach one subject in great depth or five subjects more broadly, you must spend time getting to thoroughly know your subject area. If you don't know it, you can't effectively teach it!

An important companion to knowing your subject matter and possessing good teaching skills is planning; the art of melding your knowledge with the best strategies for getting your point across. Good planning is an intricate process. Many teachers have given little credence to thorough planning, believing they can "sketch out" what needs to be covered and then use their experience and knowledge to teach as they go. This technique may work, but usually not with any consistency. In the past, it was easier to plan this way than it is today because goals were not always highly specific or clearly delineated. However, with the recent focus on the standards movement, teacher planning has become strategically more effective than ever before. To meet your accountability requirements, you must become a better lesson planner. Start by familiarizing yourself with the standards for your subject area or grade level. Then, begin to match the standards with the texts and other materials that you're currently using in your classroom. If there isn't a match between the standards and available teaching materials, bring this fact to the attention of your principal, as new materials will be needed. As you discover how best to teach the standards, the more precise your written plans become and the more directed your teaching. Most teachers say it's difficult to find enough time to write thorough and effective lessons, especially when they're teaching multiple subjects. The constant demands of the busy school day allow little or no time for lesson planning, causing most teachers to work on them in after-school hours. This is truly a dilemma without an easy solution. We know that the more directed and strategic the planning, the greater possibility of student understanding and mastery, if accompanied by good teaching skills. Thorough planning may save a teacher time and effort, if he is doing less re-teaching and remedial work in the future. Try to become the most effective and skillful planner you can be and see what happens to your rate of success with your students.

Knowing your subject, possessing good teaching skills and effectively planning all contribute to understanding what you're accountable for which, better prepares you to meet that responsibility. You can't really be accountable if you're not clear about your responsibilities and the principal and community's expectations of you. One of the prime jobs of the principal is to clearly communicate to teachers what is expected of them. Through his supervisory role, the principal then monitors teacher's success in realizing these expectations. If this level of supervision doesn't happen or if you're unclear about what is expected of you, it's up to you to find out. It will be almost impossible for you to meet the accountability requirements for helping students achieve mastery, if you have weak teaching skills. If you know that you're struggling and need help, ask for it. Partner with a fellow teacher whom you respect and trust. Ask your peers for feedback on difficult or puzzling situations. Ask the principal to unofficially observe your teaching in order to give you specific feedback. Sign up for staff development opportunities. Take a proactive approach to your own professional growth, rather than trying to hide your weaknesses or uncertainties. If you work with a principal you trust, in a supportive environment, take risks and share your personal concerns about the teaching process and reaching your accountability level. If you don't trust your administrator to work with you in a supportive way, rely on your peers. Regardless of whom you turn to, ask for help if you need it. Holding teachers accountable for their student's progress and mastery is a complex task that requires open and trusting communication delivered in a safe environment.

Holding a principal accountable for teacher success and student mastery is similar to asking teachers to be accountable. The principal must know his subject area, which includes leadership, communication and management. He must also have a basic knowledge of the school's curriculum and what is expected at each grade level. Much of this information can be obtained through speaking with teachers and thoroughly reviewing the standards. Principals, too, must constantly seek to improve their leadership and management skills. They also complain that there's not enough time and they can't be away from the school. These are valid arguments, but barriers that must be overcome. A skilled and charismatic leader will bring teachers along with him on the exciting journey of personal and professional growth. He'll engage all personnel in the challenge of improving self and becoming more successful in their work. Good teachers will continue to grow in knowledge and develop their skills whether they have an effective leader or not. However, marginal or poor teachers won't grow under poor leadership and the school, as a whole, will not reach its goals. Principals are responsible for all students reaching mastery, for successful teaching in every classroom, for effective management of the systems that support good teaching, for creating and sustaining a safe and creative school environment and for binding all members of the school community into a shared vision that allows all of this to really happen.

Strategy # 2 - Reflect On Your Teaching to Promote Professional Growth

Action Steps:

- identify a "teaching buddy", at the beginning of school, to meet with on a regular basis to talk about teaching

- center discussions, at staff meetings, around teaching and professional growth issues

- receive facilitator training and form a Critical Friends Group

- keep a journal of self-reflections about your teaching or leading

- reflect upon successes and failures, questioning what you did and what you might change and ask students to evaluate at least one lesson a week

Powerful teachers and principals will not hesitate to engage in a process of looking inward to discover what drives their passion and fuels their professional life. They realize both the necessity and value in looking within to discover self. The path toward knowing yourself and understanding your motivation is a significant part of the life-long journey of self-improvement and professional growth. The more balanced and complete a person you are, the better educator you'll be. Discovering the best characteristics of self leads to a life in which you apply your skills and talents to their fullest extent. If you're self-confident and happy, you'll be stronger and more focused in your work. Difficulties and challenges don't shake your foundation when you know who you are and what you're about. Taking a serious look inward is often frightening and many will not go there. There is a risk in opening up Pandora's box of self-defeating questions. What if I'm not good enough? How can I discover my skills and talents? What if

I don't have very many? What will other people think of me if I show weakness in front of them? Do my peers think I'm a good teacher? Most educators have at least occasional doubts, about their value and effectiveness as teachers, floating around in their heads. Some live constantly with these doubts. Teaching plagued with self-doubt and fear is flawed. Looking inward is an attempt to shine an outer, bright light into an unknown, dark room in order to find the light switch and turn it on. Once the switch is turned on, a new source of light then shines outward from within. This inner light is a much more powerful form of illumination because it's authentic and belongs to the self. This new, brighter beacon is the source that lights the pathway and guides the journey. You can't find the light switch without first entering the dark inner room with at least a tiny light of inquiry.

Professional inquiry and personal inquiry cannot be separated. I teach as I am. Teachers bring themselves to the teaching process each and every day. We can't place our personal strengths, goals and fears only in our personal life. They swirl around us and spill out into our work and, in fact, they often drive our motivation for how we work. Teachers and principals who are reflective about their work and their lives are more likely to be able to make the necessary connections that allow them to meet and surpass the accountability standards that have been established for them. Reflecting upon your work includes looking at what you're doing, why you're doing it, how you're doing it, how you can improve, how it impacts others and how it affects your life. This caliber of self-questioning requires you to assume personal responsibility to begin an inquiry into self and to stick with this process when it gets difficult or confusing. Reflecting on your teaching or leadership brings up your vulnerability, especially if you are sharing your insights with a colleague. How can reflecting upon your work as a teacher or principal expose your vulnerability if you're looking at your work? It will never be just looking at your work because your work isn't separate from who you are in the world. Your work reflects some part of your being. Therefore, gaining insight about your work will also lead to insight about yourself as a human being. This doesn't need to be a frightening experience. In fact, it is often a wondrous exploration. Teachers and principals who reflect upon their decisions and their teaching and working relationships with others are often the strongest members of the faculty. They develop more assurance, as they go through deep self-questioning and face inner doubts. Teachers who aren't afraid to tackle new and unknown challenges begin to feel secure in their sense of self within the current possibilities. They become school-wide leaders even as they discover new aspects of self in quiet and unassuming ways. A principal who hopes to hold his staff accountable must serve as a role model and strong advocate for personal reflection.

Get in the habit of reflecting upon your work each day. This needn't be a lengthy and painful process. Take a close look at what you're teaching that day and ask some questions – How will I reach my students with this concept? What is my level of responsibility for every student "getting it"? Can I coast through this lesson since I'm really tired or should I have them do something else? Is this really going to make any difference and is it relevant? What strategies and activities will help get this point across? Teachers very often ask themselves similar questions just as a matter of course, not placing any special significance to this questioning beyond knowing it's a routine part of their teaching day. However, many teachers never question their motives, techniques or purpose. They show up each day, well intentioned, and teach like they've always taught. They may do a good job or not. However, they're missing the opportunity to discover, through reflection, how effective they are or how they might be able to improve. If you're not clear on what you're doing or why you're doing it, you'll have less success. Teachers and principals, in today's world of higher standards and greater demands for exemplary performance, must constantly focus on their goals and note whether they are making progress toward reaching those goals. If you're not looking, you don't see what's happening. Blindness to purpose is a weakness we can't afford to have among our teachers and leaders.

Beyond the daily reflection upon the why, what and how, lies a deeper inquiry process, typically not adopted by the entire staff. This process happens in the private moments of personal reflection as well as in the public moments of small group discussions. This level of inquiry begins with the questions, "Why am I a teacher? What do I have to do in order to significantly impact the lives of the students with whom I work? What are my personal and professional responsibilities as a teacher? What is my relationship to the subject I teach?" These questions present the fodder for discussions about the art of teaching and the teacher's role in this process. This level of self-engagement is usually embraced, initially, by a small group of teachers who are comfortable looking within and, in fact, require that level of mental and emotional stimulation. Inquiry groups sprout up in schools usually in unofficial ways and often grow as word of their process spreads to other staff members. If you wish to expand your personal inquiry, get together with a trusted friend or friends and begin talking about what you do, what you love, what you fear, what works, what didn't work and what you feel passionate about. Make sure you gather with others whom you trust and build that trust consistently. This level of dialogue can be a risk-taking process that exposes vulnerable points. Principals will often ask teachers to form advisory or critical friends groups to begin this process of shared dialogue and inquiry. These groups seem to work best when they're voluntary and meet under the guidance of a trained facilitator. Many teachers have reluctantly joined such a group only to discover how much they love the process. If you feel unsure about the value in this level of personal and professional inquiry and peer dialogue, start the process with one colleague whom you trust and like. Ask him if he'd like to meet once a week to discuss what's happening in your classrooms for the purpose of sharing ideas, solving problems and celebrating successes with students. Keep it light and fun. Focus on what's working, observe that and report back. You'll soon discover what a supportive process this can become and you may choose to increase the frequency of meeting.

These small dialogue and reflection groups form in schools that have safe environments, permitting teachers to be themselves and express their opinions. The leadership of the principal is instrumental in creating this backdrop for teacher and staff self-growth initiatives. Teachers assume the responsibility for their own accountability and are more successful in reaching goals when they have a clear idea of what they're doing, why it's important and how it fits into the bigger picture. If you're a teacher who would like to engage with a friend in self-reflective inquiry, about your teaching, but don't know how to get started or feel that you have nothing to offer, take a brave step. Open that inner door and shine a bit of light into the room. Identify one thing that you do well as a teacher and focus on that. Notice that what you're focusing upon takes on a light of its own as you place a more positive emphasis on it. Let that inner light grow and guide you. It will provide you with the courage you need to get started on this journey to self and to professional excellence.

Strategy # 3 - Develop and Utilize Ongoing and Alternative Methods to Measure Student Mastery

Action Steps:

- establish and utilize clear and regular strategies for measuring student mastery

- communicate your expectations and evaluation methods to students and parents

- create multiple opportunities for your students to demonstrate their progress and their success

- schedule regular conferences with your students to review their work and provide feedback

- focus principal / teacher conferences on specific accountability strategies

If educators are to get out of the death grip that has been imposed with standardized testing that measures their accountability on one or two summative measurements, they must focus on other indicators that are just as important or even more significant than end-of-the-year test scores. Teachers have always used a myriad of methods to determine student understanding and measure mastery. However, they have not clearly communicated these alternate strategies to parents and the school community. This has led to a questioning of teachers that presupposes they don't know if their students are succeeding until the end-of-the-year testing rolls around. The critics call out saying, "Show us the test results that indicate all your students are successfully learning, then we'll know you're teaching them." Teachers and principals must respond to this public outcry by educating parents and community members as to the various, and ongoing, ways in which they measure achievement and mastery of standards throughout the school year.

Besides using quizzes and end-of-chapter classroom tests to record student understanding, teachers use multiple forms of formative assessment in their classrooms. Formative assessment occurs when information, showing a student's understanding, is used to adapt teaching and learning to meet student needs and determine if they've met specific learning goals. Teachers use these assessment measures to monitor student work and understanding in order to make necessary changes, useful to both the student and the teacher. Feedback is an important component in this process. Unlike standardized testing where the student receives a score but no feedback regarding his strengths or weaknesses, formative assessment provides specific feedback to and discussion with the student.

Teachers have used formative feedback in their classrooms for years because it provides an ongoing picture of student achievement that can be adjusted, re-taught or re-directed, as necessary. There are innumerable forms of assessment used by teachers. Classroom discussions, debates, small group dialogue and formal oral presentations

are some of the ways in which teachers can gauge student understanding of a topic or subject area. These activities don't necessarily
always receive a grade. In fact, in most cases, they don't. Rather, the
teacher either mentally records the results in his head or writes comments down to use in the future when a grade is assigned. In the case
of discussions and oral presentations, the teacher gives feedback to
the student and also engages the student in a discussion to determine
if he can explain or justify his words, thus measuring his understanding. If a grade is not given for this type of presentation, and parents
aren't present, there is usually little, if any, feedback to the parents.
Make sure that parents understand the many ways you measure student understanding in your classroom. Periodically, send home fact
sheets that specifically describe the many specific and on-going ways
in which you evaluate your students. It's also a good idea to share this
information with your principal so that he sees your diligent efforts to
meet accountability requirements for student mastery.

Teachers are able to help bring students to a clearer understanding of their work when they take time to analyze that work with the
student. It's difficult to meet individually with every student in your
class on a regular basis. However, it is critical that you find the time to
sit with students to discuss their work. This can also be accomplished
in small groups when the students are working on achieving the same
goal. A teacher's individual work with a student includes discussing
the purpose of the lesson or assignment, reflecting, with the student,
on his work and then, if necessary, assisting the student in narrow-
ing the gap between the desired results and his performance. This
requires both teacher and student interacting with one another and
the topic or lesson. It's not a situation where a student receives a returned test with a "D" and then must figure out what went wrong,
if he even cares to. Students who are taught to become self-reflective
with their work learn the self-discipline of discovering what they did
well and determining what they could improve upon. They discover
what they know. Teachers who engage in reflectively looking at stu-

dent work with students are better able to guide a student's learning as the year progresses, noting areas of growth as well as regular stumbling blocks. If you monitor student progress every day, in your classroom, you'll more likely meet accountability requirements because of your hands-on approach to teaching and learning. It's no wonder that teachers become frustrated when the only accountability measure that is counted by the public is an end-of-the-year test. It often feels insulting to reduce a year's worth of notable teaching and monitoring to a few hours of testing.

There are numerous ways for you to determine if your students are learning and meeting the required standards. Lead them through a variety of activities, in each subject area that will provide them the opportunity to interact with and learn the skill or topic, but will also allow you to monitor their level of understanding. Some of these strategies include writing, summarizing, utilizing problem solving and critical thinking skills, developing and presenting projects, performing plays, making a documentary, explaining a concept to another student, completing independent homework, giving an oral presentation, completing an exhibition, working through math problems at the end of a lesson, writing in a daily journal, developing a hypothesis in science, speaking in a foreign language, etc. The every day ways you engage your students in learning are the methods through which you may evaluate their grasp of the concept or mastery of the skill and adjust your teaching accordingly. The key here is to interact with the student so that both he and you can reflect on his work. Even very young students can be trained to engage in self-reflective inquiry. When we've trained skillful students who are able to be self-reflective and adaptable, we're moving much closer to becoming truly accountable for the results of our teaching.

If you are a principal, you play a significant role in being responsible for your teacher's accountability in the classroom. When principals and teachers realize and uphold the principle that students demonstrate their learning and mastery in many different ways, their interactions are guided by this understanding. Visit classrooms more frequently in order to have a clear and consistent picture of the learning and monitoring that occurs in that classroom. Ask teachers to reflect on key questions about their teaching successes and challenges much as they work with their students to do the same. In the observation and feedback process, watch for specific examples of strategies used by the teacher that demonstrate how he obtains a clearer picture of his student's abilities and challenges and adapts his teaching to meet these needs. If you judge your teacher's skills based only on end-of-the-year test scores, you are acting unfairly. Teaching is a complex act. Achieving a thorough understanding of concepts and content and mastering skills is an ongoing process in which one level of accomplishment builds upon and leads to another. The teaching-learning dance between student and teacher is multi-dimensional. It cannot be reduced to a set of test scores.

Strategy # 4 - Create Opportunities for Meaningful Parental Involvement

Action Steps:

- establish a consistent school / home communication system at the beginning of the school year

- provide parents with enjoyable and non-threatening ways to be involved

- meet with individual and groups of parents to discuss high stakes test preparation and test results

- include well-informed parent representatives on important school committees

- ask for parent feedback and suggestions and use this information to make improvements

Parents are important partners to teachers and the principal in the education of their children. The parental component is one over which educators don't have much control. Yet, we know that parents play a significant part in creating a strong school culture that exudes excellence. Therefore, one of the major challenges facing educators is to find avenues through which to include parents, in meaningful ways, in their child's school experiences. An additional challenge is to engage those parents who either don't have the time, because of work responsibilities or don't have the interest. One of the ways in which parents can help the school, whether they're onsite or not, is to hold their children accountable for both their in-school responsibilities and their homework. The key to requiring this level of accountability lies in a good communication system between home and school. "Parents are our partners" ought to be a slogan at every school. It's difficult to serve in a supportive partnership role if you don't know what's going on or how you can help the situation.

Teachers who develop the most successful partnerships with parents begin building this relationship on the first day of school, or before, and continue building it throughout the year. Consistency is crucial here. If you start the year sending home a weekly communication to parents but stop after a few months because you're too busy, you will have lost important momentum. Consistency in communication with parents builds bridges of trust between homes and school. These are important bonds that will serve the school well both in good and in challenging times. Parents who know their children's teacher and have a good idea of what's going on in their classrooms will be more supportive of the goals and understanding of the challenges of that teacher. Parents better understand the demands and requirements a teacher may have for their child, if they know about the standards, are familiar with the curriculum, and follow their child's progress. Educators want parents on their side in good times and when challenging or negative situations occur. In cases where there is open and consistent communication, parents are more likely to side with teachers during difficult times. Lack of parental support or hostility most often comes from poor communication.

There are many ways in which you can engage the parents of your students in meaningful relationships with the classroom and the school. Invite parents in to observe lessons so they'll have a clearer picture of your teaching style and what you expect of their children. Hold brief parent meetings or send home newsletters that describe what the students are working on, why it's important and how parents can help. Be as specific as possible and provide a variety of ways for parents to contribute. Many parents can't come into the classroom to help because of other responsibilities. However, there are numerous ways in which they can assist you by working with their children at home. Building bridges with parents means creating an environment of trust, which is essential to a close and supportive working relationship. The best learning environments are established when principals, teachers, parents and students work together. It's very difficult, if not impossible, to develop a viable school community without parent input and participation. In addition to involvement in the classroom, parents ought to be given opportunities to have a voice in the governance of the school. This usually occurs through PTSA, Site Council, Booster Club and other such governing bodies. In some school districts, Site Councils have budgetary rights, which gives parents more power. It is the responsibility of teachers and the school leadership to find meaningful ways for parents to become involved and know what's going on in their child's classroom and school. Parents are accountable for how they raise their kids and for the attitudes, toward school and teachers, which their children bring to school. Teachers and principals are primarily responsible for all that occurs at school. There must be sharing and blending of these responsibilities that lead to students being held accountable, by both parents and teachers.

If your work life prevents you from spending time at school, stay in touch with the teacher to make sure you know what is going on and how you can best support your child. Share your opinions, concerns and suggestions with the teachers and principal. This can be done by serving on committees, meeting with teachers individually, written correspondence, at open house and through both casual and formal interactions with school staff. Find out what the strengths and weaknesses of the school are and work to build upon the strengths and improve the weaknesses. Parents need to ask the hard questions, but also support the teachers and the school. Accountability is a shared responsibility. When individuals assume personal responsibility to successfully accomplish their job within the school community, all segments of the community benefit. The ultimate benefactors of adult collaboration and assumption of personal and professional responsibilities are the students.

Accountability is about taking personal responsibility for your job and your life. Schools that support both personal and professional growth, through the daily interactions of the principal and staff, have personnel who act responsibly and are accountable for their actions in and out of the classroom. Schools in which people collaborate and consistently care for and support one another are wonderful places to work. They're fun, serious, helpful, inspiring, energizing, thoughtful, soothing, memorable, loving and successful. This harmonious environment supports both excellent teaching and masterful learning. Become actively engaged at your school in offering support to your peers and your principal. This support can be as simple as a smile and a thank you or as complex as helping a friend through a difficult personal or professional crisis. Co-create a school environment where each member of the community loves showing up every day, knowing that he will be supported whether he's having a good day or a bad one. Human growth requires meaningful connections with other humans. Make your school a center for learning that supports all members of the community.

7. RITUAL, TRADITION, CEREMONY

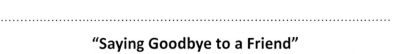

"Saying Goodbye to a Friend"

ONE SUNDAY AFTERNOON, in April, I received a phone call notifying me that one of our kindergarten students, Jessica, and her mother died in a fire that destroyed their house the previous night. Only her father survived. Tears came easily as I thought about sweet little Jessica. I pictured her sunny disposition and the open and friendly way she interacted with everyone in her class. I couldn't believe that this adorable and friendly five-year-old was dead. I thought of the twenty-five other students in Jessica's classroom. What do you say to five year olds about a friend dying? How do you explain this tragedy without creating fear? I had never had a student in my school die so I didn't feel prepared to deal with the other student's reactions. I called Jessica's teacher, who was also distraught over the news, to discuss how we would handle this situation on Monday morning with Jessica's classmates.

My school had no guidance counselor, social worker or crisis team so Jessica's teacher and I would have to handle the situation. Jessica's teacher, Mrs. Ogden, didn't think she would be able to talk to the kids about Jessica's death. She asked me to tell them. What would I say? Could I do it without breaking down? How would the kids react? I thought about Jessica and her classmates all night. I questioned the fairness of a five-year-old losing her life. I wondered if her death would cause fear in her classmates, when they went to bed the next night. I thought about going to the funeral, which filled me with dread. I wished I weren't the principal. I didn't want to face Jessica's classmates, fearing I would cry in front of them. This was too hard to do and too big a responsibility to assume. Why couldn't someone else assume this task? What would I say to the students? How would they respond? These questions and thoughts tumbled around in my mind throughout the night.

Monday morning dawned bright, cool and sunny. It was a perfect day. It somehow seemed unnatural to speak about the death of a five-year-old on such a beautiful day. I arrived at school very early in order to search the library for a book about death. The only one I found was a children's book about the death of a pet bird. It treated death in a very forthright, but gentle manner. I armed myself with this book to begin the discussion with the students.

The students arrived. The secretary made the morning announcements. Teachers took the lunch counts. Messages went back and forth between the classrooms and the office. The school settled into its daily routine. Most of the older students knew about Jessica's death. They spoke quietly in the hallways about the fire. Some students asked me about it, but most of them engaged in their usual morning activities. The older kids didn't know Jessica and they soon exhausted the topic, which held no further interest to them.

I tried to mentally prepare myself to talk about Jessica's death with her classmates. What questions would they ask? Would they feel frightened about their own safety? Would they understand? Maybe I shouldn't say anything at all. I was torn. Emotions and worries twirled around inside of me. I felt as if I were going on stage to deliver one of the most important talks of my life. I walked heavily into the kindergarten, apprehensive, sad and reluctant to face these innocent young students.

Mrs. Ogden hugged me, when I entered the room. Her puffy, red-rimmed eyes questioned me, "Why Jessica? Why did this have to happen? How do I go on with these kids today?" She fought back tears as she called the students to come and sit on the carpet near the front of the classroom. Once the students gathered on the carpet, Mrs. Ogden retreated behind her desk with her head bowed, occasionally wiping her nose and eyes. Determinedly, I picked up the black piano bench and placed it in front of the attentive students. Eager faces watched as I sat down. I took a deep breath, quietly gathering my thoughts and struggling to keep my emotions under control. Twenty-five innocent faces turned to look at me, waiting and anxious. I asked how many of them had heard about the fire at Jessica's house? Most of the students raised their hands.

"Jessica and her mother burned in the fire," called out Jeff.

"Her father tried to save them, but he couldn't," chimed in Sara.

"My mom told me that Jessica went to heaven," said Jamira.

Their matter-of-fact responses amazed me! Was death really this simple and clear cut?

"It's true that Jessica and her mother died last night when their house burned down," I said. "The firemen tried to save them, but the fire was too hot. They couldn't get into the house soon enough. I feel sad that Jessica died." Don't cry, I told myself. Keep it together a little while longer.

"I feel sad too," said David, quietly. The room was silent. No one fidgeted. They stared at me and waited.

"Have any of you ever had a pet that died?" I asked. Several hands shot up.

"One of my baby hamsters got loose and it got sucked into the vacuum cleaner," said Josh. He rushed to add, "My mom said he died right away."

"My dog, Barney, died. He was old," a little voice called out.

"My cat ran out into the street and got hit by a truck. We buried Tootsy in the backyard near the swings," said Jenny in a sad voice.

"I found a dead bird once. It was all icky," added Sam with a sigh.

"Well, I want to read a story to you about a bird that died and then we'll talk about what it means to die." I read about the parakeet that suddenly died one day. The family, in the story, mourned its death and provided the bird with a burial in the backyard.

"How did the boy, in the story, feel when his bird died?" I asked.

"He was sad," several voices called out.

"What happens when someone dies?" I asked, wondering if this was too philosophical for five year olds.

"They go to heaven," replied Bobby.

"We don't see dead people anymore," said Jim, shaking his head.

"That's right, Jim. We won't see Jessica. She won't be in our class anymore. We'll miss her a lot and we'll do something special so we won't forget her. Do any of you have any questions you want to ask me?" Here it comes, I thought and cringed. All the "too tough to answer questions" that I hoped to avoid.

"Can we go play now?"

The tension in the classroom disappeared immediately. The twenty-five little bodies, which had started out still and quiet, wiggled now. My presentation lasted about fifteen minutes. Now they wanted to play. We had discussed the death of pets, burials in backyards, sadness and heaven. Now they wanted to play.

"Yes, you may go play now," I replied. A huge cheer went up as everyone jumped to their feet and scurried to their favorite areas. They immediately and totally involved themselves in the important work of play. I felt relieved that they hadn't asked any hard questions. I was emotionally spent. I walked to Mrs. Ogen still behind her desk.

We hugged. I cried as I walked to the office. Jessica was so innocent, so young. Then I shifted to marvel at the five-year-old approach to death. They knew Jessica was gone. They said they would miss her. They believed she had gone to heaven. They seemed to be OK. Life went on. It was time to play. They had living to do. Maybe they did understand death after all. Maybe they understood it better than we adults did.

It happened that this particular Monday was balloon day at school. Before we realized that setting helium balloons loose harmed the environment, schools set off balloons with messages in them, hoping they would reach far off cities. At the end of this memorable day, all of the students were scheduled to go onto the playground for a mass balloon launch. Since Jessica's half-day kindergarten class went home at noon, I wondered if we should just skip their balloon launch. After thinking it through, I decided that we should proceed and do a launch in Jessica's honor.

The teacher and I took the kindergarten students outside to the large, grassy field in front of the school. A slight breeze pushed white puffy clouds across an incredibly blue sky. The day was so beautiful and sad and joyful! The students jumped around, rolling in the grass, tugging on each other, anxiously awaiting the balloon release. Mrs. Ogden blew her whistle and the students gathered around her. She gave each student a helium balloon with the student name and the school name attached to a long string. She instructed them to hold onto the balloon until she gave the signal to let them go. On the count of three, twenty-five, multi-colored balloons lifted into still blue the air. Cheers erupted from the students as they twirled, shouted and pointed out their balloons until they were no longer visible.

"Everyone come over here," I called out. "These five pink balloons, I'm holding, are for Jessica. Mrs. Ogden and I picked pink, Jessica's favorite color. There are five balloons because she was five-years-old. We've placed an extra long cord on these balloons so that you can all hold onto them before we let them go. When we let them go, we'll think about Jessica and say good-bye."

The boisterous and active students ran over to grab hold of the long string that held the five pink balloons. They were suddenly quiet and still. They understood the solemnity of what we were doing, even amidst the fun and play of releasing their individual balloons into the air.

"OK, does everyone have hold of the strings," I called out.

"Yessssssss!" shouted twenty-five eager voices.

The students, Mrs. Ogden and I stood huddled together near the outside door to the classroom holding five pink balloons. We prepared to say good-bye to Jessica, releasing her spirit, recalling our memories of her, and entrusting her to a greater power.

"Let them go!" I shouted.

The children let go of the string. The balloons didn't immediately rise as the others had. The bunch of five pink balloons began to skim across the top of the grass, blowing across the large field bordered by the street. The balloons were gliding along quickly but they still hadn't risen. All of the students began running after the balloons. The kids didn't say anything. There was total silence. They just ran with the balloons. They didn't try to catch them or touch them. They were one with the balloons, a unit of flowing children running with their friend Jessica! I stood in amazement as I watched this event unfold. No one had told the kids to run with the balloons. No one had told them that they had to be quiet.

Suddenly, my amazement turned to alarm as I realized that the balloons and the children were heading toward a very busy street on the far side of the field. The children would chase the low-flying balloons right into the busy street. Mrs. Ogden apparently saw the same possibility because she and I began running after the kids. Fear enveloped me as I ran as fast as I could to catch up with the students. The students and the balloons had a head start.

Amazingly, just before the students reached the busy street, the five pink balloons began to lift. They rose rapidly and flew straight up into the blue sky. What an incredible sight! The students stopped to watch. They shouted and waved as the balloons rose.

"Bye, Jessica!"

"Jessica's going to heaven!"

"Look, they're going up to God!"

"Bye, Jessica. Bye! Bye!" they shouted in chorus.

The students continued waving until the balloons were tiny dots beyond the white clouds. When the balloons were no longer in sight, the kids started tumbling, running, and laughing. Mrs. Ogden and I stood in awe, tears running down our faces. We couldn't have ever crafted such a fitting and wonderful farewell for Jessica. The students reminded me that life is but a time of play upon this earth, a time to love and help our friends, a time to be joyful. The events of that sunny, clear Monday morning are a rare gift that I've held close to my heart ever since.

A few months, after Jessica's death, her father met with Mrs. Ogden and me. The family wanted to do something special at the school in honor of Jessica. We discussed many different options, but ultimately decided to take two actions. First, we had a tree-planting ceremony with Jessica's classmates and placed a tree, in her honor, outside the classroom. We laid a small plaque in the ground in front of the tree stating it was planted in Jessica's memory. There turned out to be a bit of confusion about this plaque when one day a kindergartener asked me, "Is Jessica buried under that thing?" I found out that many of her classmates shared this misconception so we quickly straightened that out!

Jessica's father decided to establish a special end-of-the-year award for a kindergarten student who demonstrated excellence in the area of art. Jessica loved art and showed promise in that area. The selected student would receive a nice plaque and a fine set of art supplies, provided by Jessica's dad. At the end of that school year, a kindergarten student was selected to receive the "Jessica Art Award." Jessica's father, one set of grandparents and an aunt and uncle attended the special ceremony at school, which proved to be an emotional event for the family. Their loss was still raw but they seemed to take some strength from being with Jessica's classmates. I'm not sure the students fully understood that this ceremony was to honor Jessica's life, but they sure loved the ice cream that they all received at the end!

Each year, for the next six years, Jessica's father contacted me in April and reminded me to talk to the kindergarten teacher to select a student for the "Jessica Art Award." Each June, he and members of his family came to present the award and give ice cream to all the kindergarteners. When he remarried, his new wife came with him. When he moved out of state, he flew back for the ceremony. After a couple of years, the "Jessica Art Award" became a big deal in kindergarten, although the students didn't really understand what it was about since they hadn't known Jessica. They just knew that someone received a box of good art stuff and everyone got ice cream! The family decided the last year that Jessica would have spent in elementary school would be the last year of the award. This final ceremony was quite poignant for Jessica's family as it marked an ending and a separation. The annual "Jessica Art Award" always reminded me of the tenuous nature of life. However, remembering the day that those five pink balloons headed up to heaven, on that sunny Monday morning, reminds me that miracles happen every day. They're out there. We need only to pay attention so we don't miss them.

Ritual, Tradition, and Ceremony

Definitions:

Ritual: a series of actions or types of behaviors regularly and invariably followed by someone

Traditions: long-established customs or beliefs that have been passed on

Ceremony: ritual observances and procedures performed at grand and formal occasions

Ritual, tradition and ceremony together define the heart of a school. They highlight the human connections that create the daily rhythm and drive the life force of any school community. Each of these areas creates a rich backdrop for community building to occur throughout the school year. The priorities of a school are clearly defined in the focus of the rituals, traditions and ceremonies created by students, teachers, principals and parents. These school-wide activities and events help to form the organization's identity, allowing it to expand and flourish. Students, teachers, principals and parents discover more about themselves and their strengths and deepen this knowledge through these engaging opportunities. Purposeful and meaningful relationships form in schools that have histories of ritual, tradition and ceremony. The benefits of ritual, tradition and ceremony are vast and enriching to students, educators and parents alike. They present opportunities for relationship and community building, which strengthen the educational environment and have long lasting implications. Since ritual, tradition and ceremony showcase the priorities of a school, they need to be nurtured, honored and integrated into each school day.

Rituals are actions or types of behavior that are regularly followed. They typically become habitual parts of our life. Some examples of rituals in schools are:

- the teacher shaking hands with each student who enters class in the morning

- older students going to lunch in groups rather than lines

- buddy programs where older students read to younger students

- daily occurrences in the classrooms such as break time, after lunch song, etc.

- the principal making morning announcements and greeting students

Rituals are important to students and teachers because they help them feel secure by creating predictability. Learning involves quite a lot of novelty and exploration. We need to combine predictability with novelty to ensure that learners feel safer and more grounded in their learning. Predictability at school assists the many students who live in totally unpredictable worlds at home. It's difficult to focus on learning when their world is topsy-turvy and always in a state of change or uncertainty. The predictability of rituals gives a student something concrete to hang on to. It helps students clarify their identities and discover how they fit into the school setting. Predictability is also a positive force for teachers. Schools have been bombarded by numerous changes over the past few years, requiring teachers to continue making changes in their instructional methods and daily activities. Ritual lends a sense of security and routine that we all crave. Rituals provide richness to the educational scene, guiding student and teacher success.

Rituals also create feelings of stability. Knowing there are certain things we can count on every day or each week is reassuring. Teachers who have a sense of stability are more likely to engage in change activities because they know there is a center that will hold things steady during the change process. Students, who are learning to become risk-takers in their education, need stability. It's reassuring for a student to know that she can balance the uncertainty and fear of trying something new with familiar parts of the school day that are consistent. Schools with high student and teacher turnover find it difficult to establish feelings of stability for their students and staff. High turnover makes it even more imperative that schools find ways to provide stable environments in which students and teachers may grow.

When each school day is predictable and stable, students and teachers feel physically, emotionally and mentally safer. Feeling safe provides the foundation for risk-taking and exploring outside one's comfort zone, both essential components for effective learning to occur. Students who feel safe are traditionally happier in their school experience than those who feel the stress created by fear and chaos. School rituals are often grounded through interactions between students or between teachers and students. Rituals can have lasting and positive impact upon student behavior in schools. Students who engage in school rituals that show support for diversity and individuality tend to show more respect and develop friendships with students who are different from them. Behavior problems are greatly reduced in schools with a history of classroom and school rituals. Feelings of emotional safety are enhanced in these types of stable environments where students don't feel threatened either externally or internally. Predictability and stability also give teachers and staff reassurance.

Classroom and school rituals provide students and teachers with a sense of self. When a student "fits in" to a daily ritual and establishes relationships with other students and her teacher, she grows in her sense of self and discovers what she has to contribute. We all need to feel part of a community, giving as well as receiving. Ritual provides us with opportunities to see who we are in relationship to other people. This is especially important for those students who don't traditionally fit the norm. The teacher, who greets each child upon entering the classroom and asks her to share a positive strength with a peer, provides opportunities to form friendships. Ritual gives students a home place from which to practice human relationship building in a safe and predictable way. Structure is important to finding self because we need the stability and solidity to balance the feelings of chaos and uncertainty that arise when we face something new. Ritual is a structure that gives students a chance to see who they are in relationship to others and the environment in which they interact. The richness to be found through human interactions is highlighted in schools where ritual is alive and a well established part of the school environment.

Ritual offers important daily support for the learning process it-self. Teachers incorporate the richness of ritual into the learning and teaching process. Teachers who understand that effective learning occurs when students have a strong emotional link to the topic or subject matter will create ritual within their teaching activities. When emotions are engaged in the learning experience, memories are more likely to be recalled and accuracy improves. Learning experiences that include ritual (plays, chants, team problem solving, etc.) are more likely to be meaningful to students. Learning rituals ought to be fun. The use of ritual, in the classroom, indicates that teachers realize the importance of involving students in enriched learning experiences that improve recall, provide predictability and build meaningful tra-ditions.

Many rituals ultimately become traditions. Traditions are long-established customs that are eventually passed on and become part of the culture of the school. A student who attends the school where her father attended might participate in some of the same traditions that her father did when he was a student. Some examples of school traditions are;

- end of year awards program
- graduation exercises
- 6th graders going to camp
- student/staff basketball game
- special songs sung at the school opening assembly every year

Traditions become an integral part of the history of a school. They give a solid and well-established feeling to the school climate. Stu-dents who attend schools steeped in tradition become a part of some-thing bigger than themselves. Tradition helps to move us out of our self-focus to see what others have created before us. It invites us to become more solid, more significant, and more giving to something larger than our seemingly mundane daily lives. Traditions provide enriched experiences that students might not otherwise have at school. Creating new traditions, and building upon the old, is one of the fun growth processes in schools. Students, instrumental in creating new traditions, feel that they're contributing to something meaningful and lasting. Humans like to leave their footprints upon the path they walk. We can assist our children in this effort by instituting classroom and school-wide traditions that bear their imprint.

Student involvement in school traditions nurtures and expands their feelings of pride in self and in school. Students who feel pride in their teacher, school and themselves are more likely to become involved in the life of the school. Their involvement and contributions support their learning and achievement. Feeling proud about our accomplishments and contributions leads to personal empowerment. Schools rich in traditions provide students with multiple opportunities, as they pass through the grades, to become a lasting part of the traditions in which they are involved. Most students remember the fourth grade Pilgrims play or sixth grade Greek culture day. These events and activities provide memories to last a lifetime. They also tend to bring forward feelings of joy, personal fulfillment and belonging.

Feelings of belonging come with participation in and development of classroom or school-wide traditions. Belonging nurtures our need for community and purposefulness. It also makes the daily school experience more meaningful to student and teacher alike. Many students have dropped out of school or turned to drugs and violence because they have no feelings of connectivity and belonging in the school community. This is a sad commentary about one failing aspect of our educational system. Kids who, from a very early age, are known and noticed by their teachers, encouraged to be involved in meaningful rituals and traditions, and help to create new school customs are more likely to stay in school and become successful and happy students.

Participation in school traditions is also a good way for educators to get parents involved in the school. Even if the parents didn't attend a particular school, they become part of the traditions as their children progress through the grades and learn the traditions of that grade or of a particular teacher. Parents need to feel as if they belong to the school community in order to best support their children and the teachers in the educational process. Parent and teacher organizations are often instrumental in establishing new school traditions. PTAs have a long history of significantly contributing to school rituals and traditions. Schools thrive with appropriate parent involvement. Therefore, administrators and teachers must strive to find the best ways in which parents can support their children's education. Tradition provides a sense of pride and belonging to all who engage in its rich history.

Tradition gives us a larger view of the priority that a community places on education because it requires us to look beyond the day-to-day school issues and see what has transpired over time. A parent who decides to send his child to a school where excellence in education has been a valued tradition for over fifty years can feel somewhat assured that his child will be exposed to a good education. Newer schools don't have rich histories to fall back upon. Rather, they have the exciting opportunity to create new rituals and traditions as their school culture grows and matures. Whether a well-established or newer school, tradition ought to become a valued part of the school culture, as it will support student achievement, parental involvement, and teacher success.

Ceremonies provide the gift wrap for the presents of ritual and tradition. Ceremonies are formal observances that celebrate and honor rituals and traditions. Some examples of school ceremonies are:

- athletic and arts awards programs
- volunteer recognition
- National Honor Society induction
- presentation of classroom awards

School ceremonies present opportunities for the entire community to come together to celebrate the achievements and efforts of its members. They provide a supportive group of people gathered to honor students and staff for the positive work that they have done. Celebration is a public display of what we value most. Ceremonies help to institutionalize the priorities of a school because they show what the school values in a very public way. If a school focuses heavily on sports recognition programs but has few academic assemblies, this provides valuable information about the school's goals and priorities. Students and parents tend to place more importance on those programs that are publicly recognized, whether they are the most important or not. Ceremonies provide school personnel, parents and students with opportunities to be joyful and proud. They contribute to positive self-esteem for those students who are recognized. However, they can be very defeating for those students who aren't honored. That's why it's so important for teachers and schools to see that every student receives recognition at some time during the school year for something they have accomplished. Every student is gifted and contributes. These individual contributions should be noted in all areas, not just for sports and high academic accomplishments. Classrooms that are centers for ritual, tradition and ceremony will provide students with the richness that these activities present on a daily basis. Students benefit when recognized for their efforts and accomplishments. Students learn that there is satisfaction in personally acknowledging and in publicly recognizing the contributions of fellow students. An ethic of respect to be found in honoring others will be taught and reinforced in those classrooms that acknowledge the efforts and accomplishments of all students.

Ceremonies bring formality and richness to our lives. They raise us out of our mundane daily existence into a higher plane of pride and purpose. They take our narrow focus and broaden it to include other people and unique circumstances. Ceremonies often bring solemnity, respect and honor into our lives. Stand with 500 students, pledging allegiance to the flag and singing the National Anthem and feel your heart swell with pride, knowing you're part of something bigger and more powerful than yourself. Feel your spirit soar when attending high school graduation and watching young adults, whom you taught in third grade, proudly walk across the stage to receive their diplomas. These events inspire us and take us out of the daily rat race of life if only for an hour or so, showing us that we've contributed in some important way. Ceremonies elevate our spirits and motivate us to do more. They remind us of our humanity. They serve as a snapshot of all that we love and value in life. Ritual and tradition are reinforced and expanded through ceremony.

Ritual, tradition and ceremony are essential components of any good school community. Those schools, actively involved in creating and following ritual and tradition, and honoring them through ceremony, build incredible spaces for both academic and social learning experiences to occur. These essential practices promote excellence and participation in learning activities at school. Teachers, administrators and parents must focus on developing systematic support in these three areas. It is time well spent in the long run because these efforts will create a climate that supports pride in accomplishment and honor for those issues that are universally important to educators and parents. A school without ritual, tradition and ceremony is a school without a heart. Principals and teachers who wish to build a strong school culture, or change a negative school environment, need only begin to create ritual and tradition and then celebrate them. School culture will be dramatically changed and improved with the addition of these three essential components. The human spirit will be uplifted and inspired in these positive environments.

Ritual, tradition and ceremony create an ethos in schools that supports the development of innovative programs, leading to the growth of students and the realization of the school's goals. Schools, with rich traditions of positive rituals and ceremonies that support students, teachers and parents have advantages over other schools.

Strong bonds of friendship are often formed between students or between students and teachers or between teachers and other staff members and administration. Ritual and tradition promote positive interactions and reinforce the importance of the human connection in everyone's life. Students and teachers are better grounded in schools with a history. Grounding means feeling present, solid and safe. It develops in places and situations that are permanent, stable and predictable. Feeling grounded presents students and teachers with a firm platform from which to launch exploratory missions into the learning arena. When people feel grounded, they are usually calmer, feel good about themselves, act with self-confidence and handle challenges more effectively. A grounded foundation will assist students, teachers and principals in reaching their personal as well as school-wide goals. A grounded person would demonstrate orderliness, planning, and thoughtfulness in decision-making.

Ritual, tradition and ceremony enhance relationship building by giving individuals opportunities of belonging to unique groups. These groups might include the classroom, after-school clubs, sports teams, educational organizations and the school-wide community. All humans wish to belong. Schools that honor ritual, tradition and ceremony provide multiple opportunities for students and teachers to feel they belong. This is a key emotional component that will support student motivation and achievement. Students are more highly motivated to work hard, try new things and accomplish goals in schools where they feel part of the whole. Validation comes with belonging and contributing to a classroom, club or school culture. Students, teachers, administrators and parents seek recognition from each other for the job they're doing as well as for who they are as human beings. Personal and professional acknowledgement provides us with feedback that influences the core of our belief in self. While we shouldn't and can't look to others to define who we are or guide what we do, feedback from others contributes to our sense of self. Students will often seek out membership in inappropriate groups in order to be validated by other youth. That's one of the reasons it's so important for teachers and principals to create positive opportunities through which students will feel validated and become significant parts of the whole. Students who are involved and who feel that they belong do not tune out or drop out. Being a respected and validated member of a school community is a key to success for most people regardless of age or academic ability.

One of the spin-offs that we often see in schools that have tradition, ritual and ceremony in place is great enthusiasm. Most educators would agree that enthusiasm is an important partner to the learning process. When we observe excellent teaching and wonderful learning experiences, we'll find high levels of enthusiasm displayed by both students and teachers. The more enthusiastic and passionate a learner feels about a topic or project, the more she will apply herself to the task at hand. Motivation is high in classrooms where students feel they belong, are listened to and have something important to contribute. Motivation drives learning. This motivational drive allows learners to push through their fears, knock down walls and continue to move forward. Students who are motivated and enthusiastic find and identify their purpose and develop a sense of self. They openly explore various subjects and activities that help them discover what they are drawn too and what they don't care to pursue.

If ritual, tradition and ceremony together truly define the heart of a school and represent the life force that drives the daily activities of any community, then schools ought to put a high priority on developing and maintaining healthy programs in these areas. The heart represents both strength and tenderness. The heart of a school must beat the steady rhythm of academic success for all while at the same time provide nurturing and self-awareness. It's a crucial balance that is necessary for the survival of the learner and teacher alike. Ritual, tradition and ceremony can provide this balance between the mind and the heart.

The following three strategies will assist educators and parents to create schools that are steeped in ritual, tradition and ceremony.

1. Identify and introduce those rituals and traditions that reinforce learning and support the school's vision.

2. Institute support systems for rituals, traditions and ceremonies.

3. Attach physical icons to ritual, tradition and ceremony.

Strategy # 1 - Identify and Introduce Those Rituals and Traditions that Reinforce Learning and Support the School's Vision

Action Steps:

*   make a list of the rituals, traditions and ceremonies that you use to support student learning

*   ask your students which rituals, traditions and ceremonies are their favorite and invite them to co-create new ones

*   share a few of your most effective rituals, traditions and ceremonies with peers

*   establish specific rituals, traditions and ceremonies that include parents and community members

*   work with your colleagues to co-create new school-wide rituals and reinforce current traditions

There are many rituals that are introduced by teachers within the classroom. Some are for fun, others are more focused in their intention and relationship to learning. Teachers who develop rituals that support sound educational principles, in their classrooms, not only build traditions but also improve student learning. Therefore, it makes sense for educators to develop as many rituals that support learning and encourage students as possible. Teachers who stand at the classroom door every morning and shake hands with each student, making eye contact and saying "good morning" know that this ritual helps to make students feel as if they belong and that someone cares about them. This is such a simple, yet effective way, for the teacher to connect each day with every student. It also allows the teacher to gauge the temperament of students by looking at their body language and listening to their responses. Another strategy used when the students enter class is to require that homework be turned in immediately to the teacher. This allows the teacher to monitor who did work and who didn't complete it. This ritual raises the anxiety level of most students, which hopefully motivates them to complete and turn in their work.

There are several effective rituals centered around testing issues. Teachers who focus on test preparation and readiness will develop certain rituals around both classroom and standardized testing situations. Many teachers work with students to be mentally and emotionally ready for testing. Students stand up and stretch, take deep breaths and sit calmly, with their eyes closed, prior to taking the tests. This type of ritual may be effectively built into every testing situation in which the student is involved. It becomes habitual. Another testing ritual in many schools, prior to standardized and state mandated testing, is to provide students with snacks and water prior to and during the test. This helps students concentrate and think more clearly. Wouldn't it be wonderful if students had water and snacks available to them every day to assist their learning? Teachers often use the rituals of clapping hands in a pattern or singing a short verse to engage student attention. This is particularly effective when introducing a lesson but can also be useful during a lesson to refocus student attention. There are innumerable classroom rituals that teachers pull out of their toolbox and use with students every day.

School-wide rituals may also be based on sound educational and developmental principles. For example, students standing in an orderly line while waiting for the bus to load them at the end of the day presents a message of safety, respect, and control. These are all important characteristics for students to master but practicing them also sends a message about what is valued at the school. A safety ritual new to modern schools has visitors check in at the office and obtain an identification badge. Students are trained to report any adult, not wearing a badge, to a teacher or other school personnel. Teachers and school staff send any adult to the office who isn't wearing a badge. In this case, the ritual developed around a specific safety issue important to the school. There are many fun rituals that have specific purposes behind them. Among these is announcing birthdays, awards and team results over the school's loud speakers. The principal going to each classroom to hand out awards is also a favorite ritual. These "fun" rituals are designed to build self-esteem and reinforce positive effort and achievement. It might be useful for a principal and her teachers to list all of the school's rituals that they can think of and then put them in categories to see how many truly support the educational and personal growth of students. Almost all rituals have a strong communication and relationship focus. Educators ought to be more intentional in creating and implementing rituals. They are powerful tools that help to mold the school culture and support excellence in teaching and successful learning.

Strategy # 2 - Institute Support Systems for Ritual, Tradition and Ceremony

Action Steps:

- invite the PTSA or Booster Club to financially support ritual, tradition and ceremony at your school

- acknowledge the efforts teachers make to involve their students in rituals, traditions and ceremonies

- provide teachers with adequate common planning time

- inform parents and community members about rituals, traditions and ceremonies in your classroom and the school

- identify those rituals that the staff wishes to become traditions and focus support in that direction

Rituals, traditions and ceremonies don't just automatically happen on their own. It takes people behind the scenes directing and carrying out the necessary steps for these events to occur. Teachers play a significant role because they are most often responsible for the daily examples of classroom ritual that take place in a school. It requires a lot of work and effort on the part of the teacher to institute and then carry out activities that build ritual and tradition. We often don't realize or appreciate the effort that this takes both in time and personal dedication. Teachers are the key to students meeting success in the classroom and they are also instrumental in instituting the mechanisms for these successes to occur.

What does it take to support teachers in their efforts to build ritual and tradition into the life of their classrooms? First of all, it takes recognition on the part of administration that ritual and tradition lead to realizing the goals and vision of the school. Principals and superintendents must understand the power of these activities because they play major roles in supporting these programs. Initially, principals can be supportive of teachers by noticing, commenting upon and participating in the rituals and traditions in each classroom. Positive acknowledgment goes a long way to support the continuation of a program or an action. Beyond acknowledgment, there must be concrete support for teachers. This often comes in the form of providing money, materials, space or equipment for events or programs. If an awards assembly is an annual tradition at a school, there will be material requirements for supporting that program. Many rituals and traditions require financial and emotional support from administration or parent groups. Teachers often bear the responsibility of supporting classroom programs with their own funds because they know that reduced financial support might otherwise doom a viable program for their students. Administration must acquire the necessary financial support so that classroom rituals and traditions don't die.

One of the most useful support tools to give teachers is planning time. So many school rituals, traditions and ceremonies are planned and carried out by the teachers who try to squeeze that planning into an already stressful and over-worked day. Teachers tell us that one of the greatest gifts they can receive from administration is common planning time. This should not be considered a gift to teachers, but rather a right and a necessity for them to effectively complete their jobs. Unfortunately, teachers rarely find that they have adequate planning time. Teachers, parents and administrators must place their focus on creating intentional rituals, traditions and ceremonies that support the goals of the school. Much of this work could be accomplished through site councils, PTAs, staff meetings or special committees. It appears that tradition and ritual naturally form and grow in schools without a lot of conscious thought as to how they fit in with the whole school picture. If educators put more intention into these aspects of school life, perhaps they would support the educational bottom line in a more significant way.

While financial and planning support are necessary, people support may be the most important factor leading to the success of ritual, tradition and ceremony in a school.

Rituals and traditions are based on sharing actions, events and outcomes with other people. They create a common history for a school that grows each year as new rituals and traditions come forward and old ones become more firmly institutionalized. Ceremony plays an important role in recognizing the benefits of rituals and traditions to the life of the organization. If rituals, traditions and ceremonies form the heart of the school and create its history, it is essential that all members of the school community participate in establishing and celebrating them. Schools that provide quality education have a strong parent and community involvement in their school. Ritual, tradition and ceremony provide one of the best ways in which to engage parent involvement. Individual parents, parent groups and community members often become the catalysts for new traditions to begin in a school, creating a webbing effect throughout the organization, linking all members in meaningful ways.

Most neighborhood or small town communities place a high value on their schools and parental involvement in those schools. Teachers and principals look for meaningful ways in which to engage these interested citizens in appropriate and helpful directions. When parents act as partners to educators, children and schools thrive. More financial support will be available for schools when the community is behind the teachers and administrators. Parents invest a lot of time and money in schools that welcome them warmly and embrace their desire to contribute to the life of the school in significant ways. Therefore, it is to everyone's benefit when there are very specific, and meaningful, avenues through which parents may become involved. Rituals, traditions and ceremonies provide the pathways for parental involvement to flourish.

Strategy # 3 - Attach Physical Icons to Ritual, Tradition and Ceremony

Action Steps:

- give your students tangible objects to mark rituals or traditions

- share the traditions, specific to your grade level, with your students in order to build pride and unity

- work with other teachers and your principal to ensure that all students are involved in school ceremonies

- teach parents about your classroom rituals and why they're important to student learning

- co-create rituals and traditions between home and school

Rituals, traditions and ceremonies become more quickly publicized and institutionalized when they are visible. Icons or objects that represent rituals and traditions and are presented in ceremonies serve as reminders and rewards. They remind us of participation, mastery or completion, rewarding students, teachers and parents alike. If rituals and traditions are based on sound learning and socialization principles, they ought to become fixed and recognizable by all within the school community. It's not unusual in schools to find trophies, certificates, medals, banners, school t-shirts and other branded materials used for recognition and marking purposes. Many schools have spirit weeks and school pride days that are designated special days to show pride in the school. These fun events provide students with a greater feeling of being part of something that is valued and meaningful.

If you are a teacher, principal or parent involved in building rituals and traditions in your school, attach an icon wherever you can. It will more quickly result in the ritual or tradition taking hold with the students and community. Icons are symbols that people respond to because of an emotional attachment to them. They are often remembered as meaningful representations of school experiences that we've had. Most adults can remember their high school or college mascots even if they haven't been in school for years. The mascot triggers fond memories of the times spent at the school. This doesn't mean that every ritual and tradition must have a material object associated with it. Songs and poems can also be effective tools used to institutionalize and trigger memories around rituals and traditions. High School and college songs are usually remembered well into adulthood. Students will recall songs that they sang years before in elementary school. Year after year third graders will learn the same frog song for their play. A high school senior will still be able to sing that third grade song and remember her role in that annual play years later. Teachers who attach songs and rhymes to the teaching of content will find that students retain and recall the information more readily.

Icons are important for teachers and parents also for many of the same reasons they're important for students. Classroom teachers become very protective of special rituals or traditions that become attached to their grade level and they are often reluctant to let go of them. If it's tradition for the fifth graders to always present a Thanksgiving play to the school, that becomes an event that every first to fourth grade student anticipates as being their right as a fifth grader. Rituals and traditions enrich school cultures that develop in classrooms and eventually become institutionalized for that grade level. Teachers themselves become involved in rituals and traditions with other teachers, parents and the principal. In first grade, "room mom" comes in every Friday to read to the students. Retired scientists meet on a weekly basis with middle school science fair entrants for mentoring. These events create richer environments in which many share the duties of teaching. They provide teachers with supportive friendships and parents and community members with greater knowledge about school programs. Attaching icons to rituals, traditions and ceremonies "flags these events" as important to the school's priorities. Therefore, they provide useful information to the community about what is going on at the school. Icons can become great communication and public relations tools. Icons are the outward signs that educators and parents put forward to engage their students and children in the active life of the school. Icons are most often presented at and associated with ceremonies.

Ceremonies often tap into feelings of inspiration and pride. The formality of them brings majesty to the honored person or event. Ceremonies possess a strong personal component because they usually recognize or praise some characteristic of the human spirit. They may evoke strong emotional responses from both recipients and observers. Ceremonies bring ending to projects or mark passage to another level of performance or higher grade. Closure is an important component to feelings of success. Teachers often use ceremony in their classrooms to mark completion and achievement. This allows students to experience the self-evaluation that comes with closure as well as the excitement that comes with beginning something anew.

Ceremony exists to mark significant human events, recognize individual or group greatness, and honor the human spirit in all of us. Ceremonies inspire us because they encourage us to rise out of our ordinary lives and recognize people and events that impact us in extraordinary ways. Classroom and school ceremonies clearly place students at the center of the educational system. Schools without ceremony lack this awareness and focus. A rich ceremonial history brings great pride, joy and sense of purpose to a school community. When students, teachers, parents and administrators feel part of this greater purpose and majesty, they are more likely to do whatever is necessary to ensure that the learning and teaching are of the highest quality. The quickest and most effective way I know to improve the morale of a school community is to create classroom rituals, reinforce school traditions and make sure that all school community members participate in ceremonies that honor who they are as important contributors to the community. Icons are the visible sign that this is happening in a school. Ritual, tradition and ceremony unite us through shared values and human interactions. They help us to form, sustain and advance the direction of and focus on the school's vision. Schools where ritual, tradition and ceremony thrive provide interactive and enriched learning and teaching environments.

Index

A

ability 21
Accountability 207
  action steps 221, 226, 230, 234
  alternate strategies 231
  balance of programming 219
  daily supervision 214
  formative assessment 231
  local experts 212
  professional growth 210

B

balance 158
belonging 250

C

change 72
classroom space 149
collaboration 15, 17
communication 35
community building 246
critical friends groups 229

D

death 239
doing the dailies 162

E

emotional safety 13
Empowerment 95
  action 104
  action steps 102, 112, 115, 119
  feedback 107
  intuition 120
  learning 103
  students 98
  teachers 100
Environment 136
  academic 145
  action steps 148, 152, 156, 161, 163
  emotional 138
  relational 142
  safe 12

F

feedback 107
formative assessment 231

H

Haleakela 7
homelessness 168
honesty 21

I

inspiration 165
intuition 120

K

kindness 32
kindergarten students 102
knowledge base 35

L

Leadership 49
  action steps 56, 60, 69, 74, 77
  expert leaders 58
  observing 62
  people first 67
  professional and personal 59
  shared 52
  voice 67
listening 65

M

middle school students 125
mistrust 14
modeling 29
motivation 255

O

observations 196
office 44
Optimism 175
  action steps 179, 184, 188, 192
  belief system 189
  intentional communities 193
  power of choice 184

P

Parents 235, 251, 261
  consistent communication 235
  parental involvement 19
  leadership 58
planning 223
positive talk 156
predictability 247
pride 250, 252
principal-teacher relationship 18
professional growth 210

R

recognition 252
relationship building 13, 254
reliability 24
respect 13, 33
risk 74
risk-taking 13
Ritual, Tradition, and Ceremony 245
ritual, tradition, ceremony
  action steps 256, 258, 261
  ceremonies 251
  community building 246
  icons 261
  rituals 246
  traditions 249

S

safe schools 150
school climate 16
self-evaluation 111
self-fulfillment 36
shared vision 24
stability 247
staff development 27
strength 25
suspensions 130

T

teaching partner 15
Trust 11
  ability 21
  action steps 26, 29, 33, 36
  collaboration 17
  honesty 20
  relationships 13
  reliability 20
  strength 24

V

visibility 27

Y

yellow cart 82

Printed in the United States
120748LV00002B/3/P